FLAT WORLD NAVIGATION

COLLABORATION AND NETWORKING IN THE GLOBAL DIGITAL ECONOMY

KIM CHANDLER MCDONALD

First published in Great Britain and the United States in 2015 by Kogan Page Limited

2nd Floor, 45 Gee Street
London EC1V 3RS
United Kingdom
www.koganpage.com

1518 Walnut Street, Suite 1100
Philadelphia PA 19102
USA

4737/23 Ansari Road
Daryaganj
New Delhi 110002
India

© Kim Chandler McDonald, 2015

ISBN   978 0 7494 7393 8
E-ISBN   978 0 7494 7394 5

British Library Cataloguing-in-Publication Data

A CIP record for this book is available from the British Library.

Library of Congress Cataloging-in-Publication Data

CIP data is available.

Library of Congress Control Number: 2015021105

Typeset by Graphicraft Limited, Hong Kong
Print production managed by Jellyfish
Printed and bound by CPI Group (UK) Ltd, Croydon, CR0 4YY

Always, Michael

"Believe it or not, this is power."

Birdman or (The Unexpected Virtue of Ignorance). Dir. Alejandro G. Iñárritu. New Regency Pictures, 2014

"In the long history of humankind (and animal kind, too) those who learned to collaborate and improvise most effectively have prevailed."

Charles Darwin

"While consumer social like Facebook and Twitter gets the headlines, perhaps the greatest untapped potential for social networking lies in business applications."

Ryan Holmes, Founder/CEO, Hootsuite

FWN Code: To bring the walls down, it doesn't help to put someone's back up.

CONTENTS

07   Navigating the direction of the DACE   177
Peter Church, Jeff Finkle, Peter Hewkin, Philo Holland,
Giorgio Prister, Robert Joachim Schiff and Liora Shechter

**08   Is flat world navigation the game changer for women
in the workforce?**   209
Shala Burroughs, Anna Fälth, Natalie Goldman,
Louise Guido and Carolyn Lawrence

Summary: A collaborative conclusion   229
Christopher Altman and Francesco Calabrese

ABOUT THE AUTHOR

Innovation and collaboration advocate and advisor, Kim Chandler McDonald is the author of the internationally acclaimed, award-winning, *Innovation: How innovators think, act and change our world*. It is available in print, as an eBook and an Enhanced Edition/Online Ecosystem encompassing industry-leading SmartMarks and cutting-edge technology. The Co-Founder of KimmiC, a company which specializes in leading-edge innovations and robust FIA (Future of Internet) technologies, she is a globally respected thought leader in international business strategies, disruptive approaches and trans-formational trends – particularly those involving innovation and the DACE (Digital, Attention and Collaboration Economies).

The world's first 'branded' Flat World Navigator, Kim was included in the inaugural 'LinkedIn Power Profiles – Australia' list. She is a Global Ambassador for the #GlobalResolutions Initiative and currently sits on Griffith University's Enterprise Advisory Board, Knowledge Com-mercialisation Australasia's Advocacy Committee and the Board of Governors of Frost and Sullivan's Association of Growth, Innovation and Leadership Executives (AGILE) as well as being an Academy Fellow of the International Entrepreneurship Academy. Formerly, Kim was writer/editor for a number of national and international publications and host/producer of the award-winning *English Breakfast* radio programme.

Kim Chandler McDonald
Photographer: Christian Hagward

BIOGRAPHIES

Morra Aarons-Mele is the founder of digital marketing agency Women Online. Working with women online since 1999, including helping Hillary Clinton log on for her first Internet chat, Morra has launched online campaigns for the world's leading organizations. Founding Political Director for BlogHer.com, she's written for BlogHer, the *Harvard Business Review* online, The Huffington Post, MomsRising, the *New York Times*, and the *Guardian*. She's taught at the Yale Women's Campaign School, the Harvard Kennedy School, and at the World Economic Forum's Young Global Leaders forum at Harvard, as well as at the Johns Hopkins Graduate School of Communication.

For nearly 30 years, **Mary Adams** has helped business leaders conquer challenges such as growth, change, mergers and acquisitions. Having lived the shift from the Industrial to the Social Era, her passion is unlocking the collective power of intangible capital – the key asset class for companies today, providing 80 per cent of the value and 100 per cent of the competitive advantage of the average company today. Co-author of *Intangible Capital: putting knowledge to work in the 21st-century organization* and Smarter-Companies founder, Mary began her career at Citicorp and Sanwa Business Credit before founding management consulting firm Trek, where she developed the tools now in the ICounts Toolset.

Do Cool Sh*t author and serial social entrepreneur, **Miki Agrawal**, was awarded the 2013 Tribeca Film Festival's 'Disruptive Innovation Award' and named in Forbes' 'Top 20 Millennials On a Mission' list that same year. The former pro soccer player is the founder of the acclaimed farm-to-table, pizza concept *WILD* and has partnered with Zappos.com CEO Tony Hsieh to open the concept in Downtown Las Vegas. Her latest ventures include THINX, a high-tech underwear solution for women during their 'time of the month' and Super Sprowtz, a children's media company aimed at getting kids to eat more vegetables.

Scientist, diplomat, and NASA-trained commercial astronaut, **Christopher Altman** has amassed an impressive array of award-winning accomplishments, pioneering research breakthroughs and influential leadership roles at world-leading institutions including multidisciplinary 'Deep Future' research institute Starlab, NASA Ames Research Center and the Kavli Institute of Nanoscience, as Chairman for the UNISCA First Committee on Disarmament and International Security, and as part of the US Government's fast-track research programme in the global race to harness the revolutionary promise and potentials of quantum technology. As flight member and astronaut candidate, then as Director of the Board and Chief Science Officer for the world's first commercial astronaut corps, he has played an integral and historic role leading the next generation of manned spaceflight in efforts to open up widespread public access to space.

Emmy-winning former NBC and *Wall Street Journal* reporter, now connective behaviour columnist for *Forbes* and *Huffington Post*, **Kare Anderson**'s TED talk, 'The Web of Humanity: Becoming an Opportunity Maker', attracted over one million views within two months. Her clients are as diverse as Salesforce, Novartis, S.F. Giants and The Skoll Foundation. She's a founding board member of Annie's Homegrown, co-founder of nine PACs, and author of *Mutuality Matters*, *Moving from Me to We*, *Getting What You Want* and other books. Anderson is on the advisory boards of Gloopt, Raynforest, Watermark and TEDxMarin. Discover more at her blog, *Moving from Me to We*.

Karen Barnes is the Founder of Critical Shift Consulting, a firm helping clients create strategies and communications for change. Her approach incorporates the latest research and translates it into practical, applicable plans and messaging. Plain and simple, Karen brings tools and expertise to help bridge the gap between attitudes and actions, creating new, meaningful and sustainable behaviours. Clients include Boeing, Steelcase, Johnson & Johnson, Toshiba, General Mills, Energy Star, and Lowe's Home Improvement. She is also a partner in B2P Partners, a consultancy devoted to making business more powerful by making it more personal.

An entrepreneur since 1987 and founder of several companies and NGOs, **Miguel Reynolds Brandão** is an experienced international business strategist, negotiator, broker, angel and mentor predominantly focusing on SMEs and startups. Since 1994 he has been a strategic management advisor for institutions in Portugal, Brazil and the United States. An author of books and articles on the topics of strategic management systems, entrepreneurship, business brokering and teleworking, his latest work, *The Sustainable Organisation*, was published in May 2015 and co-authored by Nádia Morais. Miguel is a sought-after international speaker on topics which include strategic management, e-work, entrepreneurship and venture capital.

Saskia Bruysten is co-founder and CEO of Yunus Social Business (YSB), which she co-founded with Nobel Peace Prize Laureate Professor Muhammad Yunus. German-based YSB (with subsidiaries in Albania, Brazil, Colombia, Haiti, India, Tunisia and Uganda) enables social entrepreneurs by incubating, accelerating and financing them. It does so by providing coaching, mentoring and business planning support, as well as debt and equity financing for the most promising social businesses. Its aim: building entrepreneurial ability and business infrastructure – in parts of the world that have formerly relied on development aid and philanthropic donations – by building bridges between impact investment capital and high-potential businesses that solve social and environmental problems.

Shala Burroughs is the co-founder and former COO of CloudPeeps.com – a marketplace that connects businesses with experienced, social media and online community managers. She loves the freelance economy and can't wait to watch it grow. She was a 2013 Startup Leadership Program Fellow and member of Barnard College's Athena Management Masterminds of 2014. She holds a BA in Government from Dartmouth College where she was a 2007 Rockefeller Leadership Fellow. She lives in Long Island City with her husband and beagle.

For over 55 years **Dr Francesco A Calabrese** has brought innovative and practical technical and leadership results to private, public, and academic client enterprises. His work includes membership in the International Visiting Faculty established by Bangkok University for Thailand's first PhD programme in Knowledge and Innovation Management, being a Senior Fellow at the George Washington University Institute for Knowledge and Innovation since 2002 and its Managing Director and Associate Director for Research and Business Alliances. Since 2014 Dr Calabrese has been Founder/Executive Director of I2KI and Founder/President of ExMG, a Management and Mentoring Consulting firm he created in 1990.

Lorraine Carrington has not founded any organization, but has instead volunteered for many – helping out the underdog is a passion of hers. She does this in her spare time as she works as a Programme Director managing complicated and usually difficult programmes of work – something else that inspires her. A lot of time is spent with her family and friends and she loves to crew for friends for fun sporting events – be it the Murray River marathon or an Audax ride. Along the way new skills are learned as the day that stops is the day she will stop. To relax a book is necessary and the crochet hook is never far from her side.

Sandy Carter, IBM General Manager Cloud Ecosystem and Developers, is responsible for IBM's worldwide focus on building and expanding the Cloud ecosystem for ISVs, entrepreneurs, developers and academics. Author of three books, including *Get Bold*, Sandy is a recognized leader in social business, receiving numerous awards such as: Forbes Global Top 40 Social Marketing Masters, 10 Most Powerful Women in Tech, Women of M2M for Internet of Things (IoT), CNN Women of the Channel, Top Nifty 50 Women in Technology, Top 50 Social Business Influencers, and Top 10 in Social Media. Sandy can be reached via Twitter @sandy_carter, or her blog socialbusinesssandy.com.

Peter Church is an Australian lawyer, corporate advisor and author who has spent almost all of his 40-year career living and working in South East Asia and India. He holds degrees from the University of New South Wales, the University of Sydney and the University of London. In 1994 he was awarded the Medal of the Order of Australia (OAM) by the Australian Government for his services to Australia in

Asia. His current roles include chairing corporate advisory firm, AFG Venture Group, acting as Special Counsel to the English law firm of Stephenson Harwood and is a non-executive member of the board of the Indian investment bank, Elara Capital. He is the author of numerous books on Asia including a history of South East Asia and on the life stories of Asian business leaders.

Trilingual **Marc Dufraisse** has over 25 years of professional experience as a management consultant, trainer and executive in various European countries and industries. His focus is on the human dimension in organizations, such as people's capacity to communicate, work in teams, change and be efficient, creative and innovative. His goal is to reconcile individuals with companies for the good of both parties and deliver results in a WIN-WIN alliance.

Innovation leader, speaker and teacher of Collaborative Innovation, **Jeanine Esposito** is a 25+ year innovator across business, education and the arts. After 10 years with Unilever in Marketing and five in Strategy Consulting, Jeanine founded Spark Consulting to drive innovation for Fortune 500 clients. In 2013, Jeanine started Innovation Builders for education. She and her team create collaborative cultures by teaching 21st-century Collaborative Innovation Thinking, facilitating teams to re-think, re-imagine and rejuvenate, and helping 'make space' that invites and inspires collaboration and innovation every day. Within this supportive space and culture, she implements Excitable Learning™ programmes that use real-life issues and learner passion to build truly collaborative innovators.

Anna Fälth is the Manager of UN Women's EmpowerWomen.org. She initiated consultations for this global online platform in February 2013, and brought it to its global launch during the high-level segment of the UN General Assembly on 23 September 2013. Anna has over 17 years working on women's economic empowerment issues. She started in the refugee and immigration service in Sweden, and then joined the United Nations system in 1998. She has since then held economic advisor positions in UNCTAD, UNDP, UN-DESA and now in UN Women. Anna holds a Master of Science degree in

Economics from Lund University, Sweden, and a European Master's in Law and Economics from Hamburg University, Germany. @Empower_Women, @afalth

Co-Founder/Convenor of Meeting of the Minds (the premier international leadership conference for sustainable cities) and Director of Urban Innovations at Cisco Systems, **Gordon Feller** has worked with and advised leaders of multinational companies, cities, NGOs, foundations, and national governments on urban development issues for nearly 30 years. He has written hundreds of articles for newspapers, scholarly journals, and magazines and was formerly executive editor of *Urban Age* magazine and *Planet Earth* magazine. In June 2014, Feller was appointed as a Global Fellow of the Commons Lab, Science and Technology Innovation Program at the Woodrow Wilson International Center for Scholars.

As COO, **Aria Finger** oversees the business development, finance and campaigns departments at DoSomething.org, the largest organization for young people and social change, with 3.5 million members and counting. Finger is also the Founder and President of TMI, a strategy agency that advises Fortune 500 brands and top NGOs on how to reach young people. She was one of the first ten World Economic Forum Global Shapers, is an adjunct professor at NYU, and was the youngest person named in the 2012 Crain's NY Business '40 Under Forty' list.

As President and CEO of the International Economic Development Council (IEDC), **Jeffrey A Finkle, CEcD**, is a recognized leader and authority on economic development. Jeff previously served as Deputy Assistant Secretary in the US Department of Housing and Urban Development, and has received numerous awards over the years for his commitment to making sustainable economic development a priority in communities of all sizes. He received a Bachelor of Science degree in Communications in 1976 from Ohio University in Athens and pursued graduate studies in business administration at Ohio State University. He maintains a strong connection with Ohio University's Voinovich School for Leadership and Public Affairs.

Chris Gabriel has delivered extraordinary results in telecommunications and technology companies across five continents. His success arises from his inclusive leadership style, cross-cultural sensitivity, intuition for customer motivation, and a sense of humour that keeps everything in perspective. Chris is now an angel investor and mentor and holds various strategic roles including senior advisory roles with several global equity investors and leading Australian universities. He has funded several startups in the mobile applications, wearable technology and infrastructure sectors and enjoys jazz music, collecting art and wine, his awesome red Cinquecento and a regular dose of Monty Python.

Natalie Goldman is driven by making a difference in this world, through her passion for helping people. This is evident in her 20-year career through Learning and Development, Coaching, Organizational Development and Technology. It has now transformed with the birth of Launch Pod, which combines her career and her passion for empowering women. She is a believer of challenging the norm, being curious and innovating, finding better and different ways of doing things, of connecting, collaborating and then disrupting. Her work experience spans corporate, government and the not-for-profit sector with a multitude of companies and industries.

Author of *Gamestorming: A playbook for innovators, rulebreakers and changemakers*, **David W Gray** is co-founder of Boardthing, founder and CEO at Limini and board member of Rosenfeld Media. In each of these endeavours he is able to bring his experience and expertise to assisting organizations, including numerous Fortune 500 companies across all industries, to solve complex problems related to culture, innovation and change. He does this through connecting people and facilitating groups to help them collaboratively develop new strategies, launch products and services, and design as well as deliver organizational change initiatives.

Patricia Gene Greene holds the Paul T Babson Chair in Entrepreneurial Studies at Babson College, where she formerly served first as Dean of the Undergraduate School and later as Provost. She is the

Academic Director for the Goldman Sachs 10,000 Small Businesses and 10,000 Women programmes. A founding member of the Diana Project, a research group focused on women's entrepreneurship, Patricia is a federal appointee to the National Advisory Board for the SBA's Small Business Development Centers. She loves to talk about entrepreneurship and changing the way the world does business with anyone who will listen.

Louise Guido is CEO and Managing Partner of ChangeCorp, Inc, a mobile solutions company providing services to people in emerging markets. Its products build communities to support empowerment, such as SmartWoman, SmartFarmer, MoneyMatters, SmartHealth, Business Intelligence, Life Skills and MyFamily – all designed to improve the lives of people in emerging and developing countries. Its flagship, The SmartWoman Project, providing expert content with social networking and impact, is an international women-only 'mobile movement' connecting women and providing life and business skills, career, leadership, health care, relationship advice and much more.

Senior Advisor at the United Nations Trust Fund to End Violence Against Women, **Carolyn Hardy** has more than 20 years' experience and has worked internationally across marketing, communications, advocacy and partnership development and governance in various senior roles in the UN and the private sector. A passionate advocate for women's and children's rights, along with her current work with the UNTF, Carolyn is an International Board Member at Amnesty International. In 2014 she was awarded the Distinguished Alumnus award from CQ University.

Peter Hewkin, Founder of the Centre for Business Innovation Ltd (CfBI), is a serial entrepreneur and business leader. With an impressive international network, deep connections within the world-class Cambridge high-tech cluster and a robust record of successful technology and innovation facilitation, Peter's areas of expertise include micro-fluidics, open innovation, graphene/nano-carbon, social media, Big Data, Internet of Things, smart cities and medical devices. Over the last 15 years Peter has led three technology-contingent companies, including the CfBI, facilitating top-tier engagement in disruptive technology and new business process opportunities by linking global movers and shakers from business, government and academia.

After a career start with a subsidiary of Apple Corp Korea in SFO, **Philo K Holland III** spun off a tech firm architecting a multilingual learning system with Stanford and the world's first online automobile configurator for Ford dealerships in northern Bavaria in 1996. As senior PM at T-Systems HQ in Frankfurt, Philo integrated intercultural resources with 30 countries, forming a company-wide Organizational Development service framework. Today, Philo is an advisor and adjunct professor on collaborative productivity. He earned a BEc from the University of Utah and a MBA from JMU Wuerzburg. A native-born Californian, Philo now lives in southern Germany with his wife and 15-year-old son.

Megan Kachur is a Creative Leader and Trend Forecaster with over 12 years' experience in merchandising, innovation, and product development for Disney Theme Park Merchandise. Her expertise resides in synthesizing external market patterns, behaviours and trends and building them into innovative retail solutions. Using Creative Problem Solving and Design Thinking-based tools, she leads teams that generate highly differentiated products and compelling retail solutions for the Disney Theme Parks around the world. In addition to her Master's in Business Administration, she also holds a Master of Science degree in Organizational Creativity, Innovation and Creative Leadership.

Mie Kajikawa is Founder of Sport For Smile and has led the first-ever platform in Japan to promote social inclusion through sport, collaborating with the UN, WEF speakers and the World Bank. Previously she worked for the Tokyo 2016 Olympic Bid and global consulting and financial firms. Her company, which advises on Sports' Social Responsibility, received an EY Groundbreaker Award. Additionally, Mie was selected as a TEDx speaker, a ScenaRio2012 panellist and a US Embassy, Women's Leadership Program mentor. She earned her Master's degree in Sports Administration from Ohio University as the first-ever female, Japanese NBA intern.

Managing Director at People Innovation Partners, **Edmund Komar** is a Blogger, Speaker, Coach and Facilitator focused on a strength-based approach to foster growth of business and people. His broad range of experience includes leadership roles in HR, IT, Business and Consulting as well as working with small to large Euro-Stoxx or DAX companies such as AXA and Deutsche Telekom, as well as acting as a principal of well-respected consulting brands like Towers Watson. His mission: building bridges from tradition to innovation, offering know-how and know-why transfer from highly dynamic industries and startups as well as supporting leaders to translate business challenges of tomorrow into today's leadership actions.

Owner and Principal at Kummer EcoConsult, **Katharina Kummer Peiry**'s work is focused on aiding her clients to develop that win-win solution: industrial development, which protects the environment and creates jobs, turning environmental problems into solutions. She has worked in international, environmental law and policy for many years in a variety of roles including: academic writer and teacher, negotiator, analyst, facilitator and leader of an international institution. Her book, *International Management of Hazardous Wastes*, first published in 1995, is still considered to be the standard work on the Basel Convention.

President and CEO of Women of Influence, **Carolyn Lawrence** has committed her life's work to influencing women to reach their career goals and evolving corporate culture to shatter the glass ceiling. Women of Influence inspires an international community of 120,000 women across multiple platforms with four key focus areas: events, media, corporate diversity consulting and professional advancement centre. Prior to Women of Influence, Carolyn worked at TD Water-house producing Economic Outlook events for high-value clients. She blogs for *Huffington Post* and the *Globe and Mail*, and sits on the Executive Committee of the International Women's Forum.

Amelia Loye is a social scientist specializing in stakeholder and community engagement, and cross-government collaboration. For more than a dozen years she has worked with and for governments in Australia, Canada and New Zealand, engaging stakeholders and citizens in policy development and programme delivery. During this time she has worked on changes to legislation, major infrastructure projects, and community education, social marketing and behavioural change programmes. She also helped drive online engagement and OpenGov initiatives in British Columbia QLD and NSW, and actively supports local and international engagement, stakeholder management and Gov2 communities of practice.

At twenty **Donnie Maclurcan** gained his place in the *Guinness World Book of Records* for completing the fastest journey on foot across Australia, crossing the country in 67 days. He hasn't stopped since! Co-founder of the Post Growth Institute, his career has included co-developing the (En)Rich List, organizing International Free Money Day, lobbying for Aboriginal justice, assisting Sydney's homeless and coaching the Fijian sailing team. A Fellow of the Royal Society of the Arts, an Honorary Research Fellow with the UTS Institute for Nanoscale Technology, and a Distinguished Fellow at the Schumacher Institute, his two books, *Nanotechnology and Global Equality* and *Nanotechnology and Global Sustainability* have been translated into 20 languages.

As the Founder and Chief Executive Officer of WordSmithRapport™, **Karima Mariama-Arthur** brings more than two decades of comprehensive, blue-chip experience in law, business, and academia to the field of professional development. A leading authority in cutting-edge adult education, Karima is distinguished by her commitment to excellence and extraordinary talent for elevating executive brands. As an expert facilitator, executive communications consultant, and strategic leadership advisor, she trains, coaches, and consults individuals and organizations on the dynamics of complex communication and high-performance leadership competence.

CEO at The Royal Women's Hospital in Melbourne, Australia, **Sue Matthews** is an internationally renowned, transformational health care executive. Before her move to Australia, Sue spent three years as interim President and CEO of the Niagara Health System and prior to that she was the Provincial Chief Nursing Officer for Ontario, leading the development, implementation and evaluation of Ontario's

Nursing Strategy. In 2012, Sue received the Margret Comack Award for Nursing Leadership. She has also received the Canadian Nurses Association's Centennial Award in 2008 and 2004 saw her named as one of Canada's 100 most powerful women.

Joan Michelson is Founder, CEO, and Host of Green Connections™, an innovative media platform about energy and the green economy. An adept media personality focused on innovations in energy, sustainability and the amazing people involved, she is an award-winning, creative business and communications leader/reporter/producer, having generated millions in revenue and branding for top companies, government agencies and non-profits through creative, strategic and integrated media relations, branding, events, advertising and marketing initiatives. She has been an Adjunct Professor in the Communications and Journalism Department of Columbia Union College in Maryland, and actively promotes growth in clean tech and the advancement of women.

Servane Mouazan is the founder and director of Ogunte CIC, an award-winning organization that contributes to 'building a better world powered by women'. Ogunte has helped thousands of women social entrepreneurs, as well as their ecosystem of support providers, to make a positive impact on people and the planet, by enabling them to learn, lead, and connect. Servane created Make a Wave, the first UK incubator for women social entrepreneurs and developed the International Women's Social Leadership Awards, which focuses on the achievements of women-led businesses. At Ogunte, she offers a gender lens on ways to change people's world.

Blair Palese is Co-Founder and CEO of 350.org Australia, which is building a movement to stop new fossil fuel projects and rapidly reduce greenhouse emissions to address climate change. A current board member of Greenpeace Australia Pacific, Blair has held senior management positions in Greenpeace International and The Body Shop as well as working as a consultant for the Antarctic Ocean Alliance, Greenpeace in Australia, China and the United States, The Climate Institute, The Green Building Council of Australia, the Climate Group, Planet Ark and two sustainability programmes with Australia's NSW Government.

Ms **Saundra Pelletier** is CEO of Evofem, Inc, a privately held innovative biotechnology company that develops novel women's health products for global markets. She is also CEO of Woman Care Global, a sustainable non-profit dedicated to helping women get access to high-quality, affordable health care products. Ms Pelletier has launched pharmaceutical brands worldwide and expanded indications for brands in multiple countries. Previously, as Corporate Vice President and Global Franchise Leader at Fortune 500 companies, Ms Pelletier reorganized companies, managed worldwide partnerships and optimized licensing agreements. She is a board member for several organizations focused on education, philanthropy and women's empowerment.

Giorgio Prister has been President of the independent association of European Local Government CIOs, the Major Cities of Europe Organization (www.majorcities.eu), since 2008. Prior to this Giorgio worked for IBM for over 30 years in multiple positions in manufacturing, sales, marketing and finance. In 1991 he took on the leadership of sales and marketing for Europe's IBM Local Government Industry and in 2006 he began his work as an independent strategy consultant in collaboration with Items International and the Italian Association of Telecom Users.

Digital communications and social media strategist, professor and thought leader, **Alan Rosenblatt, PhD** has over 25 years' experience at the digital intersection of politics, advocacy, media, and education. Senior VP of Digital Strategy at turner4D and Co-Founder of the Internet Advocacy Roundtable and Take Action News, he taught the world's first university course on digital politics at George Mason University in 1995 and he's been teaching it ever since. Adjunct professor at Johns Hopkins, American, Georgetown and Gonzaga Universities and the former Associate Director for Online Advocacy at the Center for American Progress/CAP Action Fund, Alan regularly blogs at SocialMediaToday.com and can be found across the web at @DrDigipol.

Robert Joachim Schiff gained his Doctor's degree in Mathematics in 1978. In the same year he was hired by the Municipality of Saarbrücken. In 1982 he became Head of the Electronic Data Processing Department of the City Administration of Saarbrücken.

In 1994 the IT Services of the Municipality of Saarbrücken were out-
sourced to the city-owned institute, IKS, and Dr Schiff became the
head of this. In 1991 a second company was created, of which he
also is the director: IKS Kommunal GmbH, a private company which
is owned 100 per cent by the Municipality of Saarbrücken.

Sylvia Scott is the Founder of Girl's CEO Connection, an organization that sets teenage girls on a path toward fulfilling lives as
successful entrepreneurs and leaders. She launched the Realizing a
Vision conferences that bring high-school girls together with female
entrepreneurs, role models and prospective mentors. Sylvia's background includes MBA studies at Babson College and a long career
in PR and event production. Driven by the passion to help teenage
girls build brighter futures for themselves, Sylvia began designing
programmes to mentor in the development of entrepreneurial traits
and skills women determined essential to grow a venture.

As CIO of the Tel Aviv – Jafo Municipality, in the past four years,
Liora Shechter's challenges have included developing the Digi-Tel
platform, which offers personalized, location-based information,
services and benefits, including city-wide free wi-fi, to its residents.
This approach won the coveted 2014 World Smart City Award at
the Barcelona Smart Cities Summit in November 2014. Ms Shechter
has a BSC in Computer Science from the Technion and an EMBA
with Excellence from Recanati Business School at Tel Aviv University;
in the Israeli army for 21 years, she retired with the rank of Lieutenant
Colonel.

Wendy Simpson is the Chairman of Wengeo Group, an innovative
diversified investment group, and was the founding Chairman of
Springboard Enterprises Australia, Australia's only internationally
focused business accelerator for women entrepreneurs seeking investment capital. Previously Senior Vice President of Alcatel Asia Pacific,
Wendy was responsible for a budget of €4.2 billion, the sale of major
mobile and broadband services to 17 countries and was part of the
negotiating team bringing the internet to China. In 2013 Wendy
joined the World Vision Australia Board, received the Medal of the
Order of Australia for service to the community and, on International

Women's Day, was inducted into the Australian Businesswomen's Hall of Fame and was listed in the Australian Financial Review's list of 100 women of influence.

Erik Starck works with innovation and growth for enterprises and entrepreneurs as the CEO of Startup Studio Malmö. Currently he is busy organizing a startup accelerator focused on health and drawing lean growth canvases on whiteboards for agile teams. Erik started his first company in 1998 and has been in love with entrepreneurship ever since. He has a Master's degree in Software Engineering. He lives in Malmö, in the south of Sweden, with his wife and two daughters. Ping him on @erikstarck to grab a coffee if you're nearby.

Cameron Tuesley is the founding director of Integral Technology Solutions (Integral), which has been operating in the Australian market since 2001. He specializes in managing and leading teams of technology professionals as well as providing executive-level guidance and architectural direction on technological projects. In 2012, Cameron founded TeamArrow, which focuses on the development of high-end engineering and environmental sustainability skills in young people, partnering with leading Brisbane companies and the Queensland University of Technology (QUT) on technology including the development of a solar-powered race car.

An original and visionary thinker in the field of innovation who has focused on understanding and enabling innovation since 1992, **Dr Bettina von Stamm** very much enjoys her role as a stimulator, provocateur, 'inspirator' and catalyst to enable different ways of thinking around, and understanding of, innovation. Her company, Innovation Leadership Forum, is a Think & Do Tank which supports leaders and decision makers in their efforts to create more innovative work environments. In addition to public speaking and delivering bespoke, custom workshop and seminars Bettina contributes to executive and post graduate programmes at prestigious universities and organizations throughout the world.

Media entrepreneur, company director and philanthropist **Deanne Weir** has more than 20 years' experience in media and communications. Deanne chairs the boards of four private companies, is Deputy Chair of Screen Australia and a board member of the International Women's Development Agency, Playwriting Australia and the Australian Women Donors Network. Deanne is a director of WeirAnderson.com, which is home to the WeirAnderson group of investments in media and communications companies. Deanne is also a director of the WeirAnderson Foundation, a Private Ancillary Fund with a particular emphasis on projects that will improve the lives of women and girls.

Adrian Westaway's backgrounds in electronic engineering and industrial design, combined with the fact that he is a full member of the Magic Circle, help him to understand how things work, and how they will work in the future, while at the same time keeping a strong focus on interaction and experience. The first ever James Dyson Fellow in 2007, he was made a fellow of the Royal Commission of 1851 in 2010 for his work on interactive lighting systems. A senior tutor at Queen Mary University of London and the Royal College of Art, he is also a visiting faculty member at the Copenhagen Institute of Interaction Design.

Clara Gaggero Westaway is the co-founder and creative director of Special Projects, an award-winning design consultancy based in London. She previously co-founded and ran the design studio Vitamins. Her design experience spans from digital services to physical products. Clara has designed for companies including the BBC, BlackBerry, Nokia, Samsung, Burton and global startups, and has worked on projects including wearable technology for pro snowboarders, an internet-connected calendar made entirely out of Lego, and designed the only mobile phone user manual to be featured in the MoMA New York. Her philosophy is to treat each project as a unique challenge, yet focus the process and the solutions on the user. Clara is a visiting senior lecturer at the Royal College of Art and at Queen Mary University of London.

THANKS

In creating and collating this collection of essays, interviews, features and facts I have had, as with my last book, the opportunity to meet a myriad of fascinating, frank and forthcoming individuals.

What I found, in each of them, was a willingness – often an eagerness – to connect, communicate and explore potential adventures and ventures to share. Equally sociable and strategic, their ears are finely tuned to pick up on potentials as they are fully engaged in exploring the advantages being made available to those ready, willing and engaged in doing business in the global DACE – the Digital, Attention and Collaboration Economies.

They are fully aware of the advantages their bridge-building abilities bring to any organization or business venture – regardless of whether that business is being done within the walls of a multinational conglomerate or a multi-departmental local entity. It makes no difference if the connections made involve a non-profit NGO, a multi-tiered governmental organization or a sole-proprietor SME – what matters is that strategic collaborations and profits, both tangible and intangible, are being made.

My deepest thanks go to each of the Flat World Navigators who joined me in this project. Their open-hearted willingness to share their stories and tell their tales has left me awestruck at their gracious generosity. As with my last book, I am exceedingly pleased and profoundly honoured to now be able to call so many of them my friends. There is a wonderful Greek word which, to me, sums up what they have given. That word, '*Meraki*', means doing something with soul and creativity, sharing a piece of yourself in what you do. They more-than-*Meraki*'d!

Additional thanks to MYOB CTO Simon Raik-Allen, Dan Keldsen of Information Architected, Inc. (and co-author of the great book, *The Gen Z Effect*!) and Ernst & Young's Andrea Prieto Losada for their enthusiasm and input.

I wish to also thank Thomas L Friedman, author of *The World is Flat: A brief history of the twenty-first century* for the initial 'compass point', which started me on this journey across, around, through and within the Flat World.

I was remiss in not doing so in my last book, so I must take this opportunity to thank all of the support staff – Flat World Navigators in their own right! – who did so much to enable the participants (in both books) to carve out the time to connect and collaborate with me. Without them these publishing projects truly would not be possible. With that, special thanks must go to Camille Alexander, Richard Berman, Patrick Berzinski, Jane Cochrane, Katharine Dill, Jenny Greaves, Carla LaFever, Yves Leboulenge, Melissa Lukach, Ella Maschiach, Becky Michel, Cathy Olofson, Andrew Pinelli, Jason Riggs, Gabriele Ruttloff and Jade Ulrich.

I'm so fortunate to have an amazing team at Kogan Page working with me to produce a product we're all proud of. Thank you! They knew what they were getting into with this second book, and they got into it anyway. In particular, my thanks go to Jenni Hall, Lucy Carter, Philippa Fiszzon and Sophia Blackwell, for whom, it seems, no question is too odd or time difference too annoying.

And now for the 'mushy stuff' – of course my thanks each and every day go to Michael, my cohort, companion, co-founder, co-conspirator, colleague, champion and chum. Most importantly, he is the love of my life and I would not be who I am today without him.

I do not thank them enough, but I think Jenny and Keith McDonald know that their consistent support is something that I will always be beyond grateful for.

To friends, old and new, who have stayed close and kept the fires going in heart and hearth while I've been navigating – you know that my heart is always with you and, wherever I am, I stand by your side. In particular I must thank Shelby Piton, Elaine Hutton, Sharon Pinney and Jason Revere, who never fail to pick me up if ever I am flagging. Michael and I will be bringing a party to a few continents and coasts this time around, so I hope I'll be able to thank all of you in person, while we share bubbles, babble and a barrel full of fun.

Cheers!

Kim

ps Thanks to De La Soul for keeping it real – your authenticity and joy in connecting and collaborating is an inspiration!

ABBREVIATIONS AND COMMONLY USED PHRASES

Attention Economy: The value apportioned to the attention, by the Enduser audience, to a business, brand, product, service, etc.

B2B: Business to Business.
B2C: Business to Consumer.
B2ONE: Billion to One.
Big Data: Generalized term used to describe massive data sets comprising structured and unstructured data.
Business Intelligence Software: Analysis/analytical software-based tools that can be applied to a company's data to gain insight.

C2C: Consumer to Consumer.
C2B: Consumer to Business.
CEO: Chief Executive Officer.
CIO: Chief Information/Innovation Officer.
C-Level: High-ranking executives within an organization whose titles begin with 'Chief'.
Cloud: A network of internet-based, remote servers on which users can store, manage and process their data.
CMO: Chief Marketing Officer.
CMTO: Chief Marketing Technology Officer.
C-Suite: The group of high-ranking executives within an organization whose titles begin with 'Chief'.
Collaboration Economy: (aka Peer-to-Peer Economy/Collaborative Consumption) Doing business through dynamic cooperation and collaboration.
Collaboration Platform: Historically focused on small collaborations enabling people to share ideas, work and/or documents, together they have evolved into technologies that can connect multiple individual departments, companies and countries.

CRM: Customer Relationship Management systems for maintaining customer information and managing your communication with them.

CXM: Customer Experience Management.

DACE: Digital, Attention, Collaboration Economies.

Digital Economy: (aka: Internet/Web Economy) the economy based on digital technology.

Dual Licence: Software that can be used as an Open Source project; there can also be a commercial licence treating the software as commercially available.

e-Commerce: The buying and/or selling of goods and the exchange of data or funds over the internet.

Enduser(s): The individuals or group of individuals who are the intended (or unintended) users of a service, product, idea, etc.

Enterprise Hardware/Software: Hardware and software focused on supporting extremely large and complex companies.

FIA: Future of Internet Architecture.

Flat World: Phrase coined by Thomas L Friedman contending that the world of business, commerce and connections is a level playing field affording all competitors equal opportunity.

Flat World Navigators: These are the connectors and bridge builders who make and maintain dynamic networks and business relationships.

FWN: Flat World Navigator.

Google: (v) to search online.

IoE: Internet of Everything.

IoT: Internet of Things.

IP: Intellectual Property (aka KA).

JV: Joint Venture.

KA: Knowledge Assets (aka IP) – a piece or pieces of information, which 'you' know and someone else doesn't.

KPI: Key Performance Indicators.

Knowledge Management System: Systems that attempt to capture, categorize and utilize information to benefit company performance.

Majority World: Where the majority of the world's population lives.

Maker Movement: Involving groups or individuals who create products using already used or discarded materials and computer-related device(s).

MOOC: Massive Open Online Course.

OpEd: Opinion Editorial.

Open Source: Software, which has its 'source code' made freely available by its authors.

ROI: Return on Involvement.

Semantic Web: A common framework enabling data and processes to be shared, combined in a machine (computer)-readable format.

Smart Data: Data, big or small in size, which has been made useful through the implementation of context and insight.

SMB: Small to Medium Business.

SME: Small to Medium Enterprise.

Taxonomy: The classification and categorization of information.

The Third Billion: Referring to the one billion women who will enter the global workforce in the next decade.

UGC: User Generated Content.

VUCA: Volatility, Uncertainty, Complexity and Ambiguity.

Also available by Kim Chandler McDonald: *Innovation*

Any organization looking to succeed in the global digital economy of today – and tomorrow – must innovate. *Innovation* introduces the global pioneers whose ideas and products have driven the changes that have revolutionized our world. It showcases thought leaders who have broken the mould and led the pack in every field from business and technology, government and social policy, food, culture, media, medicine and more. Drawing on exclusive interviews with 100+ leading innovators from around the world, *Innovation* highlights the common denominators linking these highly creative people. It presents the inside track on who's done what, how they did it, what drives them on, and why innovation is so critical to individuals, businesses and to society as a whole. This book is a fascinating, fast-paced read that will empower you and your business to be more innovative too.

BE INSPIRED TO FOLLOW IN THE FOOTSTEPS OF THE WORLD-CLASS INNOVATORS WHO'VE REALLY ROCKED THEIR ROLES

ISBN: 978 0 7494 6966 5
Published by Kogan Page

Introduction

Advantage Attention
Authentic Business Change
Collaboration Communicate Connect
DACE Digital Economy Enduser Flat World
Navigator Global Network Relationship Strategy
Success Technology Win-Win **Career CMO Design Digital**
Earning Empowered Engage Innovative Leader Marketer
Partners Platforms Potential Profit Services

Featuring

Saskia Bruysten (Yunus Social Business – Global Initiatives),
Megan Kachur (Creative Development Manager Ideation Disney
Theme Park), Cameron Tuesley (Integral and TeamArrow) and
Adrian Westaway (Special Projects, Design and Invention Studio)

Timing, if not everything, is certainly vital in organizations of any and every size: When to move? When to hold back? Are you leading the way or lagging behind; are you too soon, too late; are you engaging with your customers; do you know where your next competitor will come from; do you know where your business is headed? The questions are insistent and consistent.

Timing also goes some way to answering the questions: Why this book, and more to the point, why now? Quite simply, we have reached a pivotal point in what is a dramatically different business frontier. Dubbed by the US Army War College as the VUCA – Volatile, Uncertain, Complex and Ambiguous – age, it is fair to brand it as Business's Big Bang era. It is a time when the conventional and accustomed advantages taken for granted by those in Tier One countries and companies are often at best ill-founded, and at worst completely invalid. Additionally, in this era of quick-time communication, speedy online setup and delivery, the ever-present reality of pop-up businesses – located anywhere in the ever-flattening world of diverse, digital economies – capable of bursting the bubble of a traditional business model is here and here to stay.

> In the VUCA world, companies face increasing demands from customers they've never served with needs they've never had to meet, relentless productivity pressure thanks to competitors with lower costs, and business model threats from upstarts in new sectors.
>
> (Blau, 2014)

Along with the questions, competition is exponentially increasing, empowered by the explosion of mobile-enabled, savvy and vocal consumers, the global web and the vastly cheaper and simple-to-use, next-generation Cloud services. Something must be done; decisions must be made; capabilities must be uncovered, embraced, engaged with and taken advantage of. Your success or failure is only a few empowered Enduser mouse-clicks away.

Size is definitely not everything... in fact, it could be argued that the smaller the organization the more agile and able they are to adapt to the changing environs. Regardless of the size of the organization, what is without doubt is that doing nothing is not an option for anyone at this time. As Dan Keldsen, President of Information Architected, Inc and co-author of *The Gen Z Effect* shared:

> ...companies who had been able to just run their businesses as they'd continued to do for decades, have realized they can no longer afford to NOT take advantage of both modern technology infrastructures (networks, collaboration/knowledge systems, processes) and modern management techniques around incentivization and employee engagement, if they are going to survive.
>
> (2013)

Luckily, there is something that can be done, regardless of who you are, where you are, or the size of your organization. It is a flat world of global business and international economies, but it is a flat world that can be navigated. In fact, it must be navigated, by all those who play a part in it. This book gives you the information you need, not only to access, accentuate and develop your own flat world navigational skills, but also to engage and empower the Flat World Navigators within your organization – those people who excel at building and maintaining authentic relationships and dynamic networks – in such a way that they can be leveraged to expand the distribution footprint of your product, service or idea.

DACE details

In the current business environment, brought forward through the Digital, Attention and Collaboration Economies (DACE) there are certain givens:

1 The traditional business world has forever changed and regardless of the size of your organization – be it a basement-based, one-person initiative, holed up in the hinterland, or a multinational behemoth with offices in every urban and suburban arena – empowered consumers, clients, colleagues and competition are able to connect to you wherever you are and whenever they want.

2 These empowered consumers, clients, colleagues and yes, even competitors – who are now your potential joint venture partners – are increasingly interested in exploring the possible benefits brought about by a collaboration with you and your organization. This is particularly important in an economic reality which demands that to commercialize efficiently, everyone must do more with less: less cash, less time and customers with less patience and less reluctance to change suppliers, without telling you, if they are unhappy.

3 The greater the ability you and/or your organization have to connect and collaborate the easier it will be for you to take

advantage of the fact that geographic boundaries and traditional market barriers have become increasingly meaningless as the business world becomes ever more flattened.

4 Be it cross-culturally, 'cross-cubically', cross-country, internationally or with your neighbour just down the street – the necessity to connect and collaborate is mandatory for the organizations and individuals looking to thrive in a world of global networks and networking.

These connections and relationships are necessary for successful navigation of this flat world of the global DACE, and require skilled pilots to steer you and your organization through the cacophony of clutter that can clog any misguided business strategy. A Flat World Navigator (FWN) is necessary as they are skilled in using systems strategically to build dynamic relationships and bridges to enable you to effectively engage with your consumers, clients, colleagues and potential joint venture partners so that all stakeholders are em-powered to generate bigger, better business.

> I used to be a management consultant working for the Boston Consulting Group. One day, about six years ago, I heard Professor [Muhammad] Yunus [Founder of the Grameen Bank] speak in London and I thought, 'Wow; that guy is so cool!' After that, everything happened pretty quickly. Two to three weeks later I jumped on a plane to Berlin because I'd heard that he was speaking there. I just walked up to him and said, 'You don't know me, but I really want to get involved.' That's how we started working together.
>
> I moved to Germany to start things off and, because of my background at BCG, to get corporate entities involved. Over time our business relationship has grown and we've created several joint ventures with corporates. About three years and a half years ago, I said to him, 'Why don't we help bring social businesses to other countries in a positive, venture capital kind of format?' He said 'Why not!' and that

was the beginning of Yunus Social Business. He owns 51 per cent of it and I, along with one other partner, own the rest. That's exactly how we started – and it all began by reaching out and connecting.

Saskia Bruysten, Co-founder and CEO at
Yunus Social Business – Global Initiatives

The FWN is a new role and core capability, which is essential to the success of any and all organizations – this is not a 'like', it is a 'need'; it is not a rebadging of a current box on your organizational chart. This is new and pivotal to your company's near-, mid- and long-term future success. Together we will explore not only what this new world encompasses, but how best to take advantage of the plethora of opportunities it is creating and continues to make manifest.

Along the way I will introduce you to a profusion of experts who bring an extensive and extraordinary range of experience and expertise as it pertains to flat world navigation, collaboration, networking and building dynamic relationships. A great deal of my work – and immense pleasure! – in creating this project involved connecting and collaborating with these inspiring international business leaders, indefatigable digital marketing and social media stars, award-winning astronauts and academics, empowered enablers and mobile mavens from around the globe.

It is their voices you will hear as they share their actionable insights, practical know-how and mastery of flat world navigation through quotes, features and in-depth interviews. The concentrated interviews, which close each chapter, further explore key themes addressed therein. In addition, each chapter will also include my own essays and research findings and 'Actions with Intent' segments for you to actively practise. All of these components are designed to provoke you to reflect on your own situation in the flat world, encourage you to work with the Flat World Navigators within your midst, engage your own flat world navigational skills and aid you in avoiding the potential pitfalls that lie in wait for those who believe doing nothing to embrace the DACE is an option.

Cameron Tuesley, *Managing Director at Integral and Founder of TeamArrow*

In general, I'm passionate about building talent and, with TeamArrow, specifically with young people who are focused on sustainable energy. In building teams we look for people who are both generalists and specialists at the same time. They have to have a great depth of experience in one area but also be nimble enough to apply themselves across a range of things. With both Integral and TeamArrow, we've developed teams that have natural momentum because of people that are focused on doing what they need to do in their specialized area while, at the same time, having a unified view of the whole project. We run an agile approach at Integral and in developing the [solar] vehicle, which works really well with this team structure.

As an example, in working with the BBC's *Top Gear* last year, we took three people with us – specialists in solar, electrics and software. We had a mechanical problem right before filming but it wasn't an issue because these three guys, none of whom knew anything specifically about the suspension system, applied themselves to fixing it. The group is filled with people who are willing to train themselves across the breadth of the project, which definitely makes them stand out!

They're people who have confidence combined with the fact that they don't feel a need to be upright, or uptight, about their area of comfort. They're happy to tackle any problem, big or small. It's perfectly okay for any of the team members to deal with the grubbiest, nastiest jobs. They have a willingness to get involved in areas that are outside of their comfort zone, which I think is extremely important.

This willingness is also important in business, particularly in the global, digital economy where you're really dealing with a rapidly moving environment. You need people that are comfortable being in an environment of change, living outside their comfort zones, collaborating and being willing to take on new things. All of that is critical.

Organizations that are still working through a traditional structure when it comes to collaboration and decision making – those using a top-down process with very clear lines of delineation and reporting – will find it difficult to thrive in an environment that's rapid, dynamic and changing.

I think the greatest challenge to teams, be they building solar cars or building a business, is a sense of belief. When you're dealing with people and you're asking them to do challenging things, it's completely reasonable for them to feel like you're asking them to do the impossible. That's why it's vital that the team leader or leaders believe it can happen. If the leader believes and is absolutely committed to making it happen, then everything else falls into place.

Definitions

Before we move forward, it will be useful to provide some definitions that will be commonly used in this work:

Flat World. In his 2005 bestselling book *The World is Flat: A brief history of the twenty-first century,* Pulitzer Prize-winning journalist and author, Thomas L Friedman rightly contends that the world of business, commerce and connections has become a level playing field wherein most, if not all, competitors are granted an equal opportunity for success. Additionally, and correctly, he points out that countries, companies, communities, governments and individuals must adapt to this commercial reality – this Flat World.

Flat World Navigator (FWN). These are the bridge builders, the 'connectors and collaborators' who excel at making and maintaining dynamic networks and relationships with consumers, clients, colleagues and partners through the use of both innovative and traditional tools, techniques and technologies. It is these individuals – these masters of ROI (Return on Involvement) – that bring attention to ideas, products and services. They carry the banner of business success across the flat world of the global DACE, wherein authentic connections create measurable value and positive returns with little to no marginal costs.

Digital Economy. Also referred to as the Internet and/or Web Economy, the Digital Economy is that which is based on digital technologies. As such, due to its ability to make borders and boundaries irrelevant, it is international in scope and encompasses both traditional structures such as publishing and distribution (Amazon), deal purchasing (eBay, Groupon), payment platforms (PayPal, Stripe, Monetaris), banking, etc. It also works with ever-more innovative and leading edge technologies such as Cloud-empowering initiatives like Bitcoin, collaboration platforms such as ConnekTek and integrated platforms such as those seen melding gaming and publishing. What is without question is that, as the interconnectedness of the flat world becomes ever more obligatory in doing business, the global Digital Economy and the traditional economy are increasingly intertwined and difficult to disentangle from each other.

Attention Economy. As empowered Endusers of products and services become increasingly aware that their attention is valuable, business paradigms that rely on their 'eyes on the prize' will change as an equitable trade for attention, which parlays into profit, becomes ever more contested by all stakeholders. Why is the Attention Economy important? In short, because it doesn't matter how good your offering is if no one is paying attention to it.

Collaboration Economy (also known as the Peer-to-Peer Economy or Collaborative Consumption). Increasingly, working with shared sources of knowledge/service/product creation and distribution as well as promoting the engagement and collaboration between academic, research and corporate stakeholders is an imperative when looking for commercialization success. Along with its obvious challenges, which will be addressed in subsequent chapters, commercial cooperation has the potential to create cost efficiencies, reduce financial risks and improve the potential of doing more with less as it drives productivity growth and new product/ innovation development. The Collaboration Economy is about making deals, making money and doing business – regardless of what that business is (for profit, non-profit, etc) – through dynamic cooperation.

It is also imperative that individuals and organizations that look to take advantage of the potential profits – both fiscal and otherwise – inherent in the Collaboration Economy, must be prepared to be agile and flexible in their methods of doing business, as well as in the associated business models therein. They must have the wherewithal to aim for win-win opportunities, rather than the more traditional win-lose model coupled with inflexible business practices and engagements. Though this may appear counterintuitive, particularly in a time of such swift digital demands, budget constraints and hotly contested markets, the Collaboration Economy requires those that engage in it to be prepared to 'play a long game', sacrificing short-term payments/wins for medium- to long-term prosperity and profits.

Factoid

In Australia alone collaboration is worth a whopping AUD$46 billion to the nation's economy.

(Source: Farrall *et al*, 2014)

ROI (Return on Involvement). The amount of effort, energy and enthusiasm returned, often exponentially, to the Flat World Navigator, be it through money made, time saved or additional Enduser appreciation.

Adrian Westaway, *Director of Technology and Magic,*
Special Projects Design and Invention Studio

There are so many parallels between collaboration, magic and design. When we're doing a project at Special Projects, we're desperate to take it to a point where we create a moment of delight. We want to create something unexpected and special, but it has to be anchored in something meaningful, something useful, like in the case of the Samsung mobile phone user manual we made.

When you watch people use our manual for the first time, the way they approach it is very much like a magic trick. There is a moment when they think, 'Hang on, something is not right; this is funny, this is not normal'. And they turn to the next page and the next and they're in a new universe. They're smiling and giggling, but they've also set up their phone and they didn't even know they were doing it. As with magic, it's the ultimate user-centric design.

There is no way you can fool someone into believing something magical has happened until you fully understand how they are going to perceive everything you do. With magic, you have to really understand how you release information to the audience; how they are going to perceive every movement, every smile, every look, every word. In a way, it's the same with design. You have to fully understand, contextually, how they are going to experience your invention, your product, before you can begin to pull them into your universe.

Traditionally, when you mentioned the word digital, you'd have thought of separate digital agencies and product design agencies. Product design people would make the 'plastic boxes' and, the digital people would do all the software. Now, with the Internet of Things where everything can be connected, you really have to do both. It's now very rare to design a physical object that doesn't have some form of connection to the digital world and vice versa.

We love our projects and all the crazy tech things we incorporate in them, but we try to make that technology as invisible as possible.

It's the job of the magician to make things invisible, so that all you are left with is with the experience. That's the feeling we want people to have with our designs. You shouldn't feel like someone's dumped a bunch of circuit boards on your lap; you should feel like you're able to do something you couldn't do before. It doesn't really matter how it works, that's the part that's invisible. That's the magic.

Issues addressed

This book will address the issues involved with the successful navigation of the Flat World and the global DACE through the successful creation and implementation of some simple strategies and easily attainable skills. Issues addressed, through interviews, insights and real-world examples, will include:

- How globalization and innovative tools and technologies have changed traditional business paradigms.

- How Flat World Navigators and flat world navigation can be utilized to effectively build business bridges and a competitive advantage in the global DACE.

- The differences between social media – wherein intellectual assets are freely shared – and collaborative business platforms where knowledge assets (KA) are highly valued and, as such, shared selectively and securely at both a micro and macro level.

- The changed balance of power due to the emergence of the empowered Enduser who, through the effective use of flat world navigation, can be capitalized on to add to the value chain and the likelihood of a product and/or service's successful entrance into the market.

- Flat world navigational skills acknowledged as a core competence and key differentiator for organizations wanting to thrive in the DACE and for the individuals within those organizations whose roles are being retooled, redesigned or made redundant.

- The importance of effective interdepartmental collaboration when wanting to ensure delivery of a service, product or idea; and how to integrate solutions and business models which focus on getting the most out of win-win strategies.

- What these seismic shifts in the business culture means for legacy infrastructures, businesses and business people who want/need to expand their markets, networks and pool(s) of potential joint ventures, and cooperation/collaboration partners.

- Entrepreneurially minded men and women looking to learn both the value of their innate flat world navigational skills and how to direct colleagues, managers and C-Level leaders, etc to value and respect these same skills.

- How flat world navigation affects business and socio-political economics from a global perspective, including its potential for a demonstrable increase in profits for business, communities and individuals alike.

Introductions

However, at this point, it may be useful to know something about my own connection to this arena. I am the world's first brand Flat World Navigator, having been so designated in 2009 as I prepared to relocate to Australia. Long before I took on the title I have comfortably exercised my connection skills – reaching out to connect, communicate and collaborate is what I have always done, in one way or another. It is what I continue to do, on a daily basis, with individuals and organizations all over the world. This network, my 'little black e-book' if you will, includes nationalities which have, in many instances, particular and/or preferred ways of communication, both personally and professionally. Knowing how to engage with each of them in a way that engenders an authentic connection that brings something positive to each person involved is the very basic foundation of all the bridges I have built.

I think we get lost in likes, shares, tweets and page views and forget that what makes the Internet magical is the human connection, and the vastness of our ability to learn and engage with each other. Just because platforms don't have a feeling, doesn't mean we have to change our humanity.

(Malik, 2014)

Without embracing my 'inner Flat World Navigator' it would have been impossible for me to reach the international innovators and innovative thought leaders who participated in my first book, *Innovation: How innovators think, act and change our world*, nor would this new book be filled with my fellow connectors and collaborators. Additionally, flat world navigation has been, and remains, integral to the business strategy of KimmiC, the high-tech company I co-founded with my husband, business partner and collaborator, Michael McDonald.

Such is the focus of our work that we spent more than five years creating FlatWorld™ technology – an FIA (Future of Internet Architecture), simple, secure, multilingual, corporate-strength business platform designed for the Digital and Collaboration Economies. It is technology that enables knowledge assets from any source to be captured, collaborated with and capitalized upon. From the outset it was designed to level, or flatten if you will, the business playing field. It does this by empowering Tier None organizations, regardless of size or locale, with collaborative technological abilities equal to those that would have, until this point, been reserved for Tier One organizations who had no restrictions on their cost and capability reserves. It is a reflection of a determination to be part of the growing Profit with Purpose (PoP) business paradigm.

Using flat world navigation is also reflective of our business strategy, which encompasses connection, communication and collaboration. A strategy is irrelevant if it is not implemented; as such I am always on the lookout for individuals and organizations that have convergent interests with us. When I find them, be it through doing a particular 'key word' search, or from an article I may come across via a news thread, I reach out to them, explaining that I see similarities between our areas of interest and potential projects.

One recent case example that illustrates this is the following: on a LinkedIn discussion board I noticed a comment which intrigued me. I explored the poster's profile, saw potential and reached out to him. Rather than simply click a button and ask to be 'connected', I wrote a personal note within which I outlined not just the interests we shared, but also the potential synergies between our goals. I ended with an offer of assistance to any project(s) where I could be useful. At no point in the message did I ask for anything; what I offered was an invitation to join my high-level, high-worth network of influencers and thought leaders. As this was a DACE-based communication, I used a Digital tool, grabbed the invitee's Attention and offered to explore a Collaborative enterprise, if that was of interest. A couple of Skype calls later and KimmiC's FlatWorld technology is being featured at an international convention and we have a number of joint venture partners in the pipeline. This, all from navigating the flat world with purpose and a positive attitude.

Factoid

Effective navigation of the flat world entails building a dynamic network of authentic relationships – relationships that are based on and in the DACE.

Through the insights and experiences shared by the trove of tremendous thought leaders who have joined in this project, we will share a journey through the exciting new business frontier. Additionally, as I share my own tips and techniques, I will continue to remind you that flat world navigation is an enterprise in engagement – it is active, not passive – and through the ROI of Return on Involvement, authentic relationships engendered by flat world navigation enable both commercial efficiency and collaborative capability.

Determine what area of your work or organization is under the most pressure to 'do more with less'.

Determine which business colleagues, clients or partners – real or potential – are best placed to work collaboratively with you to find a solution to a current problem.

What three areas of experience, expertise and/or best practice could you share that would save a colleague, client or partner time and/or money?

What is the full lifecycle of your product and/or service and how does your Enduser interact with it at each of those stages? Now imagine you are that Enduser; how would you want that experience to be improved?

Creating a network is only the first step – how are you maintaining your relationships in that network? Once a day scan your lists and connect with one person to whom you can offer something, be it advice, an interesting article or a potential connection of interest to them.

INTERVIEW   An interview with a Flat World Navigator

Megan Kachur, *Creative Development Manager Ideation, Disney Theme Park Merchandise*

Megan Kachur is a Creative Leader and Trend Forecaster with over 12 years' experience in merchandising, innovation, and product development for Disney Theme Park Merchandise. Her expertise resides in synthesizing external market patterns, behaviours and trends, and building them into innovative retail solutions. Using Creative Problem Solving and Design Thinking-based tools, she leads teams that generate highly differentiated products and compelling retail solutions for the Disney Theme Parks around the world. In addition to her Master of Business Administration, she also holds a Master of Science degree in Organizational Creativity, Innovation and Creative Leadership.

Megan, it seems to me that in your role as Creative Development Manager of Merchandise Ideation at the Disney Theme Park in Florida you have little choice but to be at the heart of a myriad of connected collaborations and inter-departmental joint ventures. To my mind, that makes you a pretty pivotal Flat World Navigator – or should I say a Flat 'Small World' Navigator, after all! How did you find yourself there?

I grew up with Disney; I was very familiar with all of the content, and I loved the creative magic of the company. As a child, I remember holding my father's hand, pointing to Cinderella Castle and telling my Dad, 'one day, when I'm a big kid, I'm going to work there.'

In 1999, I was finishing a dual language degree in German and French and a degree in Marketing at the University of Michigan in Ann Arbor. One afternoon, I saw a poster for the 'Disney College Program', and I applied on the spot. That fall, after returning from a marketing and translation job in

Mainz, Germany, I arrived in Florida. My Disney journey had officially begun!

My Disney career started in the Parks, working in the Attractions, or 'Rides' as they are known. I learned about our operations from every angle. I instinctively followed my passions from the beginning; mainly merchandising and creativity – although at the time I didn't know there was any 'process' behind it, let alone a career path. In addition, I had a passion for behavioural science, looking at why people do what they do. That's one of the many reasons I was drawn to retail; it allowed me to explore the psychology of both marketing and design thinking. Such an incredible effort is made by companies everywhere to understand consumer patterns and behaviours. And while I knew I wanted a career under that umbrella of work, I did not know how many steps it would take to get there.

In time I discovered Disney Theme Park Merchandise. Here was a highly creative retail organization that lived outside of the parks themselves; I had no idea it even existed! I was thrilled, yet unsure as to how I could make the leap from my current state. However, I was fortunate to meet an incredible leader whose influence would shape my career for years to come. While I did not yet have the formal experience to obtain a role in the merchandise organization, she recognized my passion and fostered my growth. By allowing me to shadow her team for one year during my days off, my mentor empowered me to learn about product development. This opportunity changed my life. A year later, an Associate Product Developer position opened, and I was accepted. I loved it; I soon became a Product Developer and I developed headwear and a number of different items for the company. I learned one of the greatest lessons in transformational leadership – that great leaders trust, support and empower, and through this, can be catalysts for incredible change.

When you say headwear, do you mean the mouse ears?

Yes, all those ears.

Wow! I thought the ears had been there forever... I mean, Annette Funicello was wearing those ears!

Exactly!

Are you saying that there is a continual development on things like that?

Very much so.

Wow!

Disney Theme park Merchandise is a phenomenal business. There are many people who have a critical role in developing the products. Our job is to ensure the products are unique and capture the stories and themes within our parks; it's a really wonderful thing to do.

Eventually I thought it made sense to get my MBA. I believed it would help me with my strategies and platforms in regards to driving my business, and I can say that in that respect, it did. But, interestingly enough, when you go through a traditional MBA programme, there is nothing in the curriculum regarding creative thinking. Even though the word is widely used in every single major American corporation – innovation, creativity, compelling products, etc – creative thinking is not a part of our formal educational system; there's nothing about creative process, creative behaviours and, most importantly, how to drive creativity in an organization.

Some might say that 'left brain' creative thinking is discouraged in much of traditional education – certainly, as you say, in traditional MBA programmes.

To an extent it is; we are taught to focus on the data. But the beauty of creative process is what lies in the unseen. It is a careful – and sometimes invisible – integration of the data, consumer behaviour, intuition, and the magic of design. I wanted to become a creative leader: one who could drive creative process and lead teams to deliver immersive retail experiences, but I needed to learn the processes and tools before I could make it happen. So I went back to get a Master of Science degree in Organizational Creativity and Innovation. It was a sacrifice, going back a second time, but it was worth it. I simply could not do the work that I do today had I not completed that programme of study.

Where I am today is exciting! I'm constantly developing and growing. It is a thrilling place to be: when I say, 'I live in the grey', I really do! The work that we do in our research lab is constantly developing and, for me, that's very exciting. My role is to lead the creative process, combine it with external market trends and patterns, then develop the content into something that is differentiated and compelling.

When you say that you work in the grey – I often say I live in the grey – I want to be sure that I understand what you mean. To me, it means that I don't need things to be defined in 'black and white' terms. It's not that things are nebulous but I'm really comfortable with them being fluid. Is that what you mean, too?

Absolutely! I'm comfortable with the fluid; I understand that when I begin any project, there will be certain variables that are unknown. Of course, there can be a beauty to a production line way of doing things. Believe me, on some days I miss linear thinking.

But it's exactly what you said; it's understanding that circumstances are not always black and white. They are often fluid, particularly if they're defined in terms of partnerships and responsibilities. Based on my experiences in partnering and communication, there's so much more that people want to do when they are excited about the work. They approach the project differently, they are willing to stretch further, to push beyond their responsibilities. That's why I think the success of creative process often starts with getting people excited about the project.

And, perhaps, it's also necessary to remove the fear of 'the fluid', especially as there is going to be much more of that necessary in the Digital and Collaboration Economies.

Absolutely. I believe there is a slow turning of the tide in today's American corporate culture. It's an understanding that we need to look beyond the horizontal, flat way of working and connecting with each other. It's a shift from the older corporate styles, the silos where so much is lost in terms of potential for new product offerings, new chances, new ways of doing things. This loss occurs in the translation from one level to the next, and the lack of collaboration from other business units who are not even aware that the project exists. I think a lot of companies are seeing that changing this is absolutely necessary in order to be relevant for today, for this millennium.

Speaking of fluid connections, you work at the heart of the DACE – the Digital, Collaboration and Attention Economies – and I imagine your work at Disney often consists of connecting and collaborating cross-cubically, cross-culturally, cross-country and across the world. How do you make this work?

Collaboration is a favourite aspect of my work. What makes a project interesting is the involvement of perspectives and stakeholders from all different departments.

Whenever we engage in a project, we have a handful of stakeholders who will be with the project throughout its lifetime. One of the things that we're able to do is have a very open dialogue. The stakeholders understand that, while they each may be from different departments and usually have different working styles, for the length of the project the working norms they're going to use are those of a creative process. It's about getting the team comfortable with the process, what's going to happen and what the time commitment will be.

A lot of it has to do with giving people a place where they can talk about their point of view and their concerns. I lead what we call 'Vision Sessions' where stakeholders are able to talk about what's going on within that situation, their concerns and what they want to happen. It's the cornerstone of creative process.

If you integrate the right tools, research, and data, you can come through with some powerful ideas and a business case to support them. You have to make sure you're signalling these creative behaviours throughout that entire time as well as utilizing common techniques such as recapping concepts, fostering inclusivity, and maintaining engagement.

It's important to participate in each step of the fieldwork with the team. The project leader must come to the table with information and direction, not arrive saying, 'OK, guys, go and do this and meet me back here in three weeks.' Communication, active listening, and participation are key.

As is fostering the belief that all ideas are welcome because even the most brilliant ideas, when you first say them, may sound absolutely ridiculous. But, the more you practise it, the more adept and comfortable you become at fostering and driving that creative, collaborative thinking.

Have you noticed that the Endusers of Disney products have higher levels of expectation as they become more empowered?

In our line of work, when you're developing a proposed concept for someone, the Enduser is everything. In the past 15 years, thanks to the abundance of and convenient access to information, expectations have absolutely skyrocketed.

We look at some of the challenges from a generational perspective. For instance, you have Millennials – a huge, thriving, up-and-coming generation – who always have a phone in their hand. As a result, they're used to getting what they want, at the best price possible, and without any delayed gratification whatsoever. Following them are the Gen Z babies who haven't known a time when the internet didn't exist. Their behavioural patterns approach addiction when it comes to being online and getting that dopamine feedback that comes with the buzz of social networking.

> **Factoid**
>
> Did you know that 2015 is the first year that the Millennial Generation will outnumber Baby Boomers in the United States?
>
> (Source: Richard Fry, 2014)

This is very different to Generation X. That said, I've noticed that I've become 'that consumer'. The one who doesn't want to wait, doesn't want to have to search and, more importantly, would greatly appreciate it if someone could do me the favour of climbing into my head and bringing up all the relevant options that are just a click away. The closest thing we have to it is probably Amazon and Amazon Prime. It's almost like a way of taking the thinking out of your shopping.

Taking this back to Disney, our guests have tremendous expectations of us, as they should, which makes for a wonderful environment to work in. Because we're not just challenged to deliver, we're challenged to deliver the best. We're challenged to deliver compelling, truly immersive products and experiences and that's what makes it fun. Those high expectations will only continue to grow, not just for Disney but also really for anyone in the guest service industry.

I'd suggest that, in many ways, Disney exemplifies my view on how a company can embrace flat world navigation. I say that because I believe every member of an organization has a responsibility for enhancing their Enduser's experience. Traditionally, you might say that if you had a rude receptionist greet you, that could tinge your emotional connection with a company. With Disney, I'd suggest that there is a buy-in from every employee; each of them seems to understand that they are the 'face' of the Disney brand.

Absolutely. The people I work with every day, whether they're in our offices or in our parks, reflect the best attributes of our brand. That's tied to the fact that, at the end of the day, we're there to make people happy.

Whether you are working in the park or creating a product for them, every time people think of that moment and that interface with your brand, they're going to be happy. That's a very powerful thing to do. You are part of this amazing brand that has this magical ability to make people smile.

How do you think the importance of this can be translated to, for instance, a company that isn't setting out to be a 'magic kingdom'? How can people be encouraged to buy into the role of being an ambassador for their brand?

Anyone, at any level, can be encouraged to do so when they are given an opportunity to see and to understand the difference they make. Communicating this is an important part of the leadership role. For instance, when you read a guest letter thanking you for their experience, it's special and motivating.

Those are just very simple ways that you can keep people engaged and motivated and proud of what they're doing. Making people happy is a wonderful thing to do; I think anyone can tap into that energy if they have someone communicating it.

So there has to be authentic buy-in and support for this from the executive level.

Absolutely. Leadership is essential to everything: maintaining the brand and the positivity behind the brand. And, of course, leadership and the environment it fosters is imperative to a creative organization.

I'm very fortunate to have a leadership team that says, 'It's OK to take a risk'; I'm encouraged to try new things. There are not a lot of people in today's corporate environment and with the current, volatile economy that can say, 'Yes, my leader encourages me to think differently and gives me the resources I need to make that happen'.

I believe great leadership has to do with someone saying, 'I want you to see where this goes. I trust you, so take this to the finish. What have we learned from it? What are we going to do differently next time?' These are the absolutely critical components of strong, creative – and collaborative – leadership: a willingness to take the risk, to learn from the results, and to try again.

FWN Keys from Megan Kachur

- Find someone within your organization who shares your passion and foster their growth. Conversely, find someone who is in a position to foster your own passions and progress. Connect, communicate, contribute.

- Great leaders trust, support and empower, and through this, can be catalysts for incredible change.

- Leadership and the environment it fosters is imperative to a creative organization.

In conclusion

As this Introduction makes clear, connecting and collaborating is mandatory for organizations and individuals looking to thrive in the world of global networks and networking. To avoid an organization getting lost, bogged down or meandering rudderless through the flat world of the DACE it is extremely important that leaders identify and empower the Flat World Navigators within their midst. It is these individuals who will strategically build dynamic, authentic relationships to effectively engage with consumers, clients, colleagues and potential joint venture partners.

Opting out of the DACE is not an option. In the flat world, geographic boundaries and traditional market barriers have become increasingly meaningless. Additionally the accelerated empowerment of Endusers – your consumers, clients, colleagues and competition – equates to an expectation that they be able to connect with you wherever you are and whenever they want. From their advantageous vantage point – where they are ever on the lookout for win-win, collaborative opportunities – Flat World Navigators are a key factor in enabling organizations to commercialize and collaborate efficiently, whilst under biting budgetary constraints. That they do so with authenticity, purpose and the Enduser experience at the forefront of their minds enhances a brand's message exponentially.

The next chapter, 'The tools and techniques of successful flat world navigation in practice', explores ways in which to put flat world navigation and Flat World Navigators to effective use. It delves into the advantages brought about by using flat world navigation within the DACE and personalized messages to connect and construct collaborative enterprises and experiences. In addition I will outline how I employ these facilities in my own professional life both as an author and entrepreneur.

The tools and techniques of successful flat world navigation in practice

01

Advantage Attention
Authentic Business Change
Collaboration Communicate Connect
DACE Digital Economy Enduser Flat World
Navigator Global Network Relationship Strategy
Success Technology Win-Win **Brand Build Content**
Ecosystem Include Innovation Knowledge Online Personal
Results Share Social Stakeholder Tools Value

Featuring

Miki Agrawal (THINX and WILD), Sandy Carter (IBM),
Mie Kajikawa (Sport For Smile and Cheer Blossom, Inc),
Katharina Kummer Peiry (Kummer EcoConsult),
Alan Rosenblatt (turner4D), Sylvia RJ Scott (Girl's CEO Connection),
Bettina von Stamm (Innovation Leadership Forum) and
Erik Starck (Startup Studio)

It's all well and good to talk up the title and hold a discourse on the designation – but what matters are the practicalities of flat world navigation in practice. The great news is that being a Flat World Navigator is as much fun as it is hard work. I often liken the skills in and around it to those required at a party – both from a sensational host and a magnificent guest. They're those people who either throw the parties that everyone wants to attend or are the guests that everyone hopes will show up at their soirée! It really is that simple – and that complex. It takes planning to perform, particularly if you want things to be as simple, accessible, interesting and inviting as possible.

This chapter will explore some of the many tools and techniques inherent in flat world navigation and outline how Flat World Navigators are potent points of promotion, communication and collaboration. Certainly there are aspects of sales, marketing and public relations involved in the role but, in many ways, it has evolved into a more personalized pursuit. This is in no small way due to the fact that, as is necessary in the DACE (Digital, Attention and Collaboration Economies) – where Endusers, whomever they may be, expect micro targeted attention and solutions – building, maintaining and managing positive, personal authentic relationships are assets that profit all stakeholders. Because of this differentiation Flat World Navigators can bring countless competitive advantages to the organizations they are engaged with and in.

Organizationally, as well as connections to sales, marketing, PR and customer service, there are similarities and synergies between Flat World Navigators and the relatively new role of the Chief Marketing Technology Officer. The difference being the CMTO is more focused on strategy, tech portfolio choice and organization while the Flat World Navigator is all about operations – utilizing a portfolio of tools and tech to reach out to potential or actual Endusers. One of the more interesting convergences between the two roles is that they both go some way to refining and redefining the currently struggling position of Chief Information Officer (CIO). To remain relevant and save themselves from being relegated to being seen simply as service providers, rather than setters of strategy, CIOs will need to focus externally and enhance their skill sets to include the same social/market-focused ideals and digital dexterity of CMTOs and Flat World Navigators.

Sir Francis Bacon is quoted as stating, *scientia ipsa potentia est* – knowledge itself is power. In the DACE knowledge alone is not enough; applied knowledge, the prerogative of Flat World Navigators, is where effective, directed influence lies.

Why is this important? Because it underlines the differentiation between Big Data, the arena of technologies, systems and processes, and Smart Data where, in the DACE, the 'data dump' of statistics and analytics are – with the aid of human instinct, empathy and insight – put towards win-win, personally targeted, solutions. William Eggers and Paul Macmillan, in their 2015 article 'A Billion to One: The Crowd Gets Personal', write of the B2ONE experience. They explain that 'Organizations can tap the data and brains of the crowd and use the insights gleaned to provide a highly customized user experience.'

What are you navigating towards?

From CEO to intern, there isn't a role within an organization that doesn't, to some degree, include the potential for a certain level of flat world navigation. Your aim, as a Flat World Navigator, is to connect meaningfully. The question is, will you decide to engage Endusers enthusiastically and, in doing so, build brand equity at the personal, departmental and organizational levels? I suggest you do, as this equity can be engineered into lowering the cost of Enduser (customer/client) acquisition, leading to more profitable, repeat custom. It is the human component to the technical referral revolution, which is what every data-mining business model strives for – the lack of it is their achilles heel.

> Sometimes people from different backgrounds argue even though they are really saying the same thing. Pointing this out and translating back and forth is my role. Doing it in an understanding and humorous way is important; pointing out that there is no right or wrong just a 'different' helps, as does using visual aids.
>
> Bettina von Stamm, Director and Catalyst
> at the Innovation Leadership Forum

It is necessary when working in the DACE to expand and evolve some, until now, fairly traditional business-based definitions. In the

Digital, Attention and Collaboration Economies a customer is not just someone who buys something, profit it not always measured in terms of money and investment may not be economic.

In the DACE a customer is anyone you interact with that you want to provide a service to. Though pecuniary profit will always remain a definitive way of measuring whether or not a customer values your product or service, profit can be redefined in non-monetary measurements such as ease of doing business, satisfaction of service etc. These are reflections of the ROI not of investment, but of Return on Involvement.

Flat World Navigators share their stories

Miki Agrawal, *Co-Founder/CEO of THINX, Founder of WILD*

When I moved to New York, I didn't have that many connections. I didn't know anyone with a lot of money, so I didn't actually know how to get investors. Nor did I have any relationship with the media or the press. So, I started going out six nights a week for three straight years. I built relationships with anyone I could and I offered my help and support to those who needed it.

It was really the question of 'How can I help YOU?' versus 'How can you help ME?' that changed everything. That mindset opened so many doors for a 22-year-old. 'Reframing' was also the game-changer to opening doors and meeting some of the top 'players' in the city. I told them that I went to Cornell, I worked in finance and I wanted to take some load off their shoulders. To newcomers, I told them that I'd heard about them opening a business in my area and I asked if I could help them to get more organized.

In my book, *Do Cool Sh*t*, there's a section on connecting with people, which is trying to build relationships that start with offering help. There are more interesting questions than 'What do you do?' and 'Where are you from?' Try asking, 'What are you struggling with?' or 'What are you most excited about?' instead. Cut through the crap and get straight to the source of the person's passions.

If you go into a room, put on a big smile; don't be nervous, just say something like, 'I like your hat'. When the conversation gets going, ask what they're excited about right now or if there's anything you can do to help them. After just these questions, they'll think, 'Wow, those are things that no one has ever asked me!'
Immediately you'll find that people want to be your friend.
The most important thing to remember is: don't talk about yourself, talk about them.

As the DACE is enabling an unprecedented power shift to the Enduser – be they consumer, customer, client, colleague or partner – this chapter details how to apply the skills inherent in flat world navigation and advises Flat World Navigators how to take advantage of this new business balance, rather than being a victim of it. As Patrick Dodd, Managing Director of Nielsen China, noted in a September 2014 press release, 'the growing online shopper base must be segmented as not all shoppers want the same online experience. Only by deeply understanding their key online shoppers can brands and e-tailers be best positioned for online success.'

Planning for your journey through the flat world

Referring back to the host/hostess analogy, consider how you'd look to anticipate your guests' requests and requirements: you wouldn't serve a suckling pig to a vegan visitor and it's unlikely that a 'teetotal' associate would appreciate you serving them martinis. Now, imagine how happy they'd be if you'd thought ahead, understood what might bring them pleasure, and had a nut loaf and alcohol free punch awaiting them.

I always connect people when I find a mutually beneficial reason to do so. For example if my female connections have a common interest in playing golf I make an introduction even when the women live in different areas or countries. When I find an article online I know will be of interest to a person I forward the link to them. This also includes blogs, newsletters, magazines and videos. In some cases it may be letting the contact know about a conference if I think they may want to attend or submit a speaker proposal.

It takes time and thought to build and maintain mutually beneficial relationships as well as connecting people. However I find my strategy to be the best for the Girl's CEO Connection and myself. In addition I have developed many friendships from business relationships, even those from forty years ago.

Sylvia RJ Scott, Founder and Managing
Director of Girl's CEO Connection

Successful navigation of the flat world equates to alignment, co-ordination, communication and consistent work towards the mutual satisfaction brought about through successful win-win strategies. Flat World Navigators work to position an offering – be it a service, brand, product or business proposition – so it addresses an Enduser's needs and their specific perspective. Though this may seem obvious, it is actually rather rare in relationships based on traditional roles and lines of communication and connection. Therefore, before you begin your journey through the flat world, be sure that your offering is aligned to your Enduser and, equally importantly, that you are enthusiastic in your preparedness to listen to, and engage with your Enduser and the feedback they will – if you're fortunate! – share with you.

Flat World Navigators share their stories

Katharina Kummer Peiry, *Owner and Principal, Kummer EcoConsult*

It is very important, when bringing people together, to manage things in such a way that people who fundamentally may have a common goal can reach a successful objective. The difficulty in these situations is that often these people will have very different ways of approaching or addressing a situation. It could be because of differences in culture or personality, but regardless of the reasons, it is important to influence those people – through suggestion, leadership and discussion – so as to move them towards that common goal.

An example of this, from the policy process perspective, is working towards a common objective where the stated interests of the different players are diametrically opposed and the debate is blocked. In that instance, if the pain level is high enough – in terms of finance, image, markets, etc – then they're more likely to say, 'Things are so bad now, we have to do something; we have to change our mindset and work together.' They will then work towards a compromise and that integrates at least some of what each of them wants.

Certainly there have been some instances where I have found this challenging, perhaps because I had underestimated each person's or each entity's individual interest and agenda. Where I saw their potential strength as a group the person, or the entity they represented, was still embedded in a competition model rather than models of cooperation and collaboration.

In building 'the bridge' between them, the first, fundamental step is for me to understand each side's language. I have to know how each side thinks. Of course, that in itself is not always easy because people often take it for granted that everybody thinks or acts the way they do. They might speak different languages – I don't mean English, French and German – but the corporate, NGO and government languages, for instance. One way of understanding these different languages is simply by observing and listening. This entails doing more than just watching; it is important to observe the discussion and see where things are going wrong and work to understand how this can be made right.

Another important step is to collect the views of the various participants; what do they think the outcome should be and how do they think we should get there. This works especially if you have an informal discussion with each of the people or each of the main groups involved. Then, based on those inputs, you can draft a compromise position and put it forward as your proposal, based on your consultations. It is often easier to move a proposal forward in this manner because everybody sees part of themselves – their ideas, wants and needs – in there. This also goes a long way to defuse the 'the person who shouts the loudest wins' syndrome in that that person no longer has the advantage of being able to wear others down by yelling or pounding the table. Instead, a solution can be reached in which everyone involved can feel they have some ownership. That is the art of compromise, which is an important part of collaboration.

Boston Consulting Global has predicted that, by 2016, social media will be worth US$4.2 trillion to G20 economies. To take part in that potential windfall, there are a few things that, if clarified and committed to at the beginning of your journey, will go a long way to ensuring your success in the DACE:

- clarify the social mission/goals of your company and/or organization;

- align your mission as a Flat World Navigator with that of your company brand and culture;

- be consistent in monitoring and measuring the effectiveness of your ROI with your stakeholders and Endusers; and

- coordinate a plan for communication, which serves the needs of Endusers, including during times of crisis.

As a Flat World Navigator, matching your authentic, engaged communication to your brand's mission is not as difficult as it might appear at the outset. The first thing to determine is what you want your brand to represent in the DACE and how you can imprint a positive, uncontrived attachment to that brand throughout your own flat world and beyond. This is where the Attention Economy is at its most powerful – and it is reflected not just in the attention your brand receives but, equally in the attention you give to driving favourable, compelling content and conversations around the brand.

Erik Starck, *CEO and Co-founder, Startup Studio Malmö*

Collaboration and networking have been absolutely essential in my career. Titles and places in a hierarchy have never been important to me; being acknowledged by and involved in various communities, on the other hand, has.

One of the networking initiatives I'm involved in is called Startup Dojo and, together with a network called Malmö Startups, it aims to bring the local startup community together. Startup Dojo is a 'meetup' where entrepreneurs help other entrepreneurs move their startup projects forward. Being part of it has allowed me to meet and learn from hundreds of entrepreneurs.

Running events as part of your marketing is a perfect way to build networks and connections, provide value to others and get your brand out at the same time. It doesn't even have to cost anything if you bring in sponsors for the event or charge the attendees. For example, we organize 'hackathons' and 'unconferences' – these user-driven events are of high value for the participants while still keeping costs down for everyone.

Physical meetings and events are still necessary in our ever more connected society; digital and social tools only get you so far. It's when we meet someone in person that a true connection occurs. Combining the two is the key.

Social media allows us to reach new markets. We can build an entire funnel of increasing value to our audience. A tweet can lead to a blog post that can lead to an ebook that can lead to a workshop that can lead to a full engagement with a client. That kind of sales funnel would be hard to build at scale without social media.

Attention can be both ephemeral and elusive, and as such, it takes the energy, enthusiasm, expertise and engagement of Flat World Navigators to cultivate, capture and conserve the attention and interest of current and potential Endusers who you want to buy in to your brand. It can be laborious and the attention is often hard won – not least because there is so much 'noise' in the flat world. Flat World Navigators are creating and maintaining paths of communication within an arena where your competitors are only a fraction of the cacophony of noisemakers clamouring for consideration.

Factoid

Speaking of 'noise', did you know that instead of clicking on a banner ad, you are:

- 31.25 times more likely to win a prize in the Mega Millions lottery;

- 87.8 times more likely to get accepted to Harvard;

- 279.6 times more likely to climb to the summit of Mount Everest; and

- 475.28 times more likely to survive a plane crash.

(Source: Popken, 2011)

Those 'noise' numbers pretty much wreck any reliance you may have placed on what is the online equivalent of junk mail flyers. Their volume has been pumped up so much that there is an increasing number of Endusers willing to pay money to turn the noise down – or off altogether. In its 2013 'Digital Future in Focus' report, ComScore, which measures unduplicated audience size, noted that the prior year saw more than 5.3 trillion display ads served to internet users in the United States alone. However, as noted in Brian Morrissey's article, '15 Alarming Stats about Banner Ads', click-through rates were at 0.1 per cent according to DoubleClick, and GoldSpot Media reports that 50 per cent of those clicks were made by accident. Noise doesn't sell, and if it does get attention, it's not likely to be the positive attention necessary to thrive in the DACE.

Getting attention doesn't have to entail reducing a message down to something bland, banal and aimed at the lowest common denominator. Jargon jars, so instead look to engage with your Enduser by creating a more complex message, which you tell over time and across various channels. This is about telling tales tailored to your listeners that are synergistic with your brand strategy. Yes, it takes planning and commitment, but the payoff – the ROI – in brand awareness in the Attention Economy is well worth the work.

If you're in the midst of a 'predicament' (aka crisis), having a procedure in place is of the utmost importance. Things can happen very quickly in the DACE and mid-meltdown is never going to be the time to determine how to proceed. To be sure, these situations need not be life threatening to be seen as of great import to Endusers. However, with the increased engagement and expectations your Endusers have, and their access to an immediate point of emotive escalation via social media, determining the who, how, when, where and why of responding is going to save a lot of headaches and heartaches for all those involved. Ramped up to situations where, for instance, natural disasters are involved, preparedness is a potential lifesaver.

There are certain questions which, when answered, can go a long way to creating a crisis communication plan. For instance, decide:

- What types of comment will be responded to via social media? It could be any, all or a combination of: customer service queries, criticisms, accolades and offers of assistance.

- How quickly will you respond, and when will the clock start ticking? Will you have a tight window of 60 minutes, one day or one week? Will the count begin when the query was sent, or when it was seen?

- Do you thank your cheerleaders (and how, with a reply, retweet or, perhaps, a small offering)?

- Do you engage with online trolls (someone set on starting an argument by posting inflammatory comments simply to be argumentative) or ignore them?

- Is it 'we' or 'me'; are responses to come from an individual (Kim at KimmiC, for instance) or the overarching business brand (KimmiC)?

Though each and every person will bring their own personalities and proclivities to how they navigate the flat world, there are certain habits that are common to many, if not most, successful Flat World Navigators. They include:

- Having an agreed-upon plan, which applies to the overarching business goals and strategies of their organization.

- Knowing 'what day it is', often using a 'content calendar' noting (national and international) holidays, days of interest, etc as a basis to begin relevant and meaningful interactions with their flat world and engage in 'content spiking' topical conversations.

- Bringing their authentic, enthusiastic selves to the party – passion is priceless!

- Knowing their audience. Of course it's important that they speak with their true, authentic voice, but it's equally important they speak in a 'language' that their 'tribe' will both understand and connect with.

- Ensuring their content is relevant to their network. This can be done by exploring topics such as: Frequently Asked Questions, Industry Trends and Innovations, How To... instructions and Top 5 or 10 lists.

- Getting involved by consistently engaging in the flat world; they know the importance of regular attendance and interaction online.

- Being current and knowledgeable about their areas of interest and expertise, enabling them to add extra value to their network.

- Working to be both interesting, insightful and informative.

- Sharing content, information and offers – their own and others – such as news of seasonal sales, new releases, industry news or press/peer recognition.

- Listening actively, asking and answering questions, giving feedback and even suggesting other solutions and service providers better suited to solving a certain problem or requirement.

- Congratulating others on their successes and thanking those who do the same.

- Contributing to conversations, campaigns and causes that reflect their personal and professional brand.

- Using images as often as they can – a picture tells a thousand words, and that's a lot of characters.

- Working to be interesting, informative, insightful and a little bit eclectic.

- Most importantly, using their tools.

Flat World Navigators share their stories

Alan Rosenblatt, *Senior Vice President of Digital Strategy at turner4D*

I have been working in the field of digital and social politics ever since the first web browser was launched in 1993. From the very beginning I viewed the internet as a communications revolution, where people connected with other people to share ideas and content. So from the very start of my work in this industry, I have focused on collaboration and networking. These are essential for organizing and mobilizing activists to influence policymakers and the press. Building communities to serve a strategic goal is the heart of digital and social campaigns.

At turner4D our business model is to use our campaign work to build capacity within our clients' organizations as we prefer not to have indefinite retainer relationships. We use Cloud services like Box, Google Drive, Google Docs and DropBox. Clients use these tools to share large amounts of messaging background documents with us. We then develop social media messages and share them back with the client. Using Cloud services allows us to easily go back and forth on editing these messages and quickly come to final drafts.

We use all social media platforms, especially Twitter, Facebook, LinkedIn and Pinterest to position our firm as thought leaders in modern communications and campaign strategies. We also use them to implement our projects to build relationships with activists, the press, policy professionals, and policymakers. Additionally, we use tools like Attentive.ly to learn more about our social media audiences to be more effective in our engagements with them.

Tools, techniques and tips

There is a plethora of tools which can be, and are, used by those who are successfully navigating the flat world of the DACE. Equally, there are countless websites, blogs, videos, etc, which contain an abundance of lists detailing the best ways to use these tools. There is such a profusion that if I were to attempt to bring them all together in one location, there would be no room to introduce you to the Flat World Navigators and flat world navigational insights I have the opportunity to here. This book is not a marketing manifesto or PR pronouncement; rather, it is a compilation of insights into how the skilful use of flat world navigational skills can be employed by any and all, to build business in the DACE – no matter where you are located or the size of your foothold.

So, instead of repeating what is no doubt shelves, if not bookstores worth of writing on marketing and PR, I am going to share with you how I used my skills as a Flat World Navigator to both write two books involving hundreds of international thought leaders and, additionally, launch a high-tech company engaged in many multinational joint ventures. In telling this tale I will share with you some of the tools that I employed on my own flat world navigational journey.

To begin with I should make clear that everything I do, professionally, is interrelated. Whether it's writing a book, launching some technology, building a network of allies and alliances; all of these things are in one way or another connected. Sometimes it's a 'long play', in that the correlations may not become obvious for many months or, in some cases, several years, but the synergistic undercurrents are always there. So yes, I have a plan – that is my job as a Flat World Navigator. That job was, is, and will remain, to build bridges so as to build business – and that business is two-fold: I am an author and the co-owner of a high-tech company which is a forerunner in innovative, Enduser-focused technology.

I mention this because it is integral to the story I tell. When my husband and I decided to start up a 'startup' we had a grand vision but, frankly, at that time only a handful of connections in the innovation space – which is where we knew we had to be. We wanted a seat at the table, but at that time we weren't even in the same room...

actually, we weren't even on the same continent. I knew that we were creating something that could make massive change to millions – you have to have that belief if you're focused on creating disruptive innovation – but I also knew that we would need to connect with influencers and thought leaders who, at that time, didn't know us.

While my husband, the 'code whisperer' began to build the technology, I began my life as the world's first Flat World Navigator. Little did I know that this role would take on a life of its own and take up a pivotal place, not just in our specific business strategy, but in the DACE in general.

As enthusiastic as I was then, I don't think even I was aware of how successful this strategy would turn out to be – particularly as it is not something that needs to be studied in an Ivy League business school or handed down in the hallowed halls of an exclusive society. All it took was work – involvement – to get the hoped-for returns. In sharing my step-by-step system, I hope I make it clear that anyone – that means you – given a certain level of 'gumption' and, I'd suggest, a healthy dose of graciousness, can navigate the flat world to find themselves creating connections and collaborations that have the potential to not just get a seat at the table, but own the room where the table is situated.

First things first – begin to build your network. I have been on LinkedIn since 2006 and Twitter since early 2008 – professionally, since 2010. I wasn't a 'firstwave adopter' but I did jump in pretty quickly. You'll see that I mention two start dates on Twitter, the second was started when I began my work as a Flat World Navigator.

Factoid

An ABC of acronyms for online Flat World Navigation:

AMA – Ask Me Anything

BTAIM – Be That As It May

CTA – Call To Action

DM – Direct Message

ELI5 – Explain Like I'm 5 (years old)

FF – Follow Friday

G2G – Got To Go

HTH – Here (or Happy) To Help

ICYMI – In Case You Missed It

JK – Just Kidding

LMK – Let Me Know

MT – Modified Tweet (Used if an original tweet is too long to retweet as is and therefore needs to be adjusted for length.)

NVM – Never Mind

OP – Original Poster (Used to refer to the person who originated the posted comment/article/etc.)

P2P – Person to Person (Relating to a face to face (F2F), rather than online, meeting, network, or event.)

QOTD – Quote Of The Day

RT – Retweet (Add your own comments within square [] brackets.)

SOV – Share Of Voice (The measured percentage of content and conversations happening online about you, your brand and/or company compared to your competitors.)

TL; DR – Too Long; Didn't Read

UGC – User Generated Content

Via – Referencing a sourcing site

WFH – Work From Home

XLNT – Excellent

YSK – You Should Know

'Zzzzz' – Sleepy, bored or tired

As much fun as I was having with my personal account, it was clear that tweeting for business would require something a little less personal and a tad more professional. It would still be 'me' – but with fewer jokes! So here's what I did:

- Created a profile including keywords that reflected my work and my brand and, hopefully, resonated with the audience I wanted to connect with. These keywords also made it more likely that my profile would be included in hashtag searches, therefore increasing the likelihood of connecting with those who I shared areas of interest with.

- Included some images. As the account is professional rather than personal, the company logo had to be included; but, rather than being anonymous, the 'voice' is mine, and it was also important to include my own 'headshot' too.

- Integrated my Twitter name in my e-mail signature to make it easy for people to 'click and connect' if they chose to. In fact, my business @username (@KimmiCFlatWorld) is included in all my connection collateral.

- Let my existing network know about my new technology/innovation/business-based account so they could either switch over or add in.

- Let particular followers – who, judging from their own profiles, I thought would prefer one account more than the other – know that they were welcome to 'switch' or add in.

- Searched, using keywords – in my case I looked for hashtags on topics such as collaboration, digital, innovation, Semantic Web and social media – to find individuals and/or organizations that I would like to follow and, hopefully, connect with. In some cases, when I found a particularly influential and/or insightful person, I would explore their own 'follow' list. It stands to reason that those I hold in high regard are likely to be following fairly interesting people whose content I would also find compelling.

- Created lists of areas of interest and/or expertise. By creating these groups I was better able to follow and join in industry-related conversations and connect with these same influencers.

- Decided which of my lists would be public and available to be accessed and searched by anyone. Conversely, I determined which lists – those specifically grouped around a Knowledge Asset or area of interest that I wish to keep confidential – would remain private and unavailable to anyone else.

- Integrated my accounts with other, relevant, platforms such as LinkedIn, Hootsuite, Socialoomph and my business-based Facebook page.

The next step was to create a compelling brand or at least a bridge to where I intended the branding to eventually lead. As the overarching theme in all my projects was innovation I began to write about it – first with what could be considered OpEd (Opinion Editorial) pieces and quickly moving on to writing a blog where I interviewed people who I found interesting.

I'm often asked how I selected my subjects so I'm going to share the secret with you – generally speaking, I chose to interview and write about people that I simply would have loved to have a chat with. It's that simple. My interest was authentic, my enthusiasm genuine.

Though it wouldn't make much business sense for me to give away the entirety of my 'secret sauce' I will share my basic 'recipe', which you can tweak and twist to fit your own taste and profile. I began to build a 'wish list' – often it was people mentioned in news articles or through other media mentions – and began to explore how to connect with them. Sometimes it was as easy as putting their name into a search engine and their e-mail address would be provided. Other times I'd go via Twitter or LinkedIn and send a message of introduction. Occasionally I had to do a bit more digging and connect with their 'gate keeper' before I could actually connect to my intended target. Suffice it to say, it is fairly easy to find someone, online at least, if you put in a modicum of energy and imagination.

Once found, the next step is to connect and that, again, is not difficult if approached correctly. As simplistic as it may seem, you'd be surprised how many 'yes' responses you will get if a) you ask nicely; and b) you have a reason for your request. You've likely heard the adage: you can catch a lot more flies with honey than you do with vinegar. Well I can attest to its correctness; it never hurts to ask, but ask nicely!

Mie Kajikawa, *Founder of Sport For Smile/Founder and CEO of Cheer Blossom, Inc.*

I have been so fortunate that it is hard to cite only one example of miracles that have happened in my life, especially after I left Japan for the United States in 2003. I have been given numerous golden opportunities to intern with the NBA's Detroit Pistons and Michael Jordan's Senior Flight School, as well as to conduct research on FIBA events and 'Basketball Without Borders', all of which have been both my dreams and career goals.

Following the establishment of my project, Sport For Smile, global VIPs including Schwab and Ashoka Fellows and the internationally recognized activist for racial equality, Dr Richard Lapchick – honoured by Nelson Mandela with a personal invitation to his inauguration – have generously supported me as advisors. In addition, the UN Under-Secretary-General Special Advisor on Sport, Wilfried Lemke, kindly visited our event to encourage young leaders, and we were able to host an official side event to the IMF/World Bank General Assembly in Tokyo in 2012. I have also had the opportunity to interview VIPs including Mrs Kayoko Hosokawa, Chairperson of Special Olympics Nippon, who was the first to offer help for Sport For Smile, as well as Tim Shriver, Chairman of Special Olympics, and five-time Olympic Gold Medallist Ian Thorpe.

To be honest, I do not remember what I said when asking for these opportunities and I do not know how I could possibly have thought of being so bold as a mere student or unknown social entrepreneur. But, I always learned the same thing from these experiences: if you ask, people will help you.

I believe, because I have been given so many amazing opportunities that I have a responsibility to repay this by empowering young people in whatever way I can. I am determined to pass my appreciation on to the future by directing all my efforts towards delivering messages based on social justice.

Because it is hard for women and young people to obtain trust in Japan, I went to Harvard to learn public speaking after I established my company. It was a life-changing two-week course and the best one that I have ever taken. Even though I still need to improve, I have a much greater understanding of how to deal with situations such as public speaking and cold calling.

In addition to those skills and mindsets, I personally think that in this Flat World Era you must effectively communicate to diverse audiences. It means that you have to be much more knowledgeable about various fields than was necessary in previous centuries and that you have to be a generalist whilst also being a specialist.

For a social entrepreneur who is committed to coping with authorities – particularly those with wealth and power – I absolutely rely on social media and consistently see its benefits. In addition to it helping disseminate information in massively effective ways it also serves as an efficient business partner. Without doubt it helps us make the flat world flatter, wherein everyone can be a 'YouTube star'. These changes significantly encourage my social business, as it aims to demonstrate that everyone – even people who usually need the support of others – can help one another and that even a homeless person can snatch the ball from a President and make a goal as long as they put in enough effort.

Furthermore, technologies encourage more flexible business models, especially those with longer-term goals, as they enable people – even those who do not live in the same era – to collaborate. I send my messages and deliver my projects assuming that people living in the next century will find out about, and hopefully, gain from my vision and activities.

As to the asking, explain why you're doing so. I have a note on my LinkedIn profile that specifically states: 'I do not accept any requests to connect without a personal message explaining why you'd like to connect with me. Thank you in advance for taking those few extra moments to do so.' Though I generally tend to limit my connections to those people who I: a) have worked with before; b) have a personal relationship of some form with; or c) see synergies between our interests, projects and goals, I am open to other offers. This is particularly the case when someone has taken the time to explain to me why they want to connect. It likely takes only a sentence or two, but those sentences are invaluable in engendering a level of interest from me, which could potentially lead to a profitable partnership or, at the very least, an interesting discussion.

Just making a connection isn't enough. As a Flat World Navigator my job is not just to build bridges, but to maintain them as well. This means developing an authentic relationship and genuinely engaging with the people I'm connected to. This is where those Twitter lists or LinkedIn tags come in particularly handy.

Though for many people LinkedIn has replaced their need for a recruitment company, as it is an acknowledged job board/aggregator, I use it both as a place to 'brand build' and as a point of research when exploring potential interviewees and joint venture partners. To that end, whenever I make a new connection I add some tag references such as interview potential, innovation, investment analyst, knowledge management, journalist, PR, technology, etc. That way, if I'm exploring a topic or potential venture, it's much faster for me to drill down by filtering my search parameters through those keyword tags.

Location searches are also very useful. If I'm travelling to a certain city, for instance, I will do a search to find contacts in that area, let them know I'm coming through and suggest we meet face to face. This search criteria is also something I've used during times of natural disaster. An example would be when a tropical storm hit an area where I had many connections; using a keyword search I was able to send a personal message to each person with a certain radius of the storm, letting them know that I hoped they came through it unscathed. It's often little things like that which can cement a connection and, often, turn it into a deeper friendship.

A deeper connection was certainly what I aimed for in preparing to write both my books. I see my interviewing technique as more of 'having a chat' than anything else – but for that to be possible there needs to be a level of relaxed camaraderie which only comes through an authentic connection. I think that is one of the reasons participants in my book projects are as frank and forthright as they are.

I used sites such as Freelancer.com to connect with my transcribers who, to date, have been situated in Australia, Bosnia and Herzegovina, Egypt and the Philippines. Even the original artwork for the first book cover was sourced through an online competition I set up. The winning design was from an Iraqi artist based in Morocco at the time.

Any author will tell you that finishing the manuscript is really only half the battle as, regardless of who your publisher is, the marketing of your book is a full-time, hands-on initiative. I used Twitter and Tweet Jukebox (posting selected quotes from my interviewees), LinkedIn (being an active participant in relevant groups, posting short essays, and responding to the posts of others), and Pinterest and Facebook (creating specific pages for the book). I also created a page for the book on Google+ and did an author's reading via a global Google Hangout.

Perhaps not as obvious as a platform for business, Google+ is – with over 340 million users – if not ever-present and all-pervasive, certainly an entity with a finger in a great many business pies. Google is not just a search engine, it is a verb defined by *Oxford Dictionaries* (online) as, '[to] search for information about (someone or something) on the internet using the search engine Google.' Let's face it, if you can't be found on Google it will be much more difficult for any potential Endusers – be they clients, customers, partners or interested investors – to connect with you. If you don't have the connection, you won't get invited to the collaboration table.

And this leads me back to the 'long play', which in my case was not writing a book, but rather building a business focused on disruptive, innovative high-tech solutions. Just like any other business person, I needed to tell the story of our brand and our products – and I needed the right people to hear me tell it. In collaboration with my husband we created an Enhanced Edition/Online Ecosystem format for my first book (we will do the same for all our books). It brought together the tools, technologies, experience and expertise of our collaboration and exemplified the best that we had to offer. And that is what a Flat World Navigator does – using imagination, integrity, initiative and intuition they connect, collaborate and communicate. The fun is just an added bonus!

Actions with intent

There are some simple flat world navigational Ps and Qs, which can be easily accessed and actioned by all stakeholders:

Put tools in place that monitor and measure the effectiveness of your ROI with your stakeholders and Endusers.

Plan for communication that serves the needs of Endusers, including during times of crisis.

Quality engagement, education and entertainment will be effective in increasing your ROI.

To that end:

- Be yourself. Authenticity is more effective and engaging than anything else you can bring to a relationship.
- Be both resilient and reliable.
- Engage in what personally interests you, not just where your professional interests lie.
- Return the visit. The more you learn about the visitors to your sites, posts and pages, the easier it will be to tune your messages to be relevant to their interests and passions. In any relationship, having something in common is a great place to start to build.
- Join in. If there are conversations or debates happening on other sites, pages or posts, 'dropping in' to engage in the conversation is going to be noticed and, likely, very appreciated. You can take this one step further and offer to be a guest contributor to a website or blog with high traffic and visibility.
- Showing that you have a sense of humour and humility – either as a brand or as an individual – is a great way to increase the bond between you and your Tribe of fans, followers and friends.
- Sharing something both informative and interesting may be one of the most effective ways to draw, and keep, visitors to your site. Just remember that what you share needn't – in fact shouldn't – be only about you and your business, product or service. Nobody likes to hang out with someone who only talks about themselves.
- Be gracious. Whenever possible say thank you if someone shares your own posting, article, etc – those two words speak volumes about you and your brand.

INTERVIEW An interview with a Flat World Navigator

Sandy Carter, *IBM General Manager, Cloud Ecosystems and Developers and a Social Business Evangelist*

Sandy Carter, IBM General Manager Cloud Ecosystem and Developers, is responsible for IBM's worldwide focus on building and expanding the Cloud ecosystem for ISVs, Entrepreneurs, Developers and Academics. Author of three books, including *Get Bold*, Sandy is a recognized leader in social business, receiving numerous awards such as: Forbes Global Top 40 Social Marketing Masters, 10 Most Powerful Women in Tech, Women of M2M for Internet of Things (IoT), CNN Women of the Channel, Top Nifty 50 Women in Technology, Top 50 Social Business Influencers, and Top 10 in Social Media. Sandy can be reached via Twitter at @sandy_carter, or via her blog socialbusinesssandy.com.

Sandy, can you give me an overview of how important collaboration and networking have been in your career to date?

When I got accepted to Harvard Business School everybody told me, 'Oh, the business school's great – the classes are great!' And it was, it was awesome. But what turned out to be the value point were the networks that I made. The learning did help obviously, but every five years we get back together and those connections have really helped over the years. The same is true as I've moved around and made social, physical connections – that networking has been phenomenal.

There's a lot of research on women leaders hitting a glass ceiling. And of the leaders who have become CEOs and really have made it, one of the things they prioritize above everything else is collaboration and networking. And I wish I had done more when I was younger because I think it matters so much.

As IBM's GM for Cloud Ecosystems and a Social Business Evangelist, you've taken networking to a whole new level. Looking at social business networks, has the ever-more empowered Enduser impacted the way you see business being done, and will be done in the future?

Absolutely. For instance, the other day I had customers who felt they'd run into a brick wall. They contacted me on Twitter and I got them help. They were so pleased, saying something like, 'Oh my gosh! This is the fastest help that we ever got!'

Recently we announced a lot of entrepreneurial initiatives around Millennials, whose levels of connection and collaboration are just phenomenal, especially through social networks. During a Millennial Day we held the other day, a lot of the attendees made clear that they react and respond to people who communicate like them, because that's how they feel comfortable. A lot of that communication is through text, of course, but it's also through all these social channels.

We asked them, 'If you had to change something in the way we are going to interact in the future, multi-generationally, what would it be?' They said: social is number one; number two is authenticity. You can't be social just to be social – just to be out there – it's got to be authentic. Third, they don't want to feel like part of a 'system'; they want to be recognized as individuals, not just associated with a big group.

Factoid

By 2017, social networks will reach over 2.5 billion people.

(Source: eMarketer, 2013)

In essence, from birth they've been treated as individuals. As such, I'd suggest that businesses and, in a lot of respects, organizations have to catch up to them with regards to an awareness of personal branding. You've mentioned interacting multi-generationally, which can be challenging. Millennials, GenY, Baby Boomers, academics, corporates, techies, sales people and creatives – they all have their own languages, their own taxonomies, which has the potential to lead to misunderstandings.

A fair instance of this conceivable confusion due to discordant definitions is over the word 'finished'. It can mean very different things to very different people, depending on where they are in the workflow of a project. What the technologist thinks is finished can look very different to a person who is, perhaps, in sales and wanting to demo a completed product rather than the prototype produced by the IT department – grand as that prototype might be. How do you break through those communication challenges?

That's one of the things we talked about with the Millennial work group. We actually decided to publish a glossary of terms that millennials use, how they use them and how they differ from other terms. Because I want to be more effective at communicating, I thought that was an interesting concept, and equally interesting was that they actually wanted to educate other generations about these terms. I saw this also working well with entrepreneurs who, for instance, might say, 'We talk about these five things and we need everyone else to understand us.' So, we're in the process of publishing a dictionary to help them as well.

That said, I think there are some things that go across communication boundaries, things like authenticity. That's something that goes beyond the boundaries, as does listening.

Listening is such a powerful skill; if you're not really listening then it really doesn't matter what else you're doing. There are things that cross the boundaries, regardless of whether you're using social tools, or just dealing with people.

I think intention is another one of those things, as is involvement, which I think works with your premise – let's say we should be authentically involved. People want to be heard, they want to communicate and authentic involvement may possibly make some of those connections easier to make and maintain.

I'd absolutely say that!

I also think that technology will also change a bit to make things easier. If you think about it, right now there are so many tools out there. Do I talk to you on Pinterest, Google+ or LinkedIn? Where do I go? There are too many social tools out there. I think there's going to be a consolidation or some sort of dashboard where you can see everything at once, something that helps you to really communicate well.

Speaking of communicating 'well', do you have a way to measure the effectiveness of the relationships you have?

There are multiple ways to measure relationships. One of the biggest is: how do you form the relationship, how does the relationship start? How do you become aware of that person?

Look at you and I, and how we met [I reached out to Sandy on LinkedIn]. There's another young woman I just happened to bump into on the train. She and I have now become colleagues, working for two different companies, for seven years. How do those things happen; how do you 'just run into' these people. I think part of it is planning. Where do you go? Where do you invest your time?

I think the second thing is engagement. If I was dealing with a website, I would be looking at how many people fall off – if they come to the website once and never come back. How well do you stay engaged and do you do that 'purposefully' – on purpose – or does it just happen?

And then there's the third piece of the relationship, which is about convergence. I was talking to a group of women entrepreneurs recently and I found that, at events, women are highly engaged but they really don't do well on convergence. By that I mean that they don't take that relationship and monetize it in some way. If you're a small business owner you have to be able to monetize. I think a lot of women feel that that's kind of a 'dirty' part of business and they don't want to do it. But it is an interesting metric of the business relationship.

I'm not talking about a relationship being transactional, but looking at transactions as part of a continuous relationship. Sometimes I'm going to take time out for you, and then you're going to do something nice for me and it's going to go on – that is what a relationship is about. Take my husband and me: I go to football games with him; I don't want to be at the football game but I do it for him. Then he'll go to ballet with me. That's what it is; it's about a give and a take. That's a transactional thought... a longer-term transactional thought. I think that more people would become comfortable with it if it were explained in those terms.

Absolutely! And, might I add, very connected to my conviction that the chasm between our professional and personal relationships is shrinking or at least how we approach those relationships is shrinking. In that, it's no longer necessary to look at the situation from an 'I'm going to go out there and win one for the team' perspective. Rather, it's now more about getting to know the people you are going to do business with and discovering what adventures and treasures you might explore and share together.

I'm going to add something to that. In the United States we've got this show called *Shark Tank*, which is currently the number one-watched family show. *Dragon's Den* is at the top of the charts in the UK. [*Shark Tank* and *Dragon's Den* are television programmes based around the premise that promising entrepreneurs pitch their ideas to industry-specialized investors – the 'sharks' and 'dragons'. They do so in the hope that they will receive the funding and expertise necessary to turn their ambitions into business success.]

The reason I bring that up is that there is this rebirth of entrepreneurism and I believe that entrepreneurs have really shrunk this gap between personal and professional relationships. They do it every second of their lives. What's happening with entrepreneurs is changing the value of collaboration and changing the way that people capitalize on their relationships.

FWN Keys from Sandy Carter

- Social is number one; number two is authenticity. You can't be social just to be social – just to be out there – it's got to be authentic.

- Listening is such a powerful skill; if you're not really listening then it really doesn't matter what else you're doing.

- Look at transactions as part of a continuous relationship.

In conclusion

In this chapter a variety of the actions and techniques, planning and performance enhancers that empower Flat World Navigators are outlined. The overarching importance of flat world navigational skills to the success of strategic cooperative and collaborative initiatives in the DACE is highlighted. Further to this, we have explored the competitive advantages and increased equity delivered to an organization that empowers their Flat World Navigators to authentically address and administer to Enduser expectations, while remaining an honest avatar for brand strategy.

Having been included in the inaugural 'LinkedIn Power Profiles – Australia' list of 2012, I have detailed my own methods for building and maintaining a global network of international thought leaders based on authentic communication and mutual respect. I have also elaborated on how, in building my personal and professional brand, I built a high-touch, low-friction ecosystem for those with shared interests and an openness to the exploration of synergistic, collaborative, win-win potential partnerships and joint ventures.

The next chapter, 'The foundations of the DACE (Digital, Attention and Collaboration Economies)', probes how traditional business paradigms are under threat from new challenges and competitors. It takes an in-depth look at the change being brought about by Cloud offerings and how that, along with other aspects of the Digital Economy, is empowering small- to medium-size enterprise (SME) business owners around the world. This chapter underlines the fact that, through the judicious utilization of Flat World Navigators and flat world navigational skills, an organization can efficiently and effectively leverage and profit from social channels connected to an internationally engaged and digitally distributed marketplace of business in the flat world.

The foundations of the DACE (Digital, Attention and Collaboration Economies)

02

Advantage Attention
Authentic Business Change
Collaboration Communicate Connect
DACE Digital Economy Enduser Flat World
Navigator Global Network Relationship Strategy
Success Technology Win-Win **Advocate Billion Corporate
Data Events Executives Industry Media Mentor Online
Services Social Support Tools University**

Featuring

Marc Dufraisse (AutentiCoach Partners),
Edmund Komar (People Innovation Partners),
Amelia Loye (engage2), Saundra Pelletier (Evofem, Inc and
WomanCare Global) and Wendy Simpson (WENGEO Group)

When exploring the circumstances and conditions that are the foundations of the global DACE (Digital, Attention and Collaboration Economies) there are certain things which must be taken as 'given'. For those individuals and institutions who grasp the contingencies that the DACE presents, opportunities abound. For those who do not, one need only look at the current situation of high unemployment and personal debt, which is married to a lowering of middle-class economic power, to have a fairly clear guide as to what awaits them.

For instance, there is no question that globalization and innovative tools and technologies have changed how effective business is carried out, and how business models and goals are successfully realized. Additionally, as quickly as change has happened in the last five years, the rate of transformation is set to increase – in some cases exponentially! – in the next few years. Prescribed 'profit patterns' have been realigned and the business 'playing field' levelled to such a degree that the traditional borders, boundaries and benefits taken for granted in the 'business as usual' paradigm are now under threat from unparalleled levels of new entrants, challenges, change and upheaval.

> There is a cultural change happening in companies; they're evolving and becoming more complex. They're looking to create a culture that focuses on cross-functional, collaborative teams that are capable of addressing and developing their market. They're working on getting over their fixation on having everything pre-established. It's a fixation that clashes with the culture of empowerment and collaboration because, to a certain extent, you have to get out of people's way and create a culture where you allow them to 'make and change' the products, services and approaches to business.
>
> Marc Dufraisse, Founder AutentiCoach Partners

A case in point is the global hospitality industry. This arena has been affected to such a degree that the archetypical business models and patterns that long underpinned its previously unassailable incumbents have been cut to pieces. Upstart startups and ever-more vocal and demanding Endusers, both of which having taken full advantage of the DACE, are rushing in and flooding the once quite stable playing field.

Keeping up is easier than catching up

One need only look at a company such as Airbnb – the US-based online hub connecting private citizens with a bed, bedroom or entire property to rent, with the potential paying public – to see the effect that a garage startup can have if it hits the sweet spot of being the right product at the right time. The fact that it is easily accessed, extremely economical and, most importantly, has company cheerleaders and Flat World Navigators to 'spread the word' is part and parcel of its ability to take a significant slice of the Attention Economy.

Additionally, in less than ten years Airbnb has taken a healthy bite out of the hotel industry's profitability pie. In 2012 it reportedly swallowed approximately US$250 million from the prodigiously lucrative and persistently fought-over Parisian hotel market. A year later there were more than 10 million visitors staying in one of their listed rental accommodations worldwide and by the end of 2014 the company was valued by industry sources at US$13 billion – and began 2015 with rumours abounding of their imminent IPO listing.

Hotels and restaurants are notoriously labour-intensive industries, requiring both high levels of bricks and mortar, staffing, and incidental regulatory and ancillary costs to run effectively. So imagine the effect of the DACE on those businesses that do not need such a level of input prior to an output of anything resembling a profit. This is particularly the case if they are able to engage in the enhanced savings engendered by making use of the tools and technologies ever-more easily accessed via the Cloud. It is not a question of 'if' your company should take advantage of the Cloud, it is a fact that if you don't your competitors will take full advantage of you and your error in judgement.

According to IDC, the global spend on IT Cloud services was nearly US$4.5 billion in 2013. Their CloudTrack Survey (McGrath and Mahowald, 2013), showed that more than 80 per cent of companies in the United States were already taking advantage of Cloud-based services and, of those surveyed, 46 per cent expected nearly half of their IT services to be delivered via the Cloud by 2016. The Cloud services sector is growing to such an extent it is expected that, by 2017, North American businesses alone will be spending nearly US$107 billion on IT services delivered via the Cloud.

Consumers are increasingly taking advantage of the optimized services and selection made available to them online. Statistics compiled by Statista – The Statistics Portal, reveal that international B2C e-commerce sales were valued at over US$1.2 trillion in 2013. The number of international internet users purchasing products online has grown steadily – in 2011 there was a digital buyer penetration of 38 per cent; this is expected to rise to over 47 per cent by 2018. Businesses that either ignore or only engage here halfheartedly will be relegated to a sideline that will soon cease to be relevant on any meaningful scale. No one is suggesting that 'bricks and mortar' will be completely replaced, but the move from 'bricks to clicks' is now entrenched and business models and strategies must evolve to match this.

Flat World Navigators share their stories

Edmund Komar, *Owner and Managing Director at People Innovation Partners*

Before the social media age networking was already crucial to my professional success as I got all my jobs and promotions due to recommendations from my network. While I now build and strengthen my reputation by blogging and posting throughout a set of social media channels – and this blogging does result in consulting and coaching assignments – recommendations still fuel the largest share of my business.

As Managing Director of People Innovation Partners I ensure that we use the business model canvas to support companies with traditional cultures that have to reinvent their business models but lack the skills to do so. An industry sector where this is illustrated is the German energy market, which is facing a dramatic transformation due to the shift to renewable energy.

Our approach is to develop and inspire a critical mass of leaders and professionals with the skills to drive innovation and growth by collaboratively developing and reinventing business models. We use social media and collaboration platforms to support the building of communities and to strengthen the cohesion of these tribes. In some companies we intensify the community building by linking individual careers to the business transformation which, of course, leads to a totally different approach to talent development.

During the late 1990s I began to support change and transformation via large group events such as Open Space [Technology (OST)], Future Conferences and using the World Café methodology. Since 2009 we have increased transformation by combining digital and analog (personal) elements. We call this process and these events 'DigiLog'.

The 'DigiLog' design enables the dramatic acceleration of the change process and gets rid of the annoying admin part of interactive events. This year, for example, we had the opportunity to support the German Association for People Management (DGFP), along with more than 200 participants, as they started shaping the collaboration of tomorrow.

Size doesn't matter in the global Digital, Attention and Collaboration Economies (DACE)

The figures from Australia alone illustrate what a monumental shift has taken place and how that is encroaching on what was once considered the norm. The January 2014 ACMA report, 'Australian SMEs in the Digital Economy', notes that in one month more than 2.11 million adults (aged 18 or over) conducted at least one transaction – be it buying, selling or 'shopping' (which can include browsing) – online using their mobile phone. Visa released UMR Strategic Research findings in early 2015 (Visa/UMR, 2015), which noted that 70 per cent of Australians own a smart phone and more than half of them are prepared to use them to make purchases.

Consumers will compare, share, search and explore online and, occasionally, this will translate into a trip to the store. However, these trips are becoming less frequent as local and international delivery is simple to set up and online payment platforms are increasingly easy to use and trust as avenues upon which to do business. It could be said that this alone is an excellent example of the DACE in action – a variety of stakeholders involved in delivering superior value to the consumer.

Factoid

In his March 2015 speech to the nation, China's Premier Li Keqiang focused on encouraging private enterprise. This focus is reflected in regulatory changes that move towards minimizing bureaucratic red tape and lowering costs – changes which have led to a 68 per cent increase in new businesses and the creation of 10.4 million jobs in 2014.

As SMEs constitute over 99 per cent of the Australian business arena, any changes in the way they conduct business are to be taken note of by politicians and economists alike. The Australian Bureau of Statistics paper, 'Business Use of Information Technology', underlines this when it acknowledges that in one year alone, online business income in the country coming from the sale of goods and services increased by 25 per cent. Of course this trend is in no way limited to Australia or any one nation or type of organization – the DACE will affect us all.

When looking at the Digital Economy alone, October 2014 found international IT consultancy firm Gartner unequivocal in its statement that the Digital Economy will exceed US$3.9 trillion in 2015 – this is nearly a five per cent increase on the previous year and it is a trend that is unlikely to slacken in pace. This was underlined by their Senior VP, Peter Sondergaard, in his speech to a crowd of more than 8,500 IT leaders and CIOs attending a 2014 Gartner Symposium. 'Digital businesses will impact jobs in different ways', he said. 'By 2018, digital businesses will require 50 per cent fewer business process workers. However, by 2018 digital business will drive a 500 per cent boost in digital jobs.' Again, looking at Australia with its preponderance of SMEs, and referring to the ACMA report, of those

SMEs connected to the internet, 47 per cent are using some kind of cloud computing service.

Economies can change at an astounding rate. They rise and fall for a myriad of reasons and certainly technologies and the innovative business models they support are at the heart of many of the current changes we see either occurring or, at the very least, on the horizon.

One offshoot of the Digital Economy is the 'Maker Movement', the technologically based DIY culture which is defined by Techopedia as 'a trend in which individuals or groups of individuals create and market products that are recreated and assembled using unused, discarded or broken electronic, plastic, silicon or virtually any raw material and/or product from a computer-related device.' (Janssen, nd).

This nod to computer-related devices underscores the fact that, at the heart of the Maker Movement is 3D printing, aka additive manufacturing. Through the process of creating a three-dimensional object by building layer-upon-layer of materials – be it plastic, metal, silicate or bio based – almost anything can be built… and I do mean anything; from toys to tools, models to meat, cups to clothes, living spaces to limbs. The technology is even being implemented in an innovative surgical procedure aimed at creating a nose for an Irish child born without one. Amazon is exploring the potential of furnishing trucks with 3D printers so that products could be created on demand and delivered to an ever-more demanding and increasingly impatient consumer.

As I outlined in *Innovation: How innovators think, act and change our world*, 3D printing has the capacity to:

> lower the cost of living as the price of certain items falls dramatically; but just as surely it will put swathes of skilled and semi-skilled workers out of work. The unskilled labouring jobs, which have been sent offshore, will have less relevance in 3D-adjusted economies. The economy surrounding 3D printing is likely to be more skilled rather than less – which leads to a need for more education, more apprenticeships, more training, all of which flow into and through the knowledge-based GDE.* The potential is there to shift the trade balance between East and West, but also between the Majority World and the rest of the world as 3D printing enables and empowers local control and diversity.
>
> (*GDE is referring to the Global Digital Economy)

The Majority World will have a major impact

The Majority World is so designated due to it being where the majority of the world lives and, increasingly, where the majority of the consumers within the global DACE reside. This is particularly important as 5 billion of these potential consumers – and possible competitors – now have, or will soon have, access to the online arena via a smart phone or 'dumb phones' (which cost less than US$10). The Digital Economy strikes again!

Obviously technology is not just enabling the Digital Economy, but also the economies of Collaboration and Attention. It may be that, in some form or another, we are naturally suited to some semblance of a Collaborative Economy – would we have survived as a species through the environmental calamities that have struck throughout history if we did not work together for the common good?

But, perhaps that is a wee bit too esoteric. Instead, let's take a look at something as comfortably current as carpooling – that is certainly an illustration of collaboration and working within a Collaborative Economy to save money, time or resources. Regardless of their waxing and waning popularity (and legality), it is arguable that Uber cars and others like them – those vehicles driven by private citizens that you can order online and track the progress of your requested ride – are a natural progression of the industry. Equally, aren't car sharing firms such as GoGet an expected evolution of leasing or purchasing a vehicle that may be seldom used outside of personal peak hours?

The scope of change in this 'Business Big Bang' is unparalleled as its effects, to some extent, are being felt in every nation and socio-economic tier. These forces are neither good nor evil, they just ARE; they are unstoppable and unceasing, and it is how you accept and adapt to them that will see you as either having embraced a Golden Age of Opportunity or wailing over what might have been – much of the music industry can be seen (or heard) as a simple example of the latter.

Factoid

Payment platforms are getting personal. In November 2014 Facepay was launched in Singapore. This platform needs no cards, cash or pin numbers; instead it enables payments through hand and face scans.

Clearly, as illustrated by the effect such companies as Airbnb have had on the hospitality industry, ignoring this situation and hoping that it is either a 'storm in a tea cup' or a temporary disturbance that can one can 'ride out' is beyond folly. This is a generational pivot point and from this 'Business Big Bang' there will be no reversion nor cessation. There is no avoiding the fundamental need to evolve and adapt. Turning a blind eye to this is, essentially, an acquiescence to an organization's eventual extinction. However, as much as this might all seem like bad news, it is important to remember that for every instance of misfortune, whatever its manifestation, there is also a potential 'pot of gold' for those who know where to dig – or better yet, what tool to provide to those working the mine.

Technical buzzwords such as Big Data, the Cloud, etc, are being spouted as panaceas for the professional world: take one pill and you will be okay. Unfortunately, this is not the case. Taking Big Data as an exemplar, it is a specious supposition to propose that a) this plethora of data is new; and b) having access to this data will solve the problems inherent in the ever-more connected global DACE with increasingly demanding Endusers.

Neither of these assumptions is correct. Yes, there is a soupçon of accuracy, in that without any data one is, essentially, working blind and the amount of data available to all and sundry has increased. BUT, businesses have had access to vast quantities of data for decades – and this data has never led to a guarantee of better business for any stakeholder: be they as owner, manager, employee, employer, client, consumer or colleague. For example, the telecommunications industry has had access to swathes of data for years, and yet it cannot be claimed that having this service has empowered the industry to provide useful, individually targeted Enduser products and services beyond the generic offerings that have always been put forward. No, data is not the differentiator; it is a tool, not a solution, and should be viewed and treated as such.

Use your tools widely and wisely

Speaking of tools, how many of the online tools, techs and sites listed in Table 2.1 are you taking advantage of? Each of them sets out to be a solution to one or a number of needs and challenges that individuals or organizations may face on any given day in the global DACE. Though not a comprehensive list, as there are additions to the service list coming online every day, it does reflect what is available, and possible, at the time of writing.

Further exploration as to how to best use tools to enhance the effectiveness of Flat World Navigation within the DACE can be found in Chapter 1, 'The tools and techniques of successful flat world navigation in practice'.

Certainly this is not the first time that tools and technologies, in one guise or another, have affected economies. One need only look at the effect of the Spinning Jenny on the textile industry or the Gutenberg Press on printing to see that this change has been happening for centuries. Additionally, accompanying these changes is often a phasing out of positions that were once taken for granted as only being able to be performed by people. Be honest, when was the last time you spoke to a long-distance operator or saw a filing clerk?

Such jobs have been annexed by tools and technologies which work faster, harder and longer – they do more, for less. Trying to win those positions back is, frankly, a mug's game. However, what can be done is to find the positions wherein human behaviour is the differentiator, not an algorithm. What must be found are the skill sets, the core capabilities and functions which cannot be done by tech, or at the very least not as well as when done via the 'human touch' – even if, at some point, that touch is made possible by technology. The place to differentiate will not be in the massive dump of Big Data, but rather by using the authentic, interpersonal skills inherent in the role of Flat World Navigator.

TABLE 2.1 Online tools, tech and sites for flat world navigation

Business, employment and service networking	Business/ enterprise messaging	Commerce/ retail	Finance and payment	Collaboration platforms and infrastructure	Cloud infrastructure	Influence measurement and tracking
• DesignCrowd	• Chatter	• Airbnb	• Bitcoin	• ConnekTek	• Amazon Web Services	• Jive Software
• Elance-oDesk (now Upwork)	• Slack	• Alibaba	• $Cashtags	• FlatWorld	• Google Cloud Platform	• Kred
• Freelancer	• Socialcast	• Amazon	• Paypal	• Google Apps	• HP SmartGrid	• Klout
• Guru	• Yammer	• Business on Messenger	• Paym	• Huddle	• IBM SmartCloud	• PeerIndex
• LinkedIn		• Craigslist	• Square Cash	• Lotus Connections	• Internet.org	• TweetLevel
• Monster		• eBay		• MindTouch	• Microsoft Azure	• Twitalyzer
• 99designs		• Etsy		• Salesforce	• Open Text	
• 1-Page		• Groupon		• SharePoint	• Oracle Enterprise Cloud Infrastructure	
• Plaxo		• KickStarter		• WebEx	• Rackspace	
• SoapBox Viral		• Livingsocial		• Zoho Apps		
• Sortlist		• Zaarly				
• Taskrabbit						
• Xing						

Continues overleaf

TABLE 2.1 continued

Attention and communication	Social, chat, curation and forums	Content upload/sharing	Blogging platforms	Search, research and crowd-sourced Q&A	Events	Bookmarks/ site savers
• Hootsuite	• Aol	• Box	• Blog.com	• AllExperts	• Eventbrite	• Evernote
• Tweet Jukebox	• APP.NET	• .docstoc	• Blogger	• Answer.com	• Meetup	• Instapaper
• Twitter	• Bebo	• Dropbox	• Medium	• Ask	• Paperless Post	• Pocket
• Tweetdeck	• Facebook	• Flickr	• Penzu	• BuzzFeed		
	• Facebook Messenger	• Instagram	• Tumblr	• Digg		
	• Feedly	• Picasa	• TypePad	• Google		
	• 4chan	• Prezi	• Webs	• Google Public Data Explorer		
	• Google+	• Scribd	• Weebly	• Mahalo		
	• Hi5	• Shutterfly	• Wix	• Newsvine		
	• Linqia	• Slideshare	• wordpress	• Quora		
	• Myspace	• Uberflip		• Reddit		
	• Paper.li	• YouTube		• Storify		
	• Pearltrees			• Storyful		
	• Pinterest			• StumbleUpon		
	• Pulse			• WikiAnswers		
	• RebelMouse			• Wikia		
	• Scoop.it!			• Wikipedia		
	• Yammer			• Yahoo!Answers		

I am a huge advocate for building personal relationships to help with professional growth and I teach that to the people who work with me and the people I mentor. It's not just a tactic – it's a necessity. At the early stages of my career, I sometimes felt I should play down what might be seen as more emotional traits and focus on more technical or aggressive approaches. I quickly realized that was a bad strategy. Intuition, instinct, reading situations and recognizing when to push and when to pull back are crucial business skills.

Saundra Pelletier, CEO at Evofem, Inc and
CEO at Woman Care Global

This is not news to companies such as the social networking startup Nextdoor, who raised US$100 million in venture capital for its 'neighbourhood-based' private environment. The company, recently valued at over US$1.1 billion, uses its ecosystem – consider it an online local message board – to bring community members together to share 'news and views'. Already embedded in over 53,000 neighbourhoods, Nextdoor also collaborates with 650 local government agencies to send out alerts regarding emergencies, service provisions, crime, etc. Being connected to technology is different to being connected by technology. As such, it's time that the phrase 'it's not what you know, but who you know' became a certain truism.

Technology already owns the 'what': the data. However, it is those who master the 'who' of relationships – the more genuine they are the better – who will come to the fore in the flat world of the global DACE.

Flat World Navigators share their stories

Amelia Loye, *engage2 Engagement Specialist and Social Scientist*

Essentially, my business is creating opportunities for government to work with a community and all its relevant stakeholders. Often my work involves helping the community understand the issues and problems the government has to address and then inviting the community and its stakeholders to have a role in the decision-making process and solution design. Additionally, a lot of the stakeholders need to be actively involved in the implementation of the solutions.

By helping government to tell their 'story' we look to educate, inform and inspire action in the community and, perhaps, have people feel more interested in contributing to their community. For me, democracy is about people taking on a role in a community. It's not just about participation, it's about informed participation. If we are going to solve the problems facing the world we need to understand them and participate in decision making and do what we can to help address them.

One of the techniques we use for listening is social media monitoring. Listening around a topic could be as simple as sentiment monitoring online and understanding the language the community is using around a particular topic. This can then help you identify interested parties, and reach out to them. A perfect example is urban planning. The community may talk about high-rise apartments, population growth, and where they want their families to live. They don't talk about urban renewal, revitalization, or transformation of communities – that's not their language. They talk about what they see as the impact on them. Listening helps in finding a way to communicate complex things in the language of the people you are trying to reach, and connect with them in the ways they want to be engaged.

My network is international and my business model is a network of sub-contractors who provide niche and complimentary services to me. That includes professionals who can provide digital, social media, information, communication, architecture and management services. Technology allows us to work in our relative jurisdictions, share lessons and work collaboratively on strategies, tools and materials.

For instance, a former colleague from Canada, now designing information architecture for governmental organizations out of Geneva, reviews my work with Government agencies here in Australia. I have someone helping with social media monitoring in Vancouver – which means I can provide 24-hour community and issues management support to my clients – a stay-at-home mum in

Brisbane providing writing and editing support and an Open Government and mapping expert from New Zealand who provides strategic input into my work as required.

I have a broad network around the world that I can call on as required. Through my work overseas and travel to visit former colleagues and attend events I meet people whose passions and skills complement mine, and whose approach to business aligns with the way I work. I'll then strategically build that relationship, often through a combination of face-to-face or online engagement and the use of collaborative tools to share and build resources.

Being open to flexible work hours and enabling people to work from home means they can stay at home, work around time with their families, get regular contact with others in their industry and contribute to our collective productivity. The non-exclusive nature of this arrangement means we can all work across organizations and jurisdictions, learn from these experiences, keeping our ideas fresh and building on our positions in our respective fields. It doesn't suit everyone, but for those who do value it, this approach leverages international expertise to bring both innovative and tested solutions to our clients' and each other's work.

I maintain responsibility for local business development, and my team expect the rates that justify them taking the risk of working sporadically. The older business model, with permanent employees, might provide security, but with the risk of infrequent work comes great opportunity. It gives them the freedom to work from home and to work around the hours that suit them and their family, and they can work from anywhere in the world.

The fact that these things are part of my business model is, I have no doubt, one of the reasons I'm able to attract amazing talent from across the globe for my clients. The situation is really responsive and organizations get immediate access to real talent.

This is changing the global workforce. Self-autonomous working and innovative tools are critical to us having constructive, productive, collaborative professional relationships.

These Flat World Navigators (FWNs) are the key differentiators who, using the tools and technologies of the global DACE, will lead an idea, a product or service to success in those arenas. For, particularly in these economies, it is the nuanced connections and affiliations constructed by building the bridges of authentic networks and relationships, which will engage and empower customers, clients, colleagues, co-workers, collaborators and partners.

Actions with intent

Using the list of tools and technologies included in the table above, choose at least three of them to explore, noting down how they could be brought to use in your organization.

Find those people within your organization who are most enthusiastic about working with new tools and empower them to research, explore and experiment to create a portfolio of tools.

From your portfolio of tools determine which tools are best suited for use in specific situations and for particular function(s).

Decide whether, at some point in your planning or implementation, you want to look for professional advice to create a strategic plan to map your flat world navigational journey to get the most effective use of your tools.

To stay on course in your FWN journey ensure that you remain focused on insight that can be implemented. Therefore at least once a week drill down through any Big Data to determine the three things of most importance or interest within – and act on those.

INTERVIEW   An interview with a Flat World Navigator

Wendy Simpson, *Chairman, Wengeo Group*

Wendy Simpson is the Chairman of Wengeo Group, an innovative diversified investment group, and was the founding Chairman of Springboard Enterprises Australia, Australia's only internationally focused business accelerator for women entrepreneurs seeking investment capital. Previously Senior Vice President of Alcatel Asia Pacific, Wendy was responsible for a budget of €4.2 billion, the sale of major mobile and broadband services to 17 countries and was part of the negotiating team bringing the internet to China. In 2013 Wendy joined the World Vision Australia Board, received the Medal of the Order of Australia for service to the community and, on International Women's Day, was inducted into the Australian Businesswomen's Hall of Fame and listed in the Australian Financial Review's '100 Women of Influence'.

If we take as a given the importance of connecting and collaborating when it comes to setting strategy in the corporate world then how would you suggest an individual 'manages up' and guides their leaders, their executives to recognize the importance of these key core capabilities?

The first thing I'd suggest is to try to understand what it's like to be a very senior executive. I work with a number of young people, applicants for the Monash Foundation, the premium scholarship award in Australia. My observation is that one of the differences between the applicants who win and those who are not granted a scholarship is: if you're a university student and the Dean or Vice Chancellor of your faculty doesn't know you, that should be a wake-up call to you.

It's misguided to think that if you go to university, sit in your lectures, diligently work on your assignments and try to be on top of the class, that people will notice you. A wise student also understands what it's like to be the Dean or Vice Chancellor. As University leaders, they most likely signed up because they thought they could actually help educate young people; instead often they're stuck in boring meetings day in and day out. I tell students to take their destiny into their own hands. Make an appointment to meet your faculty Dean or Vice Chancellor and say, 'this is who I am and I want to talk about what I think would be great for the university.'

Managing up needs to start at university. I believe we should encourage young people and tell them that if they've got an urge to be a nation shaper, to be someone who influences other influencers, they shouldn't wait until they've got a job. Tell them to walk around their university with their eyes open. Don't just sit in your classes or study cubicle doing your assignments, look around at the university and think about some global or industry trends and issues that you, a student, would like to put before the Dean or Vice Chancellor. Then make an appointment.

Once young people get used to that approach, then the idea of looking around a corporation or an industry with the same intent becomes much easier. Every group of talented senior executives is – or should be – interested in having observations or 'fresh eyes' on a subject. If you're articulate and respectful, fresh eyes are one of the most important and valuable skill sets younger employees can offer to a corporation and the people they are seeking to influence.

Clarity is key then.

Cultural awareness makes collaboration easier and prevents misunderstandings.

I'll tell you a story about when Alcatel was setting up China as our Asia Pacific regional headquarters in 2000. We transferred our recruited telecom executives from all around the world. China became the global centre of 3G and 4G mobile research, including hosting a visitors' centre in Shanghai. Some New Zealand-based customers, over a five-month period, planned a comprehensive visit to Shanghai. At the last minute their plans changed and they weren't able to come.

In addition to the note she received from the New Zealand customers, one of our Alcatel New Zealand representatives wrote what she thought was a highly empathetic note to our Chinese colleague in charge of the visitors' centre. In it she said that 'it was a shame that, after so much planning, the customers now couldn't come to Shanghai.' Our Chinese colleague's sharp response was to say that she'd never been more insulted in all of her life. 'I haven't brought shame to our company or your customers – I have never been so insulted! How dare you say it was a shame!' It's at times like those that you realize even the smallest words can make all the difference. The notion of shame in the Chinese culture is very sensitive.

Words can be highly emotive!

Culturally laden words are not just relevant to intercultural issues, they are important in corporate life, especially when you've got major shifts happening in a corporation. I remember when I was asked to lead the operational aspects of the largest merger between two insurance companies in Australia. We thought it would be helpful to identify the best elements of both companies' corporate cultures as part of the merger. I remember interviewing one very senior executive from the acquiring company; he was gritting his teeth and shouting, 'We don't have any culture here, we're simply an insurance company so there's no need to talk about it anymore!' So we found different ways to talk about it. 'The way we do things around here' was the easiest phrase to use when explaining culture to some of our strait-laced insurance executives!

I do have a few battle scars from trying to lead change too strongly from the front. Therefore I have some advice which, while certainly helpful for most aspects of life, is particularly useful for entrepreneurs, because we are very driven, results-oriented people. One of the ways I have found that can strengthen collaboration is to tell stories and check body language. Often we are tempted to lead from the front and 'just get on with it'. We think that taking time to tell stories is wasting time, being non-productive. I have now come to the conclusion it's an essential way to gauge who is, for instance, like-minded or not. If I don't sit with people and exchange stories about why we're all doing this 'thing' together, I may find that I've been assuming everyone is there because they are like-minded – and they may not be.

I've been caught a few times thinking we were all equally passionate about empowering entrepreneurs or transforming an industry and then, later, finding out that there were those in the group who weren't going to be good fellow travellers on the journey. So yes, when working collaboratively sharing stories is fundamental – and it really helps to be a good storyteller.

> **FWN Keys from Wendy Simpson**
>
> - Try to understand what it's like to be a very senior executive.
>
> - If you're articulate and respectful, fresh eyes are one of the most important and valuable skill sets younger employees can offer to a corporation and the people they are seeking to influence.
>
> - When working collaboratively sharing stories is fundamental, so work to tell your story well.

In conclusion

Attention has been given in this chapter to the fundamental changes within business environments made manifest by the rapid acceleration of engagement in the DACE as well as the culture change towards collaboration happening in companies worldwide. We contemplated the economic effects of Cloud-based services; how the thoughtful use of tools and effective actions based on insight rather than algorithms can change Big Data into Smart Data; and the DACE's rapid rise of influence as it empowers the Majority World.

A variety of tools were listed while acknowledging that no tool can replace human empathy and acumen. As such, Flat World Navigators, whose core capabilities involve making and maintaining authentic relationships with consumers, clients, colleagues and partners are both effective and efficient conduits to the rapidly changing, globally connected DACE.

The theme of effective engagement in the DACE is further explored in the next chapter, 'Demand and opportunity through business collaboration'. In this chapter scrutiny is brought to how knowledge assets (KA) are captured, valued, protected, shared and capitalized upon within a collaborative environment. We delve into the differences between business toys and tools – noting why this difference is important when working with KA – and bring focus to those knowledge assets which gain greater value by being shared for mutual benefit.

The benefits of communication, connection and collaboration are examined, as are some best practice suggestions for boosting the effectiveness – both economical and otherwise – of these business-based behaviours. All of these are presented with the aim of accelerating your ability to take advantage of the assets made available by addressing collaboration through flat world navigation.

Demand and opportunity through business collaboration

03

Advantage Attention
Authentic Business Change
Collaboration Communicate Connect
DACE Digital Economy Enduser Flat World
Navigator Global Network Relationship Strategy
Success Technology Win-Win **Asset Benefit Capitalize**
Cost Customers Data Engage Information Media Perspectives
Software Solve Story Systems Teams

Featuring

Mary Adams (Smarter-Companies), Jeanine Esposito (Innovation Builders, Spark Consulting and Beechwood Arts & Innovation), David W Gray (Boardthing and Limini) and Deanne Weir (WeirAnderson.com)

Business collaboration is a cornucopia of offerings and opportunities with, unsurprisingly, more than a soupçon of potential pitfalls, particularly for those individuals and organizations who aren't selective in their strategies for collaboration. Of course, as with every economy, it is imperative to know what comprises one's assets and how those assets are valued, and can be capitalized upon. Unlike tangible assets, those that can be touched, stacked, boxed and baled, KA (Knowledge Assets) – aka Intellectual Property (IP) – are more abstract and conceptual in nature. That said, they are equally significant to a successful 'business bottom line' – if not more so.

Within this chapter you will gain an understanding of what Knowledge Assets are and how you can best capture, collaborate with and capitalize on them. We'll define some of the more common terms being bandied about in this arena, as well as explain the differences between the various 'toys' of social media and the business tools and technologies that empower you not just to capitalize and collaborate, but to maintain the sanctity of your KA while being assured of tracking both the provenance and development of your work and/or idea – an imperative when working collaboratively on a capitalization-focused project.

As mentioned throughout this work, there are clear competitive advantages to selectively sharing knowledge, be it of a particular service, product creation and/or distribution process. This is as applicable in the Business to Business (B2B) arena as it is for potential collaboration between academic, research and corporate stakeholders. Sharing experience, expertise as well as tangible and intangible assets such as customer base, branding and market position, enables all parties to gain efficiency and cost savings. In this instance, we will focus specifically on the KA deposited within people, processes and technologies.

> The big innovations are coming through situations where the contract designer meets the app designer meets the device designer. One person won't have all this knowledge in their heads so it's only through bringing these different experts together that you can create something powerful.

It's important to make clear, when you bring people together to work collaboratively, that they're not there for a team-building exercise or to play games – it's not some kind of Human Resources thing. They're there because there is a problem and collaboration is necessary to solve this problem.

It's true that knowledge transfer can be difficult, even within the same company if, for instance, you've got a designer, a finance person and a project manager with different points of view on what needs to be done. It's quite likely that they don't agree on what the problem is, let alone how to solve it. They've all built up their own pictures and perspectives.

It can be likened to the story of men in a dark room touching one part of an elephant and then thinking they can describe what it is. One man touches the trunk, another the tusk, a third touches the ear – each is sure they're right and the others are wrong but the fact of the matter is that none of them can picture the whole animal so their perspective is, at best, unclear. The challenge is to help them to see from each other's perspectives and create a powerful picture, an innovative solution, together.

David W Gray, Co-Founder of Boardthing,
Founder and CEO at Limini

The Collaboration Economy is about doing business through dynamic cooperation. However, it does encompass a new paradigm, a new way of thinking and working, wherein cooperation is as important (if not more so!) as competition. The inflexible, traditional, 'take no prisoners' and 'give no ground' archetypical self-interest business strategy has no place in the Collaboration Economy. Instead focus must shift to a shared interest in easing access to, and acquisition of, new markets, customers, clients and potential partners.

Flexibility is required in the Collaboration Economy if it is to be engaged in effectively. This can include a shared decision-making process, often reflected in a flat (or flatter) management system, rather than one that is rigidly hierarchical. It is likely to encompass distributed/ shared ownership of both ideas and other assets and, undoubtedly, will include an acknowledgement that ideas can come from anyone, anywhere and, as such, open the process of ideation to creation, making it much more fluid and 'democratic' in nature.

Definitions

Let's be clear, there are differences between the toys and tools available to those looking to engage in the Collaboration Economy. So let's 'bottom line' these definitions.

Knowledge Asset (KA)

A KA is proprietary in nature and generally centred around business, be it a process, product or service. More often than not it is actually that which is kept in people's heads rather than in systems, though it can also include knowledge stored in databases. In short, a Knowledge Asset is a piece or pieces of information, which 'you' know and someone else doesn't. It can be written down, stored electronically or kept in someone's 'head'. The value of the KA is generally linked to how it gives an individual or organization a competitive advantage in whatever arena they are operating in.

Toy

Though of great use for many of the key competencies necessary for successful flat world navigation, when it comes to protecting KA, social media tools are playthings that cannot compete in the arena of a business's protected, provenance-based, proprietary information. Requisite cornerstones of successful collaborations are trust, transparency and confidentiality, and high-value collaborative business relationships can only work when underpinned by technology that supports these key drivers. Virtually none of the commonly available social networking tools/companies are able to fulfil this critical criteria and, as such, should only be viewed as useful when you are happy to be communicating within a 'public' space.

Your data, posted/shared in these spaces, is being mined, so that profit can be made from it – data 'sharing' is ever more data-selling. This is the basic business model and raison d'être of most search and social media companies, be they old favourites or new startups. The models are, generally speaking, 'quid pro quo'. Ostensibly, they give you a product or service either for free or for a very modest cost;

however they then have access to, and free use of, your data. Your data is used, along with the data they harvest from all of their users, to resell to other data miners/gatherers or to create their own profitable insights. They are working to understand your customers better than you do and to then mobilize those insights in a massive way.

Whether one reads the Terms and Conditions or not, it's no secret that information placed on a public app is 'fair game' for data-trawling/mining. This is fine if you're happy to have your business's KA shared with 'all and sundry' and for your competitors to capitalize upon it to their heart's content. If not, remember that this information is your asset – be it about your products, processes, clients, relationships and/or collaborations – and all of the insight and associated benefits held within it is of great value, and should be treated as such.

Business tool

Business tools support the ongoing operations of your business, from accounting to editing of documents to logging on to your company from a hotel room etc. The Knowledge Assets of any company are generally stored in a number of systems, which include:

Customer Relationship Management (CRM)

CRM systems focus on maintaining your customers' information and assisting with managing your communication with them. They sometimes include sales force automation and data analytics. The KA in these systems is generally information regarding customers.

Knowledge Management System

Systems that attempt to capture, categorize and utilize information to benefit company performance. The KA within these systems are generally from large organizations that have separate departments which focus on capturing knowledge from the company and storing it in these systems.

Enterprise Software/Hardware

Enterprise software and hardware generally focuses on supporting extremely large and complex companies, ie organizations that comprise extensive numbers and/or a wide range of employees, customers, products/services and geographies. Your KA here is generally operational knowledge primarily concerned with delivering products and services to customers and managing/supporting services such as accounts receivable/payable.

Business Intelligence Software

In general, this is software that encompasses a number of analysis and analytical tools that can be applied to a company's data, with the aim of gaining greater insight into company performance and their customers' needs, etc.

Collaboration Platform

Historically, Collaboration Platforms have been defined as applications that are focused on small collaborations at the departmental level, which allow people to share ideas or work on documents together. The new frontier of collaboration, following the maturation of the DACE, entails a new definition. As such, one can think of Collaboration Platforms as technologies that can connect multiple individuals, departments, companies and countries.

Taxonomy

A way of classifying/categorizing information; the way libraries label books is an example of this in action. When applied in the context of business and business tools, it is a term which becomes important due to the importance of ensuring that, when collaborating, all parties are talking about the same things, ie a cup = a mug; a pitcher = a jug, etc.

Open source

This is software which has had its 'source code' (the instructions, designed by programmers, to direct a computer and/or program to execute a function) made freely available by its authors. Though it is, as it 'says on the label' free to use, it is not without cost in that there is usually little to no support available (ie a help desk) and they are generally controlled by programmers – hence they are focused on technical requirements which may not reflect business needs. It is important, when evaluating Open Source software with a view to using it for business collaboration, to ensure that it meets the same stringent security and privacy conditions as high-end enterprise software.

Dual licence

This is software that can be used as an Open Source project or, alternatively, there is a commercial licence available that treats the software as a normal, commercially available application. The upside of the Open Source licence is that it is free of charge. However, the downside is that, like most Open Source applications, it is geared towards programmers and highly technical people rather than Endusers. Therefore, if this is a solution you are evaluating, be aware that you will need to have a technical team on board.

Flat World Navigators share their stories

Mary Adams, *ICountant, Author, Speaker and Founder of Smarter-Companies*

My work in the past decade has been in close collaboration with a small global community I founded online. The focus has been intangible capital: the Knowledge Assets that dominate corporate valuations due to the shift from the industrial to the knowledge era. Smarter-Companies, which I founded in 2013, offers training and tools to those in the community who want to work at a deeper level and, today, we have partners on five continents.

Our focus at Smarter-Companies is on creating a body of knowledge and tools that helps knowledge workers and their managers realize their full collective potential. This is a very different approach to business – viewing the purpose of business to be not extraction of value (from people, from natural resources, from assets) but, rather, co-creation of value with stakeholders. Both are ultimately about creating profitable organizations, but the path to that profitability is very different. A co-creative company builds a more sustainable future for itself as well as for its community.

We have a lot of challenges in our community around differing vocabularies, but I try to avoid too many discussions about words. It's more important to have discussions about the ideas behind the vocabulary. It's more important to have discussions about the images that have an impact. So the ultimate goal is to bridge mental models.

One of the key mental models we all deal with is the view of property as a finite asset. It's key to the decision about control versus collaboration. What must I protect and what should I share? In this case, it's really important to think about the general economic principles of knowledge: value from knowledge comes from putting it to use to solve a problem.

Solving a problem requires building a whole ecosystem. You can't protect an ecosystem by keeping it secret. So, while there is a place for trade secrets and patents, this is a relatively small part of the story. Another key principle is abundance. Selling/sharing a tangible diminishes the amount/value of the tangible. Sharing knowledge rarely diminishes value; it almost always enhances it. An example is software, which increases in value the more users it has.

Most of our tools are available, for free, on our website. What would we gain by keeping them secret? The value that we can generate (and monetize) is through training people how to use the tools and creating platforms that automate the tools. That's when value gets created: when people are able to do something with the knowledge. We shouldn't charge for the knowledge but rather the services that make the knowledge easy to put to work.

The social aspects of today's technologies are revolutionary, sometimes literally. They empower people. This means that feedback is inevitable in today's world. What is not yet obvious is that it is also an incredible resource. In the not-so-distant future, enterprise resource systems will include a social component. Why is this?

The answer addresses the core of what we are doing at Smarter-Companies: experimenting with the social measurement of organizations. It's going to happen anyway so why not get ahead of it? And the more connected you are with your stakeholders, the greater the trust, engagement, sharing and collaboration. Knowledge and connection are the keys to innovation. These are not things most companies are set up to measure; there need to be shifts in what we measure and how we measure it. But, what should we measure?

Today, 80 per cent of the value of a business in the United States is intangible. These intangibles include all the different kinds of knowledge that have increased in volume and value with the advent of computing and social technologies. The four categories we focus on are purpose, people, partners and process/designs/data (each of which represents different kinds of knowledge in different states). The key is to create specific models of the core intangibles that make up the value creation ecosystem of an organization. Talking about people is too general. Talking about particular competencies or processes is specific and directly relevant to the organization.

How should we measure it? This is dictated by both the possibilities of today's social technologies and the power of direct feedback. It is possible to measure Knowledge Assets using financial and/or quantitative metrics. But counting people doesn't tell you what's important about them. More important are their competencies and experience.

These can be very hard to measure using 'objective' metrics. But they aren't that hard to measure if you ask stakeholders about their experience with your people and how they rate the level of a specific key competency. This kind of qualitative measurement is very powerful. This is why books are rated and reviewed by readers on Amazon, why hotels are rated and reviewed by guests on Expedia and TripAdvisor and it's ultimately how corporations will be rated and reviewed by their stakeholders. Businesses spend a lot of time identifying leading Key Performance Indicators (KPIs) that they measure internally. The frontier is to measure externally. If you think about it, stakeholder feedback is the ultimate leading indicator.

We will all benefit as knowledge comes to be better understood as an economic asset. Smarter-Companies works to try to create tools and training to advance this understanding. Knowledge has value when combined in a value creation ecosystem to solve a problem. This is the essence of collaboration.

> Our experience is that the creation of value is increased if people understand how their ecosystem works. What is the purpose, what are the competencies of the people involved, who are the partners needed to make it happen, what are the processes and systems that support them? The steps to understanding and optimizing this ecosystem are to model it, measure it (as a baseline and beyond), manage it for optimum performance, and deliver results that matter to your stakeholders.

Why collaborate?

It's a fair question, and one that has a fairly simple answer. In short, the Collaboration Economy is an effective way to save you and your company time and money in the highly contested race to win commercial success and provide customer and client satisfaction. This is true regardless of the size of the company, or the country for that matter, because there is no doubt that collaboration can affect the economy and budget of a nation as much as that of an organization.

Let's take Australia as an example of a nation becoming more aware of the importance of collaboration to the nation's GDP. According to Deloitte's 2014 'The Collaborative Economy' white paper (Farrall *et al*, 2014), companies that have positioned collaboration as a prioritized, key component of their business strategy are twice as likely to be profitable and outgrow their competition. These companies are, in fact, worth AUD\$49 billion a year to the nation's economy – and this is a nation with more than 99 per cent of its businesses classified as SMEs.

What's lucky for all those SMEs is that, in point of fact, collaboration is much more likely to save money than cost it. It's a fact that SMEs have smaller pockets than larger enterprises – of course they do. However, some quite simple strategies, tools and techniques are available to enable anyone to take advantage of the cumulative positive effects, such as time saving and improved product and process quality, brought about by collaboration and engagement in 'win-win' solutions rather than the traditional 'command and control' confrontation strategies. As referenced in the Deloitte white paper, small measures such as those that are affordable to SMEs have a '\$9.3 billion potential – bringing the Collaboration Economy [in Australia] to \$56 billion.'

Additionally, and as importantly, the effect of collaboration on the process of innovation cannot be overstated. It is with the cross-fertilization of ideas and knowledge, inherent in collaborative communications, that the potential of bringing a product from ideation to realization and commercial success is made exponentially more likely.

Connect and communicate

Collaboration is cemented by communication, therefore, ensuring ease of communication can only enhance the potential for positive collaboration. With that in mind the following are quite easy and, generally, inexpensive ways to boost collaborative potential:

- Add a common area where staff from different departments can congregate, socialize and easily exchange experience, expertise and ideas.

- Redesign the layout of office space to incorporate more 'open plan' areas or, if that is not possible, enact an 'Open Door' policy wherein office doors must remain open, and their occupants accessible, unless in the midst of a meeting, etc.

- Explore introducing a low-cost, highly effective Collaboration Platform which could become, in essence, a One Stop Shop for shared resources such as:

  - Commonly used documentation, ie standard IP agreements such as Easy Access IP, 'a selection of intellectual property that is made available to companies to develop for free, using a simplified one-page agreement. The objective is to reduce the traditional barriers of engagement and build trust to foster long-term relationships' (NSW Business Chambers, 2014).

- Best Practice experience when dealing with issues such as how to effectively and economically assess business tools and technologies, assistance in engaging in a marketplace and, of course, how to make best use of Flat World Navigators and/or flat world navigational skills.

- Access to mentors and advisors, either on a one-to-one basis, or in the form of a 'Mentor Information Bank' where accredited Mentors would commit to answering a certain number of questions per week/month, within their field of expertise, which have been posted on the Collaboration Platform.

- Provisioning and publishing online (live and recorded) forums, webinars and training seminars.

- As basic business education is an imperative – and available free of charge from a variety of MOOC (Massive Open Online Course) providers – online courses could be made available on this platform and include items such as small business planning, entrepreneurship and accounting for businesses.

- There is even the potential for it to be a resource for locating potential clients and Joint Venture partners.

Collaboration Platforms require a number of key components if they are to be ubiquitously used on the global stage that encompasses the DACE. They must be simple, secure, multilingual, vendor neutral, mobile, platform agnostic and, of course, inexpensive. These platforms, along with all the tools and technologies being made available in this arena, must be – in terms of cost and capability requirements – as accessible to the SMEs and 'Tier Nones' of the world, as they are to the Tier One companies and countries. It is only then that they can truly empower the collaboration between these groups, which is essential to both the global Digital and Collaboration Economies.

Jeanine Esposito, *President-CEO at Innovation Builders and Spark Consulting, and Executive Director at Beechwood Arts & Innovation*

I've spent the last 20 years leading teams in big companies – such as Pepsi, my first client – through the innovation process by facilitating a collaborative effort between diverse individuals in the corporate structure, to come up with a new product or service, develop it and launch it. I learned a lot about what makes good collaboration, true collaboration, versus working in teams.

I've run hundreds of collaborative sessions with executives at all levels, and every single session has one or two people who either don't want to be there or have decided they're not going to participate. They may even have decided, consciously or otherwise, to be disruptive. I've even seen one or two CEOs walk into the session and say, 'I'm going to sit in the back of the room and listen in while all of you come up with ideas.' (Of course I've always invited/insisted they join the team!)

The people who are reluctant to 'play' at first are actually my favourites! Because, in the end, they always end up being the best collaborators. Part of being a facilitator is giving them the creative confidence to participate and freeing them up to show them that it's safe for them to give up on the idea of having to find the 'answer' or be in control. That's really important.

There's a big difference between networking and collaborating. Networking with people is kind of like shopping for people that match with you in some way and marketing yourself. But that's not collaborating. When you collaborate, you need to put together teams that have a common purpose but diverse ways of thinking, diverse skills and knowledge and diverse experiences. It is proven that diverse teams working in a collaborative way are most successful.

For instance, Innovation Builders brings collaborative innovation and the design thinking process to schools, universities, libraries, cultural and community institutions. I'm advising a STEM high school [focused on Science, Technology, Engineering and Mathematics] on how to help students learn innovation by working on a real-life problem, and am encouraging them to build an internal collaborative, innovation culture so the students, teachers, parents, community organizations and businesses can come together to collaborate. Collaboration is one of the top, if not THE top skill required for the 21st century, so we have to teach it early and often!

Collaboration is a wonderful concept but the reality of it can be complicated. If you are, for instance, looking to solve a problem, the first thing to do is to get an authentic, real-world view of the people that are affected by that problem. Talk to them, find out what they need. You have to understand what they're trying to do, emotionally and functionally; you need to see what gets in their way and how they work around things. Let them tell you their story, shadow them, watch what they struggle with. By doing this, you're developing empathy with their experience and will be able to develop solutions they themselves could never think of.

The second step is taking the insights you've gained and working together collaboratively to come up with the 'solve-fors' that really matter. Once this is done, you use these 'solve-fors' to drive an ideation, using lots of perspectives and mind-stretching exercises. Again, collaboration is critical here.

Once the ideation is complete, the hard work comes with synthesizing the ideas to create themes and turning these into concepts. Because of the different perspectives in the room, there is a lot of back and forth discussion and iterative groupings.

Once the concepts have been developed, the collaborative teams enter into yet another iterative phase, prototyping. This phase adds even more perspectives and diverse individuals to the collaboration as we bring in the 'outside minds' of the people who will use whatever the solution eventually becomes. I developed the process to be a complete cycle so that a business or a brand will introduce their new product or service in such a way that it has the best chance of being accepted by the intended Endusers.

Added advantages

There is another advantage to the use of a Collaboration Platform, particularly for a company or organization. This pertains to the need to capture the valuable information and Knowledge Assets (KA) held in 'the heads' of employees – the information that is not written down or stored in files or databases. This is the knowledge these individuals have amassed through their experience working within the organization and with its idiosyncrasies – the people, the process etc. It is knowledge, which is of great strategic and commercial value and, until recently, impossible for 'the company' to capture and capitalize on in any effective way. By encouraging employees to communicate and collaborate on Collaboration Platforms one can ensure that their eventual departure – be it from a department, company or country – does not also equate to the Knowledge Asset walking out the door with them.

The issue of Collaboration Platforms could, and to my mind should be addressed at community, state/federal, national and supranational levels. An example of this type of resource is The BusinessUSA platform, jointly managed by the US Department of Commerce and the Small Business Administration. Launched in early 2012, its remit is to act as a 'One Stop Shop' for businesses and entrepreneurs, providing information about, and access to, the complete range of government services and resources available to them.

One could also look at Australia's Coles supermarket's 'win-win' exercise in positive collaboration with the SMEs within its ecosystem who were unable to afford the costly enterprise technology stack supporting its corporate structure. In 2014 Coles began using an online Collaboration Platform/portal, the RANGEme service, which empowered its SME partners to place their products in front of multiple buyers, in one place, simply and cost effectively – increasing the potential for bigger and better business outcomes for all stakeholders.

Collaboration gives you a much bigger and richer understanding of you, your customer, your partner(s) and the market. The data generated from this can be utilized to gain greater insight, productivity gains and feedback – all of which would be much more difficult, and expensive, to get if 'going it alone'.

We cannot leave the subject of Knowledge Assets (KA) and data ownership without acknowledging the importance of data security and provenance, particularly when it is possible that your business partner on one project could be your competitor on the next. As such, while trust and transparency are imperatives in collaboration, when working within a sensitive, multi-party, commercial arena, your KA should be shared selectively and securely – in short, only those that need to know, should know.

With that in mind, it is highly recommended that your collaborative work is done on a platform, or within an ecosystem/structure, that is capable of tracking the collaborative journey from ideation to realization. If this is done then the provenance of any Knowledge Assets can be easily controlled, accessed and audited, thus making any national and international regulatory compliance requirements easy to meet.

Preliminary research highlights the fact that collaborative approaches are generating significant benefits in terms of total costs and Enduser satisfaction. While there is slightly higher effort in establishing the collaboration connection in the beginning, the delivered benefits far outweigh the initial effort.

> From the results, it is clear that collaborative project delivery systems produce a more reliable cost outcome for public owners... An informal poll on a professional networking site also indicated that CMR [Collaborative Method] is considered more cost beneficial for public owners than other delivery systems.
>
> Kulkarni, Rybkowski and Smith (2012)

Collaborative characteristics

In no way does the Collaboration Economy remove the need, or desire, for competition within the business arena. However, we no longer live in a world where there is a definitive delineation between the two; rather, it is a hybrid, a sliding scale of the best of both of them, which imparts the greatest potential for success for all parties involved.

Collaboration is employees communicating and working together, building on each other's ideas to produce something new or do something differently. A collaborative organization unlocks the potential, capacity and knowledge of employees generating value and innovation and improving productivity in its workplace.

Farrall *et al* (2014)

Key characteristics of entrepreneurial organizations and individuals well suited to working collaboratively are, of course, quite varied. However, there are some core capabilities that make the process exponentially easier. Interestingly, these are quite similar to traits shared by many innovators. They include the promotion of:

- A determination to do better. Acquiescence to the status quo has no place here.

- A willingness to listen to, and learn from, others who have diverse areas of expertise and experience.

- An openness to communicating both with others in the same department and organization, but also to forming connections outside company walls.

- Cross-department/function transparency, which encourages an open sharing of strategically useful information that can be discussed at all levels of the organization.

- An understanding that flexibility is imperative – this is particularly true in instances when Endusers are involved in driving/directing product or process development, transformation and/or innovation.

The bottom line for profiting in the Collaboration Economy is shifting one's perspective from a 'winner take all' mindset to one which works within a collaborative, win-win strategic structure. This shift in strategy results in situations where all parties gain from taking advantage of the opportunities afforded by strategic business collaborations. These gains include added efficiencies, cost savings, and the retention of commercially valuable Knowledge Assets stored within people, processes, applications and technologies, which can be capitalized on through the use of simple, secure, auditable tools and tech.

Mustering the troops to 'trounce' others on the business playing field may once have been the route to realizing business successes, but those days have been eclipsed by the empathetic energy encompassed in a perspective that looks for all players to gain ground. Regardless of the Enduser role – colleague, customer or client – all must be viewed from the perspective of a partner who works to ensure that all wins are shared and celebrated.

Actions with intent

When looking to capitalize on knowledge assets by using collaboration tools and technologies, there are certain things to bear in mind. When determining your strategic deployment ask yourself:

Does the tool/tech work with your legacy/current systems? If not, there will be added costs, both fiscal and in the time it takes to install.

Is it simple to deploy and use? If not you will likely incur the added cost of an expensive expert who will need to be onsite to ensure the usability of the tool/tech.

Is it scalable? Success can come unexpectedly and extremely quickly. If you can't quickly scale to meet demand not only will you miss out on potential opportunities, you may also lose existing customers to competitors who can.

Is it secure? There must be a high level of data security; this is highly sensitive data and as such you must ensure that only the right people can see the right things at the right time. In large and multinational environments there will be auditors and regulators so the tool must be able to satisfy their compliance demands.

Can your partners and customers access this tool as easily as you can? If not, then there is no real benefit in the tool as it really is just 'business as usual', wherein applications are hidden behind your firewall and customers and potential partners can't easily access anything – and therefore will look elsewhere.

INTERVIEW   An interview with a Flat World Navigator

Deanne Weir, *Media entrepreneur, company director and philanthropist*

Media entrepreneur, company director and philanthropist Deanne Weir has more than 20 years' experience in media and communications. Deanne chairs the boards of four private companies, is Deputy Chair of Screen Australia and a board member of the International Women's Development Agency, Playwriting Australia and the Australian Women Donors Network. Deanne is a director of WeirAnderson.com, which is home to the WeirAnderson group of investments in media and communications companies. Deanne is also a director of the WeirAnderson Foundation, a Private Ancillary Fund with a particular emphasis on projects that will improve the lives of women and girls.

Let's jump in, Deanne, and start with your career in the media – both in publishing and production. How have social media, startups and the Cloud impacted the way you do business and how you envision you're going to do business in the future?

Let's start with We Magazines. In a sense, socially, it's all about the democratization of media and saying that it's not a one-way conversation any more, and it never needs to be again.

There are so many issues in the world today that people should be able to get engaged in, contribute to and have a conversation with – and we can now have those conversations globally. What we try to do with *Birdee* and *Hoopla* [We Magazines' first titles] is to have an experienced writer provide some news and then either seek an opinion about that news or have our whole community get together to debate and comment on the issue.

Some of the comments that we get on the *Hoopla* site are things like: 'Fabulous!', 'Really insightful!' etc, but more often than not we have detailed commentary and insight coming from our community that our writers then engage with. Interestingly, there's quite a difference between *Hoopla* and *Birdee*, whose community is mainly younger women. They're less likely to comment on the website but much more likely to engage via social media – starting a conversation on their own Facebook page or Twitter feed.

That takes them away from our site, but that's ok because it's driving the conversation and allowing people to engage with and debate on an issue in their way. Traditional media simply doesn't allow that. The Six O'Clock News says, 'Here I am telling you the news', and that's it.

When they leave your website, how does that affect how you measure customer satisfaction? How do you know if you're providing something to your Enduser that is enabling their growth, for instance?

That comes back to social media interaction by retweets, mentions and Facebook shares, etc.

Which puts you at the heart of the Attention Economy, where you seem to be fearless about empowering your Enduser. Is that something that has been integral throughout your work?

I grew up in a country town in Victoria [Australia] where we had access to two television stations and the local paper. Obviously we'd get the dailies but the country-city divide, in terms of access to information in a pre-internet, pre-satellite television world, was pretty phenomenal. It was a massive divide in terms of access to information and it always struck me that we needed to find a way to increase access.

That's why I was always so excited about internet and paid television. I think that everyone has a right to be able to access as much information as they choose to, to be as curious as they can be and not have that curiosity stopped by a lack of access to relevant information.

I was very blessed to have gone to a good high school and be with a bunch of friends who just happened to have an incredible thirst for knowledge. I guess that's what has driven me and, now, I also see this from a business perspective. A lot of the media that is allegedly targeting women has deemed that, if we are women, all we're interested in is recipes and celebrity gossip. There's nothing wrong with that stuff, but to assume that that's the only thing that women have an interest in is insulting. Unfortunately, that's how mainstream media has tended to approach women, which is why I think there's a great opportunity for We Magazines.

The way in which technology allows us to access stories and content in multiple ways also provides a great opportunity for Hoodlum, a production company that is all about storytelling. We love great stories but Hoodlum is also grabbing the opportunity that new technology provides to enhance your experience of the story. If we make an hour of television, many people may well be very happy to just sit back and enjoy their quality television. But we also find other ways to leverage the storytelling environment that we're creating. The technology that's available can give somebody a much broader experience, allowing them to engage with the characters or the issues within the story at a much deeper level.

Take a show we did for Channel 10, *Secrets and Lies*, a six-part drama/ murder mystery. The drama itself was very much on television and told from the perspective of the main character, Ben. He discovers a body and, very quickly, finds himself the chief suspect in this murder. It's a story about an 'everyman' whose world falls apart as he becomes a suspect and finds himself having to try to prove his innocence. That's the drama that you can experience through television.

What we did online was more akin to a police procedural that looked at the story from the perspective of the lead detective investigating the crime. There are all sorts of little vignettes, like the interrogations of all the relevant people of interest. You found out, through that process, little bits of information that added to your own understanding of what you were watching on television. It's another way of engaging with the characters and the story and another way to think about the television experience.

And another way to enhance the experience of your Enduser. However, it must require a commitment to, if not a passion for, a collaborative process!

That's certainly very true. In the world of *Hoopla* and *Birdee*, it's an effective collaboration between the editors of the websites, the writers who write the articles and the community, who then engage in and with that process. In fact, what a lot of the writers love about writing for us is that they get that engagement from the community. On the *Hoopla* site in particular, it's quite common for there to be an ongoing engagement between the writer of the article and the people who comment on it.

So, how do you balance this freeform engagement and the sharing of as much of the content as you do with valuing the Knowledge Assets of your organizations?

This is a tricky one because, obviously, these are all commercial businesses and it's very difficult to survive on advertising revenue alone. With We Magazines, and in *Hoopla* in particular, we've gone through a few different phases.

In the first phase we created a thing called the 'Friends of Hoopla'. We said to people, 'Look, we want to keep this readily available but we need to pay the bills and our writers.' Our mission is to provide new pathways that allow people to practise their craft. We think journalism is incredibly important and it deserves to be paid for but we also need to have a revenue model.

The initial focus was on advertising and saying to the Friends of Hoopla, 'If you are fans of great writing and you like our website, think about how much you spend on magazines in a week. Why don't you throw us five, ten or twenty dollars a month? Whatever you think you can.' It was on a pure voluntary basis, which was nice but not very reliable.

So then we decided to move to a straight subscription model. That created quite a lot of challenges in the social media world as people stopped sharing our stories. So then we implemented a new subscription model platform, which is used by the *New York Times*. It is a 'freemium' model, so you get three free stories and then you pay. That's been a lot better and we've got back the social media activity. We're getting a lot more tweets and Facebook shares, but of course you've got to pick the right topic because the Facebook algorithm changes every five minutes.

Factoid

- 76 per cent of journalists feel more pressure now to think about their story's potential to get shared on social platforms.

- 75 per cent of journalists use Twitter to build their own brand (and 86 per cent of them check Twitter several times per day).

- 82 per cent of journalists said incorporating an image is the #1 important ingredient for content shareability.

(Source: Rubel, 2015)

We're trying to find the right balance. It's a democratizing process; we want heavy sharing and we want people to be able to experience the content but, at the same time, we have to generate a sufficient financial return. I've got to tell you, it's bloody hard, but we will never move to a concept of not paying people for their content.

You also work bloody hard on initiatives which empower women and girls, particularly those who are entrepreneurially minded. Why is it so important to you to empower them?

Because we do not have gender equality in today's world and, apart from that, that's where my heart is. I believe every single human who is born on this planet should have the same opportunity, regardless of their gender, sexuality, their race, whatever – it's a human right issue. We're incredibly privileged, of course, sitting here in our western country with all of its infrastructure and wealth. But even in this country, today, women are still disadvantaged and discriminated against. My heart tells me it's wrong and my head also tells me that it's wrong, from a business perspective.

What rational business or rational society would want to limit opportunity for 50 per cent of their population – to hamper their ability to contribute to either making that business or that society a better place? People should have the opportunity to do and be what they want to be. It's about choice, that's what I'm focused on.

Which brings me neatly back to your focus on collaboration. It's a given that businesses will likely rely increasingly on collaboration as they are forced to 'do more with less'. It's an imperative to work together, using all the new tools and technologies at our fingertips, to share knowledge and work towards win-win strategies rather than the traditional command and control. As such, those Flat World Navigators who skilfully build and maintain authentic networks and collaborative Enduser ecosystems will be ever-more important to business strategy.

Absolutely! I'll never forget when I started a new role, this was in 2002, and I was in a meeting along with a senior, male colleague. He thought he'd give me some 'helpful' feedback afterwards because it was commercial negotiation with someone that we were likely to have a long-term relationship with.

I took the lead on the negotiation and focused on collaboration, cooperation, and mutual benefit – that is the language that I use. At the end of it my colleague said, 'Oh Deanne, that's so very nice, but you're in the big leagues now. It's not a negotiation until someone's left bleeding on the floor.' I just thought, 'Wow, welcome to last century dude!'

To me that is a very male approach to business and it is not how we are going to succeed in today's world. That type of aggressive attitude is not helpful in the world that we live in for the very reasons that you put forward. The opportunity that the world presents today is to allow us to do so much more with less. We can do this by utilizing all the tools available, which are inherently about collaboration and cooperation. Unless you can approach the world in that way, I don't think you can take advantage of that new and, I think, incredibly exciting environment!

We're creating new environments and those businesses that want to continue will have to cooperate and collaborate. Those that don't are going to fall by the wayside.

FWN Keys from Deanne Weir

- Everyone has a right to be able to access as much information as they choose to, to be as curious as they can be and not have that curiosity stopped by a lack of access to relevant information.

- Find other ways to leverage the storytelling environment.

- The tools available, which are inherently about collaboration and cooperation, allow us to do so much more with less.

In conclusion

The key issues investigated in this chapter revolve around Knowledge Assets (KA) and how to effectively capture and capitalize on them via high-touch, low-friction ecosystems and collaborative initiatives. We further looked at how these strategic initiatives can lead to competitive advantages generated by improved efficiency, productivity, innovation capacity, budgetary (fiscal/time) savings, greater insights and repeat business, referrals or channel partners.

There is an acknowledgement that flexibility, agility and adaptability – particularly when evolving from a competitive to a collaborative mindset – are of great value in these instances in particular and the DACE in general. The advantages underpinning the value of collaboration, communication and connection at a micro- and macroeconomic level were underlined as are some simple ways to engender this within organizations of any size and in any location.

In the following chapter, 'Profiting from your Return on Involvement (ROI) in the Attention Economy', we will pay great attention to the absolute imperative to engage wholeheartedly in the connected relationships and networks you are involved in. Where ROI is concerned there is no doubt that you get out of a situation what you put into it. The assumption that you can 'coast' through Enduser engagement with depersonalized platitudes is misguided and could potentially incur massive costs to your professional reputation, your brand and your business.

Profiting from your Return on Involvement (ROI) in the Attention Economy

04

Advantage Attention
Authentic Business Change
Collaboration Communicate Connect
DACE Digital Economy Enduser Flat World
Navigator Global Network Relationship Strategy
Success Technology Win-Win **Brand Campaign CEO**
Customer Development Economic Engagement Executives
Jobs Media Positive Return ROI Service Social

Featuring

Morra Aarons-Mele (Women Online and The Mission List), Kare Anderson (Say It Better Center), Karen Barnes (Critical Shift Consulting), Lorraine Carrington (ANZ Wealth), Gordon Feller (Cisco Systems and Meeting of the Minds), Sue Matthews (The Royal Women's Hospital) and Blair Palese (350.org Australia)

Historically, ROI has referred to the phrase Return on Investment – a rate of return on an investment which, all going well, benefits an investor. Frankly, once the investment is made there's not much for the investor to do, apart from wait and hope. In the DACE (Digital, Attention and Collaboration Economies), ROI now has a second definition as 'Return on Involvement', which is equally important – often more so. These altered economic states are far from passive and certainly do not find consumers, and empowered Endusers of services and products, willing to 'lie back quietly and take it' while thinking of better times. Far from it! Rather, dissatisfied Endusers will quickly leave while making as much noise as possible.

At their figurative fingertips are a myriad of 'microphones' – be it a smart phone, dumb phone, tablet/phablet (the hybrid phone-tablet) or any other device being carried in the pocket or purse of most of 'connected society'. The Endusers are not just connected, they are savvy about what they can expect, demanding ever-more targeted products and services designed to meet their personal needs. This is particularly important in the context of ROI, wherein Endusers are intensely impatient with regard to the speed with which they expect their needs to be met. A 2014 Hootsuite white paper, 'Social Customer Service: The Future of Customer Satisfaction', noted that '42 per cent of consumers complaining in social media expect a 60-minute response time.'

Now contrast these presumptions with a traditional business strategy of engagement, wherein cumbersome systems support an inscrutable bureaucracy with little-to-no interest in Enduser empowerment other than providing a scripted call centre. Suffice it to say, the potential disconnect is massive and a possible 'company killer'. Paul Keen, IT Manager for electronics retailer Dick Smith, puts it plainly in his profile for the CXO Challenge, stating that his typical customer knows 'as much about a product as our employees do and knows the competitive pricing better than our employees do' (Head, 2015).

For companies and organizations looking to harness the opportunities afforded them in the DACE, they must leverage the benefits made available to them via their ROI. The key differentiator between those companies that succeed and those who falter will be their level of engagement with their Endusers. As such, one of the chief capabilities a successful company must deliver in the DACE will be the simple, secure enablement of interaction between it and its Endusers. This interaction must be on the Endusers' terms, which means it must be directed and authentic; spin, jargon and irrelevant platitudes will not win the day.

> The whole arena of outsourcing comes with its own language and requirements and I have seen millions wasted in this space as the inherent management layer that is required to lead this was left out. This issue now seems to be getting attention in some of the larger organizations that have outsourced; however, there is an increased need for specificity.
>
> The value of knowledge is only useful if the knowledge is shared, although this is only effective if there is common terminology. One of the benefits of todays' 'toys' is that people – and there are many more participants in the collaborative economy – can easily ask, 'what does this mean?' It's important to be open and break things down to suit the audience; however, I dislike the approach of providing information in the 'lowest common denominator' format. Rather, learn to understand who the participants are and be prepared to work to deliver that.
>
> Lorraine Carrington, Senior Project Manager at ANZ Wealth

Understanding this shift in power is key to succeeding in this digitally empowered, attention-demanding, collaborating economy of massive scale. Those organizations that do not adhere and adjust will quickly be marginalized and, ultimately, forgotten – it's a time of 'present tense is present tension' in these days of online stress and attention deficit demands.

'I don't want to get involved' is not an option

Those competitive advantages that for so long have been taken for granted by Tier One and Two companies (and countries, for that matter) are, if not completely gone, diminishing at a notably rapid rate. To engage in the Digital Economy, for instance, no buildings, billboards or broadcasting – at least in the traditional sense of

TV/radio advertising budgets – are required. An individual, if they understand and undertake the required involvement, can be as large as a multinational corporation on the web. Frankly, with enough effort, they can be more successful, and have a larger ROI, when measuring their level of Enduser engagement.

Here are some of the ways I'm a Flat World Navigator:

- I couldn't do my job without today's technology.

- I'm a partner in a consulting firm with two guys I've never met face to face. We connected through LinkedIn, got to know each other through Skype calls, share files on Google Drive and serve clients around the United States. We're located in California, Connecticut and North Carolina.

- I'm often asked to provide services that I don't personally offer, so I've created a Cloud Network of experts I trust and have worked with before to supplement my offerings. I have everything from writers to project managers, video editors to media buyers, strategists to art directors. And it's all virtual. No overhead.

Karen Barnes, Founder of Critical Shift Consulting

By taking advantage of the tools inherent in the Social Media arena and making effective use of the profusion of Cloud-based technologies and applications available, individuals and SMEs are in a position to shift power from the hands of traditional Tier One and Two titans who do not have a strategy in place to, equally, empower and actively engage with their Endusers. This engagement includes reaching, connecting, converting and keeping Endusers – be they clients, customers, colleagues, or any others involved in the relationship. Fortunately, this can be done less expensively and more effectively than ever before due to the confluence of affordable Cloud technologies, smartphone penetration and the easy access to social media, the web and web-based tools. This is a unique, new frontier and a golden opportunity for those with the wherewithal to energetically and effectively immerse themselves in the potential pot of gold inherent in investing in ROI.

So what does all this mean? It means that you must engage, you must be involved and you must be as mobile as your Endusers. Though a big budget is not a necessity to successfully pursue positive dividends from ROI, one cannot ignore the fact that, particularly when it comes to the mobility of the message, megabucks are being spent by those who can – and this doesn't look to lessen anytime soon.

A 2014 BI (Business Insider) Intelligence study ascertained that the rate of spending on mobile advertising in the United States alone will exceed US$42 billion by 2018; this is based on an expected, exponential compound annual growth rate (CAGR) of 43 per cent. However, even with all this money spent, search and social media still remain the largest segments in this sector – and this, too, will likely continue as results become more targeted due to the convergence of the Internet of Things (IoT).

Why, you may ask, is social media so important? The answer is simple – people are more likely to believe a recommendation from an authentic brand advocate (in other words, a brand's Flat World Navigator) than from a random advertisement; according to US market research firm IDC (International Data Corporation) the conversion rates are from four to ten times higher.

> I wanted to work with organizations that understood the power of women because women vote more, we give more frequently to charity and we advocate more. Women are the advocates to drive change and increasingly, women use social networks to do that.
>
> Morra Aarons-Mele, Founder Women Online and The Mission List

Authenticity is key in connecting into this conversion rate. Endusers are inundated with a cacophony of noise – be it auditory or visual – and they're acutely adept at tuning it out, particularly if they smell something implausible, untrustworthy or false. Your promises to them must be matched by reality; it's a business basic of the DACE: your promise is a contract of trust. What you say is what you do; what you say your product will do – whatever 'it' is – then do it, it must. If you break the promise you've made to an empowered Enduser engaged on social media you'll hear about it, and so will anyone else listening in.

This level of expectation in service provision is unprecedented, as is the demand for resolution of any question or complaint. It may have been possible in years past to ignore an individual or small number of complainants, but this is certainly no longer the case, as those individuals have the megaphone of social media to create a clamour around their complaint. Thus, what could have been an easily resolved issue has turned into a corporate calamity.

You, your organization, your brand – you're all involved in a relationship with your Endusers and, like any relationship, you're going to get out of it pretty much the same level of attention and authentic goodwill that you put in. The days of 'churn and burn' as a relevant strategy are gone, in no small part because these days you're likely to be the one who gets burned by the increased volume – both in quantity and 'digital decibel' – that dissatisfied clients and consumers have through social media.

> I don't believe in cold calling because if it's a cold call you've done
> nothing to learn about them at that time and you don't deserve it.
> So warm yourself up by learning something about them.
>
> Kare Anderson, Emmy winner and Say It Better Center
> founder whose TED talk on Opportunity Makers
> attracted over a million views in two months

By putting in the effort to enhance an Enduser's experience, you engender a far greater level of 'stickiness', reduce 'churn' and optimize potential earnings. Additionally, particularly when connecting this positive determination to colleagues and partners, you elicit a far greater likelihood of successful collaboration and innovative initiatives throughout your organization.

This attitude and effort must be company-wide, and not delegated to one individual. If each member of a team, department and organization has the enhancement of the Enduser journey at the forefront of their mind, and their successful involvement in this is a KPI in the function of their role, the aforementioned enhancement becomes a deliverable that everyone is committed to. This, in turn, can become a key differentiator between you and your competitors.

Sue Matthews, *Chief Executive Officer at The Royal Women's Hospital (Melbourne)*

Health care has evolved significantly in the last five years. Empowered consumers are taking a more active role in their health care and, with the advent of new social media, etc, consumers are sharing their knowledge and experiences with wide audiences.

If you Google 'breast cancer', you will get several million results. The empowered consumer needs support to determine which sites are valid, reliable and trustworthy. This has changed significantly in the last five years. The organization I work for sees 10,000 unique visitors to our website per day. This allows us to ensure that good health information is available across the globe.

As a specialist hospital, we take our responsibility for this very seriously. We know that we are a trusted source of information and much of our business is focused on ensuring our information stays accurate as health care changes. Health care itself has changed exponentially since the advent of these technologies and tools and I believe that it causes us to have an even greater responsibility (since so many people have access to our information). We must also ensure that we maintain a strong brand and that we participate in a variety of media to do so.

With a more empowered consumer, we have moved towards a more patient and family-centred approach. This ensures that we value the preferences and needs of those we care for. Consumer satisfaction is measured through patient satisfaction surveys. These surveys are standardized for hospitals across Victoria. However, we use much more than the standardized surveys. We ensure that we share our patients' stories in a variety of ways.

We start each board meeting with a patient story. This may be a positive or a negative experience, which ensures that those making decisions are constantly reminded of our core business and prevents them from getting bogged down in things. We engage in leadership walk-arounds where we talk with both staff and patients, asking them what we could do to improve – it is here that we hear many of the stories. The results of these walk-arounds are themed, with actions identified as needed.

A more focused, patient-centred approach has been critical to ensuring that we meet the expectations of our consumers. The health care system was designed around the providers and not the patients. Many of our systems and processes are focused on the needs and schedules of those who provide care.

This is changing because of changing expectations of consumers, and the changes in modern medicine, such as a shift to day surgery and shorter lengths of stay. However, the culture of health care has a long way to go in order to meet these expectations. This is mostly because health care professionals have traditionally been trained to know, in no uncertain terms, that they are the experts. Thus, when patients and families challenge their knowledge or expertise, many feel uncomfortable.

The culture in our organization is shifting to one where we see the patients as the experts in their own lives. We, as health care professionals, provide our expertise in order for them to make the best decision for THEM. For example, a woman with breast cancer may be given a choice of a mastectomy, or a lumpectomy with chemotherapy and radiation. It is not the place of the professional to tell them what to do but, rather, to give the patient all the information available in order for them to make their own decision.

Everyone needs to navigate ROI in the flat world

This commitment to putting the Enduser first, whoever and wherever that Enduser may be – across the globe, or across the room – must be central to an ROI strategy. Unfortunately, to date there has been a decided lack of participation and understanding about the importance of involvement with, and empowerment of, Endusers from the C-Suite (CEO, CIO, CFO etc).

In some cases, this invokes the 1950s era of decidedly strong delineations between what was the work of one member of an organization, group or family ('women's work' for instance, which saw the female members of the family expected to do the cooking, cleaning, etc, while the boys worked in the yard). Just as that old-fashioned and quite arbitrary characterization of what constituted roles and requirements has evolved, so too has the awareness that engagement in social media is a shared exercise to be engaged with by all stakeholders in a given ecosystem.

Awareness is yet to mature into activity in far too many cases as of yet. This is underlined by results from the '2014 DOMO Social CEO Report' by CEO.com, which summarizes the situation as one where little movement at the C-level has actually taken place. Though, unsurprisingly, younger CEOs are more likely to have a social presence than their older counterparts, when looking at the CEOs of the Fortune 500 listed companies, 68 per cent are conspicuously absent from any involvement on any of the 'Big Five' social networks (Twitter, Facebook, LinkedIn, Google+ and Instagram).

Perhaps somewhat predictably, '74 per cent of CEOs who only participate in a single network join LinkedIn first.' (Bucking the trend, as is his wont, the only Fortune 500 CEO on all five is Facebook founder, Mark Zuckerberg.) This lack of engagement on the part of those absent executives leaves their organizations at a decided disadvantage as it is questionable how clearly the impact social media has on their Endusers' mindsets and behaviours is understood. That lack of engagement and understanding dovetails into an information shortfall which will, without doubt, affect their business strategy and fiscal bottom line.

Social media is neither fad nor fashion, it is a business reality which must be engaged with; an organization's level of involvement has a demonstrable effect on its performance and success. There are millions, and soon to be billions of potential Endusers who have social media at their fingertips. To ignore them would be like being in the transport industry and only speaking to users of buggy whips. These potential Endusers, who are located around the world, are quite literally holding a wealth of information.

Factoid

According to unofficial ComScore figures measuring monthly unique visitors (desktop use only) the global audience for Facebook is more than the next eight of its competitors combined. The Top 10 List is:

Facebook:	823 million
Twitter:	178 million
LinkedIn:	173 million
Pangaea:	110 million
Hearst:	93 million
CNN:	89 million
BBC:	80 million
Mail Online:	60 million
New York Times:	44 million
The Guardian:	43 million

(Source: Sweney, 2015)

Endusers hold the key to a relatively unexplored frontier of opportunity for creating business for you and your organization. However, to gain from it you must be involved. You must engage with them via the medium of their choice, which is more often than not social media, at least in the initial stages of communication.

Connecting and conversing with your Endusers via social media improves sales, customer service and marketing all at the same time. Unfortunately, far too many C-level executives still don't understand the importance of being proactively and positively involved in social media and how this involvement affects their bottom lines. Again I must make clear, to get a Return on Involvement, one must be active, and that includes being active on social media.

Of course, busy CEOs are not expected to spend their days posting tweets and 'selfies' – however, as evidenced by the DOMO report, five of the Fortune 500 CEOs that are on Twitter have never actually posted a tweet, and half of those that have 'tweeted' have done so less than 100 times. That is not engagement, it is lip service.

When looking for examples of effectively engaged C-level executives – other than Mark Zuckerberg, who may have something of an advantage – one could look to the CMO of Canadian communication company Mitel, Martyn Etherington. He makes clear how important engagement is through his Twitter headline, 'Passionate about Creating & Keeping Customers, Innovation & all things Digital.' Adding, it seems with some pride, that he is among the 'Top 100 CMOs on Twitter'.

In a November 2014 interview with Carroll School of Management at Boston College Associate Professor Gerald Kane, who was also guest editor for MIT Sloan Management Review's 'Social Business Big Idea Initiative', Etherington explained his longstanding passion for digital and social business as they enable deeper customer understanding, better customer service and greater brand awareness. Not only does he tweet, but his leadership has seen the number of employees tweeting on behalf of the company rise from 30 to 1,600 individuals. Though there are no hard and fast rules, the Mitel messaging has been made simple for employees to engage in. As he explained to Kane, 'Whenever we put out an announcement, we put out a whole series of canned tweets that our employees can cut and paste or edit.'

Another exemplar of social media engagement at the upper echelon is Live Nation's Michael Rapino, who has posted more than 1,200 tweets and is muscularly using platforms such as Instagram to promote his company. He has grabbed the opportunity to build his company's brand, influence its relationship with Endusers and, through social media specifically, the relationship that Live Nation has with media in general.

Enduser engagement is not only good for a company's brand, it also benefits the personal brand of the CEOs themselves. According to Weber Shandwick's 2013 report 'The Social CEO: Executives Tell All', the advantages of a social CEO are reflected in a number of ways. These positives include using social media to share company news with employees and Endusers and opening an avenue of communication with the C-Suite – both of which are good for building business. Additionally, there are positive perceptions and associations that accompany the use of social media by C-level executives, such as the assumption that the executives and/or the brand they represent are communicators, authentic and accessible as well as being innovative and technologically adept. It's a pretty stupendous payoff for taking a few moments to send a 140 character tweet!

Engage with your Endusers on their terms

The facts are unequivocal – we are accessing social media sites via our mobile platforms more and more; as noted in the 2015 Cisco Visual Networking Index mobile Cloud usage will increase '11-fold from 2014 to 2019, a CAGR of 60 per cent'. This equates to billions of social media mavens who are potential partners in your promotion portfolio, if you engage with them purposely and positively. Launched in December 2002, LinkedIn (at the time of writing) has more than 300 million users in 200 countries using 20 languages on the platform. Facebook is only 10 years old and has a whopping 1.25 billion users while Twitter, the 'baby' of the bunch, having been launched in 2006, handles more than 340 million tweets and 1.6 billion search queries daily.

Use of social media crosses borders, boundaries, general interests and generations. Mary Meeker noted in the 2014 edition of her highly influential annual 'Internet Trends Report' that the number of internet users continues to grow year on year at an average approximate rate of 10 per cent, with the fastest growth rate coming from the Majority World. When you add that growth rate to the findings in the 2013 'Global Trust in Advertising Report', which brought together Nielsen's survey results from 28,000 people in 56 countries, something striking becomes apparent. The report was unequivocal; it is 'earned media' in the form of recommendations from friends, family and trusted 'avatars' that consumers trust most – to the tune of 92 per cent!

Factoid

According to the MassMutual Financial Group, women over 50 in the United States control a net worth of US$19 trillion and own more than three-quarters of the country's fiscal wealth.

(Source: she-conomy.com, 2007)

Frankly, consumers trust strangers rather than ad campaigns that are, to their minds, tainted by 'spin'. They look to User Generated Content (UGC) on platforms such as blogs and websites, or posts and pins on Facebook, Twitter, Pinterest, etc, for authentic reviews rather than paying attention to pop-up ads or their ilk. This is particularly true for Millennials who, according to a 2014 joint survey conducted by the social influence marketing platform Crowdtap, media analytics firm Ipsos and the Social Media Advertising Consortium, find UGC 20 per cent more persuasive than a professional influencer/media campaign, 35 per cent more memorable and 50 per cent more trust-worthy (Crowdtap, 2014).

Millennials will soon be the holders of the greatest purchasing power in history and, rather than retailers, they – along with a wide swathe of other consumer groups – increasingly look to their peers for what they perceive to be honest, unbiased reviews and knowledge about products and services. When asked how much trust they had in product information from a variety of sources, the results were conspicuously clear: TV – 34 per cent, radio – 37 per cent, print 44 – per cent, social networking – 50 per cent, peer reviews – 68 per cent, and finally, 74 per cent for conversations with friends.

If your core business market segment does not focus on Millennials – or the 'Centennials' coming of age (at 18) this year – don't feel this means you can relax. Have no doubt that Baby Boomers, for instance, are insistent that they are given quality customer service and if they don't receive it, they are not backwards in coming forward to state their opinion. They will take to their Twitter feeds and Facebook pages to be vehemently vocal about the disappointing service/product/ appreciation/understanding they have been, at least in their eyes, subjected to. In fact, they may actually start a social media account just to complain.

But you know what? This relationship can be saved and be an exemplar of ROI – Return on Involvement. It is inevitable that, in the grand scheme of things, some Endusers are going to begin their relationship with you from a critical position. But, and this is a BIG BUT, if managed correctly, this fraught affair can change from one that could have been a brand fiasco to one that trumpets your success. Turning your critic into your cheerleader is positively priceless. It is this 'emotional capital' that is brought forward by Flat World Navigators, who are adept at leveraging online communities by responding authentically and at the pace expected, on the specific platforms being employed, by Endusers.

Flat World Navigators share their stories

Blair Palese, *Co-Founder and CEO, 350.org Australia*

The most important collaboration that I do is to work closely with other environmental organizations within Australia and with 350.org in the United States and internationally. This is done to share campaign strategies, material, ideas, challenges and contacts who can assist in our efforts to stop the expansion of the fossil fuel industry. Due to our comparatively limited resources, collaboration is our only hope of winning the climate change battle.

I also have a large network of friends and colleagues – particularly women I have worked closely with over the years – in the environmental, activism, NGO, sustainable business and social change sectors as well as in the arts, where we have found support for 350 since our founding in 2008. These networks are in Australia, the United States, UK and Europe. In addition, due to 350's focus of targeting Australia's coal export market, we also have colleagues in India and Asia. I depend on my networks for support, professional advice, skills that I can tap and a knowledge of what's happening here and around the world.

The impact 350.org has had in Australia and around the world is, in large part, possible because of social media. Outlets that are particularly important include Facebook and Twitter (for me via

Tweetdeck), and online tools that we've picked up as they've become available such as YouTube, Vimeo, Dropbox and a range of others.

In our early years we worked directly with the Google team to develop event maps as part of a global campaign, and now use that technology for events such as the global People's Climate Mobilization, to integrate the registration of events, sign-up capacity, location maps, details and contact information in one easy-to-use online tool. This system has also been helpful in maintaining an effective global database of those interested in remaining active with 350.org on climate change issues. In addition, we have worked with system developers on database management tools that are adaptable to the needs of the organization.

I can't overstate the importance of Facebook and Twitter in helping us develop strong and active networks of organizers, volunteers and participants as part of our climate change campaigns. The open source nature of 350.org has meant that we have been able to collaborate and bring together people and organizations that, in the past, have not worked beyond their one organization.

Examples of this include working with Avaaz, the Australian Youth Climate Coalition (AYCC) and GetUp! on the People's Climate Mobilization. That collaboration brought together 30,000 people at a climate change march in Melbourne, more than 80,000 to events in Australia, and 400,000 at the largest global event in New York – the largest climate change rally in the world. In addition, traditional media communications about our campaigns and the issues is still a very important part of our outreach. Our global fossil-free divestment campaign has gained significant momentum due to the incredible coverage and debate within the Australian and international financial press.

Interestingly, 350.org was named for two key reasons: to have more and more people ask what 350 is (the amount of greenhouse gases, in parts per million, that scientists say is the safe level in our atmosphere – we are now above 400 ppm) and to use a number, rather than a name that would have had to be spelled out and translated. To avoid having to translate the content, our 2009 launch video had graphics and numbers only, no words, so that it could be easily understood around the world. This has been highly effective in making the organization and its mission accessible outside of English-speaking countries.

Maintaining large networks of contacts does take time and we are time poor, so we try to be effective – we use every 350 event as a chance to invite those we know are interested in our campaigns or the issue to join us. We use campaign successes as a way to thank funders, partners and those who contributed in any way and we make sure we are supporting our networks personally so that we maintain good ongoing relationships. For new people that we want to reach out to, we're not afraid of the cold call and e-mail. We depend on volunteers to help manage incoming cold contacts, which minimizes the time needed and ensures that we can respond in some way. And while it's great to get asked to speak at events, we do have to be strategic as to what we say yes to!

For me personally, I find keeping up with e-mail – approximately 400 a day! – is my biggest challenge. E-mail is really just not working any more and people everywhere are terrible about tightly managing how they use it. I'd guess that half of the e-mails that I receive are mindless 'reply all' messages that I simply don't need to read. I don't have a PA to manage this; for me a PA is an extra layer between me and my networks that I don't really want. So, for those of us who don't have PAs, something has to give to make this e-mail situation more manageable!

The 350.org model as a not-for-profit is quite different from older, more traditional organizations and because of our small team, flat structure, our small budget and our desire to rapidly respond to climate change campaign opportunities, everyone does everything, including social media and communications. Because of this, some refer to our structure as 'the 350 model'. We work on short-term contracts rather than open-ended salaried positions; not only because the work and skills needed can shift rapidly, based on our focus, but also because most on the team prefer to have flexibility. This means we can be nimble, ensure we have the skills we need when we need them and that those we bring onboard grow and shrink based on the funding we raise and our campaign foci. We're open about this approach and find that, for now, it works for us.

350.org is a small outfit – about three full-time staff and about six part-time – and all of us work in the flat world, maintaining contacts across a variety of levels, actively involved in social media and in contact with a range of organizations that operate in the same NGO environment using the most effective tools to win campaigns. Developing and supporting these skills means ensuring training for new tools is possible, either professionally or through a trained team member, including the use of the most effective tools in campaign strategies and valuing the skills to work in this environment in all hires for new positions. As an NGO, rather than a company, it's important to evaluate and demonstrate the importance of these skills as part of successful campaigns as a way to ensure everyone in the team understands their importance.

Women are GREAT at establishing and maintaining huge and varied networks – the Flat World Navigation approach. And this skill, in today's world of ever-changing technology and rapidly changing strategies, is invaluable. It's critical that this skill set be valued and when it is, women do very well wherever they are. As a not-for-profit run by two women – one older and one very young – 350 avoids many of the gaps between women and men that are often seen in the business world. The best thing that we can do is to talk up the benefits and the amazing women who are part of our team. In addition, we try to ensure women in the team get support to deal with the challenges they face outside when working with companies or other organizations where that balance is still a challenge. I do feel that the flat world we now work in lends itself to so many of the things women do well, and for that I'm grateful and believe it will continue to be a game changer.

I believe those who know the benefits of the ever-evolving technological advances available, must push governments at all levels to do more to make the many tools coming online more accessible to all and to make training on how to use them a priority at all levels as well as to support funding for better and faster internet access. Better access and training to learn how to use these tools effectively will benefit all those who take them up, as well as the workforce as a whole. Unfortunately, for many, these skills and the technology – including fast internet – are completely inaccessible and this makes working collaboratively in communities that do not have access very difficult, creating a huge imbalance. The benefits are easy to see – the commitment to making them accessible to as many as possible has to be a priority!

Flat World Navigators, the masters of real-world ROI

Flat World Navigators are an organization's authentic avatars and, as such, they are essential when looking to promote trust, familiarity and confidence in a brand. They combine and leverage both traditional and internet-based networks to reach out, communicate and collaborate. Their vision PoPs – it has a Purity of Purpose and the purpose is to engage, enable and empower the Enduser.

Flat World Navigators do the work, get involved and discover ways to meet customer demands – which is key to business success in the Attention Economy. Because they're engaged and involved, they're in a perfect position to look for patterns of unmet needs and unnoticed opportunities. Once those potentials are acknowledged the likelihood of being able to leverage them towards commercial success is enhanced exponentially.

You could ignore your critics and complainants, but don't think they won't talk... and keep on talking. Instead, use the Flat World Navigators within your organization – or the flat world navigational skills you hold within your own tool kit – to engage with your Enduser and begin to manage the conversation and take control of any negatives within the situation. There is no doubt that failure to respond can lead to a loss of customers; this loss, according to Gartner VP Carol Rozwell, can be up to 15 per cent (Gartner Newsroom, 2012).

Now no one is saying that every missive and misstep must be responded to. However, it must be acknowledged that social media platforms are equally, if not more important than telephone and e-mail communication in the role they play in reaching and responding to Endusers. When determining your ROI strategy here are a few arenas of involvement, underlined in the 2014 Hootsuite white paper, referenced earlier, which should be taken into account:

- Customers who are acknowledged quickly and effectively via social media are three times as likely to have a positive perspective on a brand.
- How quickly customers get a response to their queries and complaints matters.

- Endusers prefer to communicate about their complaint on the platform of THEIR choice.

In a nutshell, Endusers know what they want, when they want it and how they want it delivered. Flat World Navigators traverse the arena of the Attention Economy and, by authentically engaging with Endusers, they customize the journey from complainant to cheerleader and ensure that, on this journey, neither the brand nor the Enduser get lost.

Actions with intent

Decide what you want your return to be when you invest in the ROI of Return on Involvement (ie to increase sales, increase traffic to your website, communicate with your current Endusers or connect with potential new partners).

Determine what online sites your typical Endusers visit regularly, then create an action plan to ensure that you, or your organization's representative(s), are actively engaged/integrated on each of these sites.

Set a measurable 'time frame timetable' for expected engagement with your Endusers on your social media sites to answer their queries and, where appropriate, respond to their comments.

Find ways to differentiate your social media sites: what makes you and your product/service unique?

Brainstorm ideas for incentives, which you could share with current Endusers to encourage them to refer others to join your portfolio of social media sites. Referrals will continue to grow in value as the DACE matures.

Collaborate whenever possible, this could include sharing information and selected networks with press and media professionals or event participants.

INTERVIEW   An interview with a Flat World Navigator

Gordon Feller, *Director at Cisco Systems and Co-Founder/Convenor of Meeting of the Minds*

Co-Founder/Convenor of Meeting of the Minds (the premier international leadership conference for sustainable cities) and Director of Urban Innovations at Cisco Systems, Gordon Feller has worked with and advised leaders of multinational companies, cities, NGOs, foundations, and national governments on urban development issues for nearly 30 years. He has written hundreds of articles for newspapers, scholarly journals, and magazines and was formerly executive editor of *Urban Age* magazine and *Planet Earth* magazine. In June 2014, Feller was appointed as a Global Fellow of the Commons Lab, Science and Technology Innovation Program at the Woodrow Wilson International Center for Scholars.

Gordon, let's start our chat by exploring Meeting of the Minds, which is the eminent international conference for sustainable cities you co-founded in 2006. Why did you decide this was where you were going to put energy?

At that time we saw a lot of focus on climate change, but inter-governmental negotiations around [the subject] were not succeeding... and of course they haven't succeeded in the years since. The idea was to get public sector leaders, particularly from cities, and representatives from the private and NGO sectors – though these three 'worlds' normally have a hard time collaborating with each other – sharing a common framework, which was this meeting. The first of which was convened in California in 2007.

We convinced Toyota to be the lead corporate, the city of Oakland, California to be the host, the University of California, Berkeley to be the co-host and we convinced the World Bank and the Rockefeller Foundation, along with a few others, to chip in some money. So we had a group of partners and we had 20 to 30 journalists who were serious about understanding our experiment. We also had [Steven Chu] the Nobel prize-winning head of the Lawrence Berkeley National Laboratory join us before President Obama recruited him to be the US Secretary of Energy.

So we managed to cut across a lot of boundaries, which was the theme of the program. We looked at the boundaries that separated cities and got in the way of them exchanging knowledge with each other, and that separated them from companies and the non-profit organizations that need to share their best practices. Then we tried to practise what we preach by creating an environment where a lot of the collaborations could develop. We ended up with about six or seven of them that emerged from the discussions: creative, cross-cutting, border-crossing-type collaborations which were quite successful. This provided the fuel for the program to go to the next level, which we were fortunate to be able to do. Because it was originally just a 'one-time' experiment to see if this would be impactful enough that it would be worth continuing and the judgement from the initial group of 300 that participated was that there was real value there.

Is there an end goal in sight or is this something that will iterate, evolve and grow, depending on the current crisis in need of attention?

It's morphing; like all living things, hopefully, they learn, they grow, they adapt. In Detroit [at the October 2014 Meeting] the macro focus was on how cities respond to global crises like climate change, which was the originating impulse.

To take that down to the micro level, how do we take a neighbourhood in Detroit, which is in distress and has not only natural resource challenges, but also human capital challenges... how do we take that to the next level using the creative inputs of partners from multiple sectors, who normally don't partner with each other.

We are attempting something different in response to the demands, which we are constantly measuring. We are constantly taking the temperature, not only of the sponsors and partners, but a host of others – many of whom show up when we convene the physical meeting. So the idea is to have virtual collaboration that leads to a typical event that leads to virtual collaboration, that leads to a physical event – and to keep that rhythm. That's how the thing's evolved and hopefully that will allow it to be constantly adapting.

Does that mean that you're also evolving or adapting the tools that you use to enable the project to move forward?

Yes, that's why we've adopted WebEx, for instance, as a daily tool. So today, we convened a conference call, using video and audio from multiple devices, with about 60 people who are participating in some of the initial work around the 2015 program. That's a nice chance to use collaboration technology that's designed to enable people in multiple locations from non-compatible devices and non-interoperable networks to have a common platform.

You mentioned your partners coming from different arenas – they come from NGOs, the not-for-profit arena and from the commercial arena. They could also come from the political arena, which may have some of the greatest challenges as they not only have to ensure that something moves forward, but they have to do it in such a way that they are able to get reelected. So there are all sorts of different translation layers that need to be drilled through to get to the potential communication and collaboration. How do you address those challenges?

Yes, it's a great question. And it goes to the heart of what we're trying to do of course. One of the things that we learned is that the technology companies have been successful because they tried to solve this problem of interoperability, sometimes in ways that have been surprisingly simple. For instance, the way the TCP/IP [Transmission Control Protocol/Internet Protocol – the first networking protocols/languages set for the internet] was constructed in the '70s by a peer group of volunteers, who then made it possible for the emergence of the internet in the '80s, as what we know today. Much of it is still based on TCP/IP, so we look to what happened in the days before it became the global, open standard.

In fact, it is actually the originating impulse behind the founding of Cisco. A husband and wife team – Len (Leonard) Bosack and Sandra (Lerner) – were both based on the same Stanford campus, but they couldn't communicate with each other because they were on two separate, incompatible networks. So they co-invented the first Cisco product, which was a box that enabled multiple protocols that were incompatible, to communicate with each other.

I think a lesson from that is that you improvise as needed in ways that may be messy and not particularly attractive and maybe not totally scalable, but you build a solution to suit the problem and you hope that that's the basis for a wider, more broadly applicable solution that can be replicable and scalable. And it turned out that Cisco was able to do that with this multi-protocol box.

The bottom line is that necessity is the mother of invention. Right now, the necessity that all of us have to face is figuring out how to create a common framework to allow the multiple vernaculars, languages and lexicons within the different sectors to converge around problem solving in common, rather than problem solving in silos.

So Meeting of the Minds is a small attempt to try to mirror the larger effort that is starting to take place. We're seeing signs that there is some real momentum in this direction, which is keeping me optimistic, amidst all the other pessimistic signals.

It seems to me that you're extremely aware of the importance of the Enduser, which is not necessarily common in the technology sector. Additionally, it appears that you look for ways to bring the Enduser in at an early stage of a project.

Yes, in fact I've a sign on my desk, which says, 'The Enduser is our R&D Department'.

What led you to that determination and how has that perspective affected how you do your work?

It's funny, it goes back to the 1960s. My father's father ran a shop for ladies' underwear, called Feller's Lady Shop. Of course for a young boy, it was always fascinating to walk into his grandfather's shop and see all the brassieres. I asked my father how his father got in to that business, and it turns out that, actually, he was a very active listener.

He would listen to what he heard when his wife, my grandmother, had friends over and they would have their 'lady conversations'. They thought that he was not engaged or listening, so they'd talk about things like, 'Oh my God, I can't find the bra that fits me very comfortably, and this is horrible!'

He was always listening very carefully. Not just because these were his customers and he needed to know what they wanted but because he believed that the way to live your life was to constantly be listening to nuances. And to figure out not just what people want, but why, when and where they want it – all those things behind the demand or act.

In our case, we're talking about the need and demand for collaboration solutions that are easy to use, that are acceptable all the time, anywhere, from any device or in any circumstance. That's something that we'll get to pretty fast... but it depends on being able to hear it, before you know that it's a need.

I would imagine, not just with Meeting of the Minds and Cisco but also in your work with the UN Habitat World Urban Campaign, you've faced a range of challenges bringing a myriad of stakeholders, potentially with divergent goals, together to solve problems. How do you address and overcome such challenges?

There's one hurdle at the beginning and then there's one hurdle at the middle, so I'll pick those two to start with.

The one at the beginning is creating realistic expectations at the same time that you're recruiting people to an idealistic vision for an alternative future. It's a challenge because you're saying to people: 'we need you to work together in this unique way because we've some mega-challenges that we want to confront. And, if you don't do this, our kids and grandkids will live in a much, much less appealing world, maybe even a very, very tough world.'

So, we have to step up to this idealistic challenge and, by the way, let's get realistic about the modest goals that we have while we're being uber-idealistic.

So there's that conundrum: saying to people, let's shoot for the moon and let's be modest about how and when we're going to get there. At the very beginning of the process, we're telling them: 'Focus like a laser beam to work with us on something that has not been done before. And, we can't guarantee that your time investment is going to pay off at the level that we hope. We are hopeful, but we're fighting every moment because you're distracted and we need to get your attention and your commitment.'

That's the first hurdle. We have uber-ambitious, global goals for transformation and we want to focus you in a way that is pragmatic and realistic, because a moonshot takes lots of little steps to get to the Moon.

At the beginning it's a process of handholding. I'm letting people know that they're not the only ones taking a risk and nobody is going to chop their head off even if they stick their necks way out, because we're watching their back.

In the middle of the process we're constantly trying to keep our 'double vision', the big mega goal and the modest strategy, so we can achieve little accomplishments along the way to give us encouragement. Because we're doing things that are really hard. And it feels lonely; even when you're collaborating with a lot of people, you're often surrounded by doubters.

The middle half of this process is tough because of the scepticism of people about whether this is doable or not – the Doubting Thomas. It's a voice in our head. Even in those of us who really believe we can make a difference, be the transformation and have the impact... there is still the doubting voice in our heads. It doesn't help if you think you're doing something that has defeated everybody who's come before – the great advocates of collaboration – so who do you think you are? We just have to confront that 'Doubting Thomas Mind' in the middle of the process, to keep the energy high and keep the focus on the goal.

Those are the two big hurdles. In both cases it just requires constant practice of the discipline of making the impacts visible and measurable – because if you can't measure it, you can't improve on it and you can't manage it. In Silicon Valley, where I am, if you don't measure it, it's not real; because you're surrounded by engineers and technologists who want to measure everything. Even if you're dealing with an unquantifiable like collaboration, which is hard to measure, you measure through the impact and outcome.

Something else that can be measured by its impact and outcome is strength of communication. You seem to bring a high level of personal authenticity and engagement to your connections and communication; is that something that you do consciously?

There's an old saying in sales – I'm not a salesman, but I've been told this by expert salespeople – which is: A B C – Always Be Closing. I've adapted that to 'Always Be Collaborating', because there's no closure to this. Collaboration is an open-ended process that starts on a certain day and never stops. If we can communicate that 'collaboration is the way to operate, the way to live', I'm hoping the authenticity of that comes true.

It's not a conscious approach to make myself feel like a partner... but to actually practise it, like a daily meditation practice. It's definitely a hard thing to do. I'm now in my 38th year of consciously trying to do this. And I'm hoping that the 'hum' in my head is not something I've got to restart every day, but it's there in the background when I wake up, when I go to sleep and presumably when I'm dreaming.

It's very clear that collaboration is extremely important to you, as it is to me. I've no doubt that the people who enable and engender collaborative occurrences are going to be increasingly important as we move forward in the Digital, Collaboration and Attention Economies and can be game changing for organizations and companies regardless of their size or where they are. With that in mind, what is your perspective on the valuing and sharing of knowledge assets – particularly as this pertains to businesses, governments and society as a whole?

Great question to conclude on, as it goes to the heart of what Cisco is going through as a company, which is the open knowledge exchange. Not just with customers and partners but with the broader technology industry. We've discovered that the businesses that have the greatest success are the ones that are focused on open source and global open standards and that are built on common platforms that everybody can utilize together and share.

> ## Factoid
>
> By 2020 it is likely that:
>
> - the 'connected living' sector will reach more than US$731 billion;
>
> - tens of millions of people will be connected by trillions of things and applications.
>
> Looking further forward, by 2025 there will be:
>
> - 3.7 billion smart phones, 400 million laptops, 700 million tablets and 410 smart appliances;
>
> - 80 per cent uptake of BYOD (Bring Your Own Device) by US enterprises;
>
> - 15 million interactive kiosks and 25 million Cloud servers.
>
> (Source: Vidyasekar, 2014)

I made the case internally that our best partners and customers – where we deliver the most value to their customers and their partners – are the ones that are also adopting open knowledge exchange and open innovation as the fundamental business model. You know, we've seen lots of companies in 'the Valley' disappear that built proprietary closed systems.

Everybody who is anybody in the technology world sees how powerful open source is and cannot deny the fact that it's changed all of the ways we operate in the technology industry. Cisco turned 30 years old in December 2014 and this has been a long process of unlearning old habits and relearning new ones. So we're the poster child for the fact that old dogs can be taught new tricks – in Silicon Valley, 30 is really old!

The Internet of Everything [IoT] initiatives that we have around cities are our frontline effort to implement this learning because cities will not tolerate proprietary – they've been burned in the past. They're very cautious now because in the past they bought things that were closed and then they discovered that those things 'went away'. They – the cities – then had to, quite literally, throw stuff out that they'd invested their 'treasure' in.

This is an important lesson learned by a lot of companies and by a lot of cities: Principle Number One is, you can't get away with anything but open in the near term and that'll be a truth... maybe forever.

The Second Principle is that open makes possible things that are amazing, surprising and unexpected. Because, you're not programming it, you're not in control of it. And the first rule of serendipity and synchronicity is that the most creative outcomes come from places that are unexpected, or in some cases, the least expected. Like, for instance, people under the age of twenty who haven't graduated college. They can create the most amazing, world-shaking innovations; we've seen that time and time again.

Those are our guiding principles – whether it's a small non-profit organization like Meeting of the Minds or a large multinational company such as Cisco, the rules apply equally. Open is not just a revolution for big technology companies and small startups, non-profit or for-profit – it's relevant for everybody.

Whatever part of the world you're in – whether it's an emerging economy, less developed, industrialized – and whatever type of organization you happen to be in, open source, open innovation and open platforms are going to be the rule of the day. You only have to look at how Amazon and other amazing ecosystems work.

Open does create a vulnerability. When you look at the places where Amazon has been assaulted the openness of the ecosystem is a vulnerability. So we have to address that, which means better security and better institutions that enable the openness to be preserved and to be successful.

We're [Cisco] building open innovation platforms around the IoT for cities, one of which is called City Protocol. It's built on the idea that as the Open Internet Protocol enabled us to make things happen in the internet, we can have an Open City Protocol that enables cities to go through the transformation they're wanting to go through.

In conclusion

This chapter primarily put a spotlight on how critical high-touch involvement with your Endusers is. This need for engagement cannot be understated nor can the necessity for it to be embraced by as many members of the organization, at all levels, as possible. Your Return on Involvement (ROI) is both measurable and palpable. The value that social media delivers in this realm is explored in detail, as is the importance of Flat World Navigators. They are the translators between any number of various stakeholders. FWNs are the key differentiators between those organizations that thrive or barely survive the juggernaut that is the oncoming DACE and its billions of connected devices and engaged, empowered and expectant Endusers.

These Endusers are at the heart of the next chapter, 'New business models built by flat world navigation'. They need only be connected to the internet and their global reach is as immediate as it is immense. It explores how changing business models are altering business strategies and roles, such as the CTO (Chief Technology Officer) and CIO, within enterprises of every size. As an 'old guard' layer of digital deniers is swiftly being swept away, agile approaches that empower and embrace connection and collaboration are increasingly being seen as important KPIs regardless of whether the business is a one-man, solo venture or a multinational, mega-sized enterprise.

New business models built by flat world navigation

Advantage Attention
Authentic Business Change
Collaboration Communicate Connect
DACE Digital Economy Enduser Flat World
Navigator Global Network Relationship Strategy
Success Technology Win-Win **Audiences CIO Culture**
Dolphin Economy Engage Experience Idea Listen
Management Market Share Shark SME Stakeholders

Featuring

Aria Finger (DoSomething.org and TMI Agency),
Donnie Maclurcan (Post Growth Institute), Joan Michelson (Green
Connections Media), Servane Mouazan (Ogunte CIC) and
Clara Gaggero Westaway (Special Projects and Royal College of Art)

Location, location, location – in the flat world of the global DACE (Digital, Attention and Collaboration Economies), where you are matters less and less as long as you've got connectivity and haven't moored your business in the swamp of digital denial. Digital, attention and collaboration: mastering these three things will be a key differentiating factor for organizations looking to stay afloat and occupy the best business berths and real estate of the future.

Don't just take my word on it. The situation is made quite clear in Gartner's 2015 forecast CIO Agenda Report 'Flipping to Digital Leadership' (Aron *et al*, 2014), the largest annual CIO survey in the world. It includes the responses of more than 2,800 CIOs, with a reach that encompasses all major industries and 84 countries. Together the CIOs surveyed have a corporate and public sector IT spend of nearly $US400 billion and approximately $US12.1 trillion in revenue/public sector budgets. Put plainly, CIOs are being told in no uncertain terms by their CEOs that they have no choice but to adapt to the 'digital now, digital first' era – frankly, they need to evolve and replace command and control 'with vision and inspiration' or they'll soon be extinct. Additionally, and with reference to our new understanding of ROI to be Return on Involvement, those CIOs deemed to be high performers are using an extra 5 per cent of their time to engage with their board, senior leadership and, perhaps most importantly of all when exploring new business models and strategies, their external customers/Endusers.

Factoid

Navigating the changing role of the CIO:

- CIOs must adapt to a new age where digitalization is rapidly undoing the traditional relationship between the business and the IT department.

- CIOs must build and nurture relationships with partners and suppliers.

- 92 per cent of respondents said enthusiasm for business units buying their own technology is eroding the central IT department's budget and control.

- Nearly two-thirds of organizations now expect CIOs to show creativity – they can do so by using mobile, Cloud and unified communication technologies, which are seen as critical to delivering commercial results for business.

- 96 per cent of CIO respondents said the evolving needs of customers are impacting their roles.

- 92 per cent of employees responding want access to an organization's data when working remotely.

(Source: BT, 2014)

Nothing floats on digital denial

Business as usual through steering by traditional 'command and control' methodology will not only fail to move you forward, it won't even allow you to maintain your current position. You will be left behind and out in the cold. In the fast-moving DACE current, tools such as mobile and social are not optional, they are imperative – they're your ticket to ride. Without them you're left on the shore with fewer and fewer Endusers standing there with you.

Now is the time to explore the flat world and engage with the technologies, such as the Cloud, Collaboration Platforms and the Internet of Things (IoT), which empower you to capture the business you want to win. By piloting these waters with focus and a firm grasp on the benefits brought by flat world navigation and Flat World Navigators – the collaboration facilitators, market makers, revenue builders and Enduser engagers – in your midst, the necessary changes to your business models and strategies will be much easier to implement. Additionally, far further reaching benefits can enhance your bottom line sooner and with much greater effect.

I am certainly not suggesting that you rest the entirety of your strategy on any one thing in particular, even if that thing is, for instance, Big Data. One need only look at the 2014 'Tesco tumble' to see the folly in that model. In that year, what was once the largest supermarket chain in the UK lost half of its market value due to, among other things, its considerable dependence on the data dump inherent in an over-reliance on statistics, analytics, and predictive percentages. Rather I propose you gather a portfolio of tools, technologies and techniques together that focus on high value for all stakeholders and which are capable of delivering early and often.

It is true that Endusers are increasingly demanding, with an expectation of instant outcomes accompanying anywhere/anytime, agile service delivery. Additionally, they have a level of technical savviness that is accelerating at a pace that brings with it both great challenges and opportunities. However, there are certain sought after outcomes which all stakeholders share: reduced costs and increased revenue. If the solutions your chosen portfolio supports are linked to your Endusers' business drivers and KPIs, your chances of success are multiplied many times over. One way to move this forward is to ensure that all stakeholders, regardless of their role or function, see themselves as problem solvers and solution providers. In essence, establishing a company culture where everyone is encouraged to access their innate flat world navigational skills, goes a long way towards empowering connection and collaboration.

> The main challenge is working with people who have the tendency to navigate solely in groups closely related to their main-interest topic. Therefore, when I organize events I make sure to bring together people from various communities and interests. The exercise is to coach people in how to talk, to communicate, in ways that strangers will understand – and that they won't be repelled by!
>
> I first focus on making them share the impact they want to make, their vision, their purpose. (I avoid technical details at that stage, because you tend to 'lose' people in the conversation.) Then I encourage people to talk about their passion and motivation to pursue such a purpose. The next step is to make them speak about their DNA, their theory of change.
>
> And finally, I make them share an ask. People always forget to ask for specific things that they need. When they do, it makes them more human.
>
> Servane Mouazan, Strategic Social Innovation Consultant,
> Women Social Entrepreneurs Advocate & CEO Ogunte CIC

Re-running present conventions is not the path to future successes

Connection and collaboration are becoming ever-more central to the Digital Economy, particularly as, increasingly, companies and those that work within them are opting for more flexibility regarding where and when work occurs. Digital platforms are supporting a myriad of means for organizations large and small to take advantage of a flexible workforce accessing affordable, apportionable tools and technology either provided by the organization or via the proliferating BYOD culture.

Taking it one step further, MYOB's CTO Simon Raik-Allen envisages – quite reasonably I might add – holographic workers being commonplace in 25 years' time. In his 2015 white paper, 'The Future of Business Australia 2040', he explains further:

> The holographic projection of people and things will be the biggest change to the workplace since e-mail. Seminars, that became webinars in the '90s, will now become holonars. You will sit in virtual auditoriums, next to three-dimensional light-based images of your colleagues from around the globe, watching a hologram on the stage of someone giving a talk. And you will do this just as easily as you gather in the office today. Launching a new business and hiring 500 people could be done in minutes. Your company could be just you and a couple of project managers: the thinkers, controlling every aspect of the company through new digital interfaces.

All stakeholders and Endusers, be they employees, co-workers, colleagues, management, C-Suite, partners, clients, or customers, will have increasing access to new tools and technologies. There has been a trend towards the integration of this access into business strategies and it is a modus operandi that will multiply exponentially. Both individuals and organizations can take advantage of the benefits and opportunities that go along with their participation in the Digital and Collaboration Economies. In particular, this can come from securing a meaningful position in the two-way knowledge flow characteristic of the cooperation and collaboration occurring between different people, departments and organizations through the synching and sharing of information either on premise, platform or via the Cloud.

An example of one of the ways that this can be operationally efficient and fiscally significant is by using these tools to bring Endusers into the R&D&D phase of a product/service build cycle. This extra D denotes the extension of the definition from R&D (Research and Development) to include Design, which is now equally important to consider in the early stages of a build. Through an engaged relationship with an organization's Flat World Navigators, Endusers' knowledge can be applied to a wide range of issues. These include comparative pricing and purchasing options, as well as opinions on the usability of any item looking to find a position in their portfolio of solutions and tools.

Flat World Navigators share their stories

Aria Finger, *COO DoSomething.org and President, TMI Agency*

The focus group is dead. In this new world of technology, getting the opinion of 20–25 people who you paid $50 to sit around for an hour seems silly. Instead, you can be creating MVPs (minimal viable products) of your new product idea and getting it out into the marketplace, or into the hands of those 20–25 consumers, as soon as possible. At DoSomething.org, instead of just focus-grouping a new campaign idea, we put the campaign up on the website, send traffic to it and monitor, in real time, how our members are responding. We can test if they'd prefer a different tagline, a different picture or need more information. Using real-time feedback helps you get products to market more quickly and truly gives you a sense of the customer feedback for your products. And, perhaps most importantly, it saves you the time of building a whole new full-featured product, only to have it fall flat on its face because no one likes it.

We now have the ability to go directly to the consumer. Large media channels like TV, magazines, outdoor, etc are still relevant, even to the younger generation, but we now have great tools to complement those firehoses. With the power of social media, we can, on a zero dollar marketing budget, reach millions of young people with a good idea. Similarly, with the power of mobile and SMS (young people rarely use e-mail to communicate with each other any more) we can have these young people become members of DoSomething through an identifying characteristic – their cell phone number – that is much less likely to change than their e-mail address.

Our company culture has always been flat. We love that ideas come from anywhere. Every Wednesday morning at DoSomething. org we have an hour-long 'innovation meeting'. Anyone can offer to present – from the CEO to a newly hired high school intern. We want to hear new ideas from all segments of the organization. The idea is presented and the whole staff then asks questions, brainstorms, cheers, and sometimes, of course, rips the idea apart. It's a great way to make sure that new (read: crazy, scary, big, hairy, audacious) ideas have a chance to bubble up.

Accessing Enduser insights and opinions can be as simple as engaging with them on a website, Facebook page, mobile application, online store or onsite kiosk. As the digital world becomes ever-more accessible there is no doubt that integrated, secure connections will also come via collaboration architecture such as wearable tech and internet TV. According to a CCS Insight forecast of the global wearables market, the number of devices shipped will jump from 29 million in 2014 to 172 million by 2018.

Traditional incumbents of the Tier One and Tier Two categories risk a serious erosion of their revenue base if they ignore these trends. Equally dangerous would be for them to discount the power and positioning taking place by those entering the arena from the Majority World or arising out of a nominally niche position in their own backyards. When you bring into play digital technologies such as 3D printing, entire industries could be upended. As I made clear in *Innovation: How innovators think, act and change our world*:

As the technology advances and the requisite components become smaller and more affordable – not unlike the evolution of mobile phone technology – it doesn't take a great leap of imagination to see this innovation as part of every wired household... How will it affect the retail industry if ever-demanding customers can order exactly what they want directly from an industry-sized 3D printer or make it themselves from the printer they keep at home?

This is not something on the horizon you need to pay attention to 'at some point'. It is happening now and it will, without doubt, have a massive impact on economies at local, national and supranational levels. Take TechShop as just one example of the change already in action. It is the epitome of an organization benefiting from the opportunities embedded in both the Digital and Collaboration Economies. A 'Maker Space', part of the 'Maker Movement', TechShop gives access to and use of machinery – ie lathes, welding equipment, 3D printers, etc. It empowers its members through use of multi-millions of dollars' worth of industrial-grade equipment for a monthly fee equating to no more than that normally paid for a gym membership. That's pumping up some serious business muscle!

Having traditional barriers to entry either lowered or, in some cases, eliminated altogether, means that individuals and organizations that would have had a massive hurdle in the way of their taking their product or service from ideation to commercialization can now move forward, often with flexible, agile strategies, to take their place in the emerging economic landscape.

Of course 3D printing and the like will not answer all challenges and it is likely that the Collaboration Economy will come into play here. For instance, traditional Tier Ones and Twos could provide major infrastructure that can be a support system used by a wide range of newcomers – thus creating a 'win-win' sharing ecosystem. This has the potential to grow exponentially and be instrumental in increasing knowledge and skills bases – banks of experience, expertise and excellence – as well as the speed of improvements hoped for in the technology and policy arenas.

Organizations of any and every size can take advantage of the savings – in time and money – inherent in the Collaboration Economy. Late 2014 saw big players in the banking sector, Barclays and CommBank, unveiling a plan to work together on an ETL (Extract, Transform, Load) software development. It is an expensive and extensively complex tool to develop, so by working together their aim is to alleviate a number of pressures and problems such as ongoing maintenance and implementation hiccups. This is certainly not the traditional behaviour of big banks, who have long sought to protect their systems and sector positions by keeping their cards – and code – close to their chests. However, as Cisco Director Gordon Feller made clear in Chapter 4, 'Everybody who is anybody in the technology world sees how powerful open source is and cannot deny the fact that it's changed all of the ways we operate in the technology industry.' Furthermore, Cisco's best partners are 'adopting open knowledge exchange and open innovation as the fundamental business model.'

Flat World Navigators share their stories

Donnie Maclurcan, *Post Growth Institute Executive Director*

In 2014, my Post Growth Institute colleagues and I established the Post Growth Alliance: 49 content-producing organizations, collaborating with a shared vision for a flourishing future not dependent on economic growth. Given the member organizations are extremely busy and often seeking widespread impact with limited resources, the Alliance seeks to save them time whilst increasing their online reach. As part of the Alliance's offering, each group is able to submit up to four pieces of content annually to an online template we designed using the latest research on what makes a good Facebook and Twitter post. We then edit the content into a final format and share it with all Alliance members via e-mail. The 49 social media managers, representing each of the organizations, can then customize the message and share it through their organization's Facebook and Twitter accounts, or re-post and retweet the original message that we launch via the Post Growth Institute's social media accounts.

This content curation service has proven incredibly successful because it lessens the amount of time people need to spend finding high-quality, relevant content, and simultaneously uses our collective reach to maximize individual group impact. For instance, one of our recent Facebook posts received 125,000 views – something none of us would have been able to achieve working alone, especially in the age of declining organic reach.

Another example of how I use collaborative methods is by running 'Offers and Needs Markets'. In this process, a group of individuals meet to share what they are willing to offer and what they need from each other, both personally and professionally. Participants are also able to share descriptive information about how available or urgent these offers and needs are, and what remuneration they are seeking or can offer.

I ran my first marketplace with 100 participants in Sydney. In just 90 minutes, more than 500 offers and needs were matched, although the room was filled entirely with strangers! At that event, I asked if there was anyone who wanted to 'shout out' a particular need they had. Someone said, 'I need a bus for my community project!' Amazingly, an older lady on the other side of the room shouted out, 'I've got a bus; it has been sitting in my backyard for five years, it works and I've been wanting to give it to someone for a good project!'

I encourage people to share their 'blue sky' need or want with the group and see what happens. In one marketplace experience I had a participant say, 'I want a Porsche!' While no one had a Porsche in their backyard that they were willing to share, one woman in the room had a partner who regularly ran a high performance vehicles day on a local racetrack. She subsequently arranged for the man to drive a Porsche, for the whole day, at her husband's racetrack.

These are fun stories, but the greatest lesson we have learned with the Offers and Needs Markets, and I think this is true whenever you're engaging in collaboration, is that when you begin with what you are offering first, rather than starting with what you need, it builds trust and a human relationship; you can then be even bolder with your needs.

Flat world navigation – building bigger, broader, better business

If this sharing of knowledge and risk can be so profitably engaged in by two banking behemoths, imagine what benefits can arise from, for instance, sharing cross-departmentally within the same organization. Problems and their solutions, as well as the opportunities that may present themselves, such as increased performance capabilities and capacities, will come from a business culture centred on the free flow of knowledge, experience, expertise and analysis and being a positive player in a secure, sustainable free flow of non-siloed knowledge and resources, wherever they reside.

Woolworths and eBay are another tag team which makes sense both for them and their customers. The companies released a joint statement in February 2015 noting that, 'new research shows that one in five online shoppers in Australia buys online at least once a week, yet almost half (47 per cent) are not permitted to receive personal deliveries at work' (Philipson, 2015). No doubt seeing this as a great business opportunity, the collaborative agreement enables eBay purchasers to collect their online purchases from their local Woolies. It's not a great stretch to think that, while there, customers may be enticed to make a grocery purchase – win-win-win.

Unsurprisingly, I've no doubt, I am a wholehearted supporter of building as many effective business bridges as possible. This is as long as the connections are useful for all stakeholders and manageable in a strategic ecosystem, which is:

- Multilingual. It should encompass human and computer languages and protocols, as well as empowering and engaging with the global digital economy in the language(s) preferred by Endusers. This also enables collaborations to include the millions of currently connected 'things' in the IoT, which will become trillions in just a few years.

- Platform neutral. This ensures that stakeholders can access the data (be it structured or unstructured), information and knowledge captured on the platform and operating system of their choice.

- Vendor neutral. Stakeholders expect to be able to use a variety of legacy systems, to work and share easily, without any added costs brought on by forcing additional spending (of time and money) on technology procurement.

- Secure and auditable. This is particularly important when the provenance of KA (Knowledge Assets) needs to be recorded and national and international compliance regulations need to be demonstrably met.

- Based on agreed upon standards. Where applicable, these can cover issues such as base-level expectations on quality and conflict arbitration practices, etc.

All of the above also ensures that there is a far greater likelihood of creating profitable and propitious relationships between large enterprises (such as banks) and SMEs. It is these smaller entities who are generally more agile, able to test and implement innovative ideas, products and services, but far less likely to be able to afford the enterprise technology employed by Tier Ones and Twos.

Flat World Navigators share their stories

Joan Michelson, *CEO, Executive Editor and Host,* *Green Connections Media*

Collaboration and networking have been crucial in my career. No one can accomplish anything alone. Networking has given me access to people and resources that have been tremendously beneficial to me, my businesses and my clients greatly, and it will continue to be so. It's how you differentiate yourself and your value, and build trust, which is crucial to getting to 'yes'. Through networking you find the best collaborators for your specific needs. Keep asking 'who else should I be talking to?'

Networking only works if you use it, though; that is, if you go to events and introduce yourself and then ask questions that are relevant and show you are listening to them – and then follow up, follow up, follow up. Persistence pays – when you are pleasant and courteous about it. The most effective 'tools' for getting your message out and engaging with audiences are:

- be authentic;

- listen to people, especially when they tell you something you don't want to hear or that makes you uncomfortable – which is often the most valuable information;

- ask for clarification if you are confused;

- admit mistakes and fix them immediately; and

- put together deals with collaborators that are truly mutually advantageous.

Do you want the best solution? One of the most important reasons to collaborate is to identify new ideas, solutions and innovations you had not thought of on your own – the adage 'two heads are better than one' – and often how to make it happen. This is especially important for companies or organizations at an inflection point, expanding into new markets, or in a new sector, such as the energy/ clean tech/sustainability space. It's also vital to finding solutions for critical global challenges such as transitioning our economy to a clean, green one to reduce the threat of climate change and preserve the natural ecosystem on which we all depend (ie water, air, energy, land and species).

Language matters. As the global economy births a host of new industries, such as the energy and sustainability industry, a host of new words and concepts enter the lexicon that most people, even highly educated people, don't know. People from different careers, training, and/or countries have different definitions of the same words as well (I've burst into laughter sometimes realizing the people I'm chatting with are using words with a completely different definition than mine!). In addition, we all have global audiences and do business with people for whom English is not their native language. (Having learned non-native languages myself, I am sensitive to the fact that English is very complicated.) Because of this we always try to define words and concepts on our radio show

Green Connections and in our blogs, including mine on the Huffington Post.

I consistently ask for confirmation that I am getting my message across, if they know what words mean, if I think they might be confused, which 'saves face' (some people don't want to ask). I often say 'There are no stupid questions, so don't leave yourself confused or in the dark about something. Ask us!'

I also ask questions that subtly probe the level of understanding of the topic under discussion, starting with the basics, so no one feels left behind. This enables me to engage with the audience, and stay attuned to them, keeping them with me. Actively engaging with the audience has other crucial benefits: (1) it helps them feel 'heard', (2) it helps them feel they gained value from your presentation, (3) it improves the likelihood you will successfully communicate your message, and (4) it increases the chances you'll be asked back or gain other business benefit from the presentation.

The mission of Green Connections Media is to grow a clean, green economy in which women have economic parity. Therefore, we raise the visibility of talented, ambitious women through the use of tools, services and connections, helping them share their expertise and grow. We do this through a podcast series of interviews with talented women (and a few men) in the energy, clean tech and sustainability space (eg, STEM, broadly defined) and related topics such as leadership and innovation, and by making it easier for industry leaders to hire and promote more women. I speak and write about these issues as well.

I am continually amazed at how many people are communication-challenged – or who think they are – and how it impedes their progress. We need to engage with the audiences and not assume they know what to do or say. Everyone has questions, everyone's questions are valid – and everyone has something to teach us. We just need to listen, ask for more clarification, listen for nuances, and follow up.

SMEs will become increasingly important in the Digital and Collaboration Economies, particularly as the Majority World becomes more entwined in the DNA of global business as consumers, competitors and potential collaborative partners. According to the European Commission's 2012 report, 'Do SMEs Create More and Better Jobs?' (de Kok *et al*, 2012) which investigated the impact of SMEs on the labour market in the EU, '85 per cent of net new jobs created in the EU between 2002 and 2010 were in fact created by SMEs.' According to both the Association of Chartered Certified Accountants (ACCA) and the Institute of Management Accountants (IMA), internationally 2014 saw SMEs experiencing increased business confidence and economic outlooks (ACCA, 2014). Though there were some disappointments due to governmental policies, there was much good news, for instance from Singapore, which was noted as being the nation with the most SME-friendly governmental policies; it was followed by the UAE and the UK.

In Australia, SMEs are the very heart of the country's economic health. They make up more than 99 per cent of the nation's businesses, and according to the ACMA 2014 report, Australian SMEs in the digital economy were estimated to make up 69 per cent of the country's workforce and 57 per cent of its 2011–2012 total business income. And, just because they're small doesn't mean they can't pack a worldwide wallop! As noted in the ACMA report:

> According to an international study of SMEs from 21 countries, including Australia, technologies such as the internet are providing opportunities to expand market reach and respond to increased global competition, with 66 per cent of respondents anticipating that over 40 per cent of their revenue will be generated from international markets within the next three years.
>
> (Oxford Economics, 2014)

Regardless of the size of the organization, it could be argued that the most important skill set moving forward will be that of flat world navigation. This is due in no small part to the fact that it will be those Flat World Navigators who create value through the relationships they build (such as that between Barclays' Chief Data Officer Usama Fayyad and Commonwealth's CIO Michael Harte) between colleagues, partners, clients and customers. This is the case at a local, national and international level and between players of any and all sizes. It is those dynamics that will be making the most difference, and the most money, in the global DACE.

Be in no doubt that these business realities include a multitude of opportunities to be taken advantage of, but your access to them is dependent upon how your organization can deliver to and profit from a collaborative value chain. The organizations that embrace this changed environment and embrace the strategic import of flat world navigation and Flat World Navigators will be well positioned to ride the waves of the global DACE rather than being drowned by them. The costs incurred in engagement are negligible in comparison to the cost of doing nothing, which could be detrimental if not disastrous to organizations led by those who erroneously believe that they can ride out the situation by bolting on a new label on an old org. chart.

This is not a 'cultural sea change'; this is a flood and for those who do not take up the buoyancy provided by flat world navigation and Flat World Navigators, it will be a tsunami that sweeps them, and their traditional business models, away. Adapting may be most difficult for those who are, at least currently, comfortably situated within the upper echelons of an organization. Decades of unquestioned belief by board members, C-Suite executives and management at the senior (and, middle) levels that 'the way it is', is the way it should be, will be difficult to shake off. But the shaking must occur so that their strategic vision on scale and scope are reframed and realigned from 'command and control' competition to the global DACE and the new business realities therein.

Actions with intent

As with any relationship, decide what you want and need from a partner and what you are able and willing to share.

Using keywords searches etc, locate and approach potential partners who appear to share a similar ethos; being in the same market domain is unnecessary.

Offer first and ask later – this may be your greatest gift in opening doors and engaging potential partners and Endusers.

Begin with one project – it's dating rather than marriage you're looking for initially – before deciding whether a long-term relationship is something to be signed up to.

Choose a project that will deliver results early and often. Look for simple, secure ways for your team, tools and tech to work together ensuring there is no unnecessary overlap and the correct person, process or tool is being used in the appropriate activity.

INTERVIEW   An interview with a Flat World Navigator

Clara Gaggero Westaway, *Co-founder and Creative Director at Special Projects, Visiting Senior Tutor at the Royal College of Art and Queen Mary University of London, Formerly Co-founder and Director of Vitamins*

Clara Gaggero Westaway is the co-founder and creative director of Special Projects, an award-winning design consultancy based in London. She previously co-founded and ran the design studio Vitamins. Her design experience spans from digital services to physical products; Clara has designed for companies including the BBC, BlackBerry, Nokia, Samsung, Burton and global startups and has worked on projects including wearable technology for pro snowboarders, an internet-connected calendar made entirely out of Lego, and designed the only mobile phone user manual to be featured in the MoMA New York. Her philosophy is to treat each project as a unique challenge, yet focus the process and the solutions on the user. Clara is a visiting senior lecturer at the Royal College of Art and at Queen Mary University of London.

Though you live in the UK Clara, you were actually born in Italy, correct?

Yes, I lived there until I was 18; I did my first MA, in Industrial Design, there. Then I moved first to Berlin for three years and then to London.

I know that you have expertise in engineering but, if you don't mind me saying, looking at your work lends me to think you have the 'heart' of a collaborative artist. You seem to take great joy in in working with different people.

Definitely! My dad had a mechanical factory, he worked in the car industry for Fiat, BMW and Mercedes. My Mom had a fashion store. Sometimes

I was in the middle of silks and sequins and the day after I'd be in a hardcore metal factory. I think that nurtured my love for both technology and engineering as well as fashion design and the more aesthetic side of things. Sometimes it's a struggle to put the two together but when it works, it's definitely a very good thing.

Certainly, both are very influenced by their Endusers. If they don't feel and look 'right', they're just not going to be used. They won't be worn or driven.

Exactly. You already see the common things in these two very different worlds.

And though they both use different 'fabrics' each, in their own way, moulds around the Enduser.

It's interesting that you say that because one year ago I was asked to do the opening presentation for a conference on the 'Wearable Future'. They asked me to frame my presentation on 'what is wearable'. To me, wearable can be things that you wear on your body but also things that surround you for a certain amount of time like a car, or even a room. We have to think about 'wearable' more broadly.

And perhaps what we're 'wearing' inside our body.

Yeah! We already have the cochlear implants.

I know you worked on some experimental wearable sports sensors for snowboarding – can you tell me a bit more about that?

Burton, a snowboarding clothing company, approached Adrian and I at our previous design studio, Vitamins. [Adrian Westaway, Clara's husband, is co-founder of Special Projects, a member of the Magic Circle, and is also interviewed in this book.] They asked us to do some investigation on wearables in collaboration with Nokia; this was in 2009 or 2010, before all the commercial wearable gadgets came onto the market. We prototyped 30 sensors in 30 days and then, of course, we involved the Endusers.

In this case these were the pro snowboarders on the Burton team. We investigated what they could wear and what information was interesting and useful for them, and for the sport, to learn more about their performance and improve their results.

Speaking of useful, the first project that I saw of yours was your Bit Planner, the internet-connected calendar made entirely out of Lego pieces. I remember putting on my 'Flat World Navigator hat' and e-mailing Adrian to tell him how inspiring I found your work. That project was a great illustration of how important the Enduser experience is to you as well as how you see them affect the research, design and creation of your products.

For us it is fundamental; we take on projects that we believe can either inspire or empower the Enduser. It is our mantra. Looking at the Enduser experience is the best way of doing that, particularly now that products and services have physical and digital elements.

For instance, you might have a website, an app and a product; we define the Enduser experience as what the person sees in all these worlds. How will the app integrate with the product? It should not be confusing, it should be an amazing, frictionless experience.

We look at the whole journey that the Enduser will have. This is from the time he or she begins to think that they may want a certain type of product or service, to the moment the decision is made on which one they want and, further, through to them finding and buying the product. It goes on to when they bring the product home, open the box, learn how to use it all the way to repetitive use.

We look at the Enduser journey through to the point at which they would recommend it to other people. That is the whole user experience; it is not just about how the product is presented but how the learning experience and out-of-the-box experience is supported.

It is a very exciting moment for an inventor. We're finally opening up and looking not just at how a person will use 'the machine' but looking at the entirety of the person's experience with multiple aspects of the product or service. I think this will give us the opportunity to improve people's lives rather than just give them a new toothbrush. We'll be able to tell them how to use the toothbrush correctly, tell if they need to go to the dentist and even tell them if their blood sugar level is too high. There is a new, magic world that can be created and it is so exciting!

Speaking of magic, I'd like to talk to you about what it's like to work with your husband in a collaborative project. I suppose part of my interest stems from the fact that I also work with my husband. We work on very different sides of the same coin – I do the text and he does the tech, he writes code and I write words, so we don't crossover. You and Adrian also seem to have complementary expertise and you've found a way to communicate and collaborate in an extremely effective way.

We met at the RCA, the Royal College of Art, on the first day of our course and we started dating two weeks later. We have two very different backgrounds but they're very complementary areas of interest and expertise.

Adrian is trained as an Electronic Engineer and he's also a magician. He brings his expertise in interaction, electronics and digital – but also in how the people react. He explores the best way to inject some surprise and astonishment into a project.

I bring the aesthetic and design element and, as I've always designed with the Enduser in mind, I take care of the Enduser involvement in the research. It's almost like we both research independently and then present our research on the topic to each other. It's then that we brainstorm together so the idea is always generated together.

Yes, it can be quite confrontational because, of course, you always have to discard some ideas and that can be a bit painful. But we know that if one of us is not fully happy with the idea, it means it's not the right idea. We really respect each other's opinion and we know that we are working towards the same goal and trying to make the idea better.

Once we've 'grown the idea' we split the responsibilities and tasks and develop the project that way. This flow of 'going away and coming back together' seems to work very well. It allows us to grow individually and then bring what we have learned back to the table.

I imagine you've developed a way of communicating with each other that gets to the point quite quickly – your own personal 'code', if you will. As you're so used to working together, is it jarring to work with other people, as they might not understand your 'shorthand'?

No, I really like to work with other people. We often collaborate with people or hire freelancers and it is always refreshing. We are very spoiled. We have a pool of talent in London, which is amazing. Every time we work with someone I really enjoy learning from them, collaborating and seeing their point of view. Of course, it might take a little longer to explain something but I never find it difficult; in fact, I always find it very constructive.

When do you bring your collaborators into the project?

We involve 3D, graphic, interface and user interface designers, video makers and photographers. So far we've brought them in either at the very beginning of the project, when we do the Enduser investigation, or when the idea is at concept stage and we need to communicate it to the client and develop it more fully.

We are trying to formalize our process; we're trying to share and teach it to other people so they can be involved in the whole project and maybe even start managing and running projects themselves.

In bringing such a plethora of different people together on a project – be they academics, artists, corporates, technologists, marketers or sales people – have you found it difficult to overcome the challenge of their disparate ontologies? For instance, I've found that many diversified groups have differing definitions of the word 'finished'. To the salesperson or marketer a finished product is one they can sell, it's ready to go to market. For the technologist, it might mean simply having a working prototype.

That's interesting; I'd never thought about the different concepts of finished before. But you're right.

I guess we always try to design products, services and experiences that are available to everyone. And we work to find ways, particularly when presenting our work, to be clear enough so that everyone can understand what we have done. We always say, 'OK, try to explain to a grandma. How we would tell her what we have done?'

That's particularly important for the new Internet of Things and connected devices. It's very important to find a way of communicating what's happening in this area to people outside of a peer group of professionals. Communicating this connectivity to the Enduser is the only way forward, particularly now that people are beginning to understand more about digital privacy and data.

I'm not saying all explanations must be simple, but things do need to be clearly explained. We often use familiar objects in explanations. A good example of this is a book we designed to explain, to all Endusers, how to set up and use a mobile phone.

It is quite a brilliant book; it's the only mobile phone user manual to be featured in the Museum of Modern Art, isn't it?

Yes; it's a really fun experience to go through it, but it actually acts as a mediator, resolving conflict between the Enduser and the device. It uses familiar objects to explain a concept, which is one of the principles of magic – giving familiar objects a little twist to make them magical.

Certainly at KimmiC we believe asking people to make too large a shift away from their comfort zone can bring about a great deal of 'push back'. However, if you ask them to only adjust by one, small degree they will still be facing in a different direction and they can still travel to an entirely new and exciting place.

The Samsung 'Out of the Box' project started with the assumption that we would have to design a 'silver' phone – a version of a mobile phone for older people. Instead we found that older people were completely able to learn a new technology, they just needed something familiar to guide them through the learning process.

So, instead of designing a new product we redesigned the out-of-box experience. Our packaging and Enduser manual guide supports their learning and also makes them giggle. Mixing analog, digital and familiar objects is definitely the way we believe we can make meaningful and magical experiences.

And it works, magically!

> ### FWN Keys from Clara Gaggero Westaway
>
> - If you want to inspire and empower your Enduser focus on how they'll experience your product or service from beginning to end.
>
> - When working collaboratively, respect each other's opinion in the knowledge that you are working towards the same goal(s).
>
> - Every explanation does not need to be simple but it must be clear and easily understood.

In conclusion

Within this chapter we explored the imperative to both understand and engage with the DACE, regardless of the size or location of your business or role. The changes being brought about by these extreme economic developments and the move away from command and control structures are underlined. So too are the advantages and opportunities presented to those willing to investigate and implement new DACE-based, flat world business models and strategies.

Equally important for organizations wanting to instigate innovation is the clarion call to seek out ideas and input from any and all stakeholders. This includes your Endusers, who can be enlisted to assist in the design of products and services. Working collaboratively, with clients, colleagues and partners you can achieve far more – including establishing a radically expanded reach – in less time, and with fewer costs, than you could going it alone.

The following chapter, 'Changing markets and competitive advantages accessed through flat world navigation', delves deeper into what development of, and within, the DACE means to your business, market, networks and pool of potential partners, clients and collaborators. This is investigated at micro/local, macro/supranational, SME and Tier One/Two levels. Additionally, we draw attention to the significance of the synergies between Flat World Navigator and SMEs and the FWN's role in generating opportunities through measurable ROI and the creation of value-based bridges between individuals and organizations.

Changing markets and competitive advantages accessed through flat world navigation

Advantage Attention
Authentic Business Change
Collaboration Communicate Connect
DACE Digital Economy Enduser Flat World
Navigator Global Network Relationship Strategy
Success Technology Win-Win   **Communities Connect**
Effective Entrepreneur Events Integrity Leverage Reputation
SME Social Stakeholder Startup Strategy Think Value

Featuring

Miguel Reynolds Brandão (Market Financed Inventions), Chris Gabriel (Alive Mobile Group), Patricia Greene (Goldman Sachs 10,000 Small Businesses Initiative and Babson College), Carolyn Hardy (United Nations Trust Fund to End Violence Against Women) and Karima Mariama-Arthur (WordSmithRapport)

Did you feel the earth move? If not, I wonder where you've been hiding yourself because the rest of us are dealing with the seismic shifts that have been steadily occurring as the business world becomes flatter and more connected every day. There's no ignoring it, no running away from it, you can't duck and cover your head or hide behind your desk – the change has come and it is as relentless as it is unstoppable.

To ensure that you and your organization – regardless of its size, location, product or service – remain standing, there are certain outward-facing and inward-looking issues which must be addressed. In particular you will need to ascertain, along with their effect on your infrastructure, what these changes mean for your market, your networks and your pool of potential joint venture/collaboration partners.

Traditional strategies and methods of building and maintaining markets are under unceasing attack. Nimble startups answering specific customer wants and needs are gaining traction and seeing growth at rates never seen in history – more often than not at the expense of established market players. Due to this it is the organizations that seize the opportunities inherent in this revolution of business structure and strategy, who will find themselves with an unprecedented competitive advantage during this time of change and upheaval.

The changing economic stage

Though there are those who may work to rebrand or refrain from stating it, those on 'the ground' are in no doubt that we are in the midst of a time of economic recession and depression. The number of unemployed and underemployed is testament to an increasing strain on national and supranational economies, and all the while every stakeholder is frantically searching for where the next economic miracle will come from. Could it be that the answer is right in front of us – centre stage, if you will – in the duopoly of entrepreneurialism and SMEs who are engaging in the navigation of the flat world?

Certainly there are a number of nations that are acknowledging this synergy. In 2014 Brazil and Europe, through the Connect organization, exchanged entrepreneurs and SME business owners with a view to expanding their worldview and increasing their international potential and possibilities. In fact it is extremely common to find entities such as the EU, OECD and the SME Association of Australia – to name but a few – consistent in their tendency to group SMEs and entrepreneurs in their case studies and development offerings.

Of course, there is no doubt that large multinationals and their ilk are important. However, internationally there is a rising trend for a large number of the unemployed and underemployed to become self-employed. They are the basis of a new surge in entrepreneurship and small- to medium-sized business owners coming onto the stage.

One clear example of this being played out was in Spain, where formidable unemployment figures – over 26 per cent in August 2013 – led to a noticeable increase in the number of people setting their sights on self-employment and entrepreneurship as their way forward. According to Spain's Instituto Nacional de Estadistica (National Institute of Statistics) by October of 2013 the number of self-employed had risen by more than 15,000; this is in stark contrast to the year before where there had been a fall of nearly 7,000 in the same timeframe. Additionally, the first half of that year saw the number of companies created jump significantly. This trend may reflect a 'push' into entrepreneurship rather than the aforementioned 'jump', but the fact remains that the move has been made and the necessity of getting off the unemployment line may have created a mother lode of new SMEs.

The 'undiscovered country' – the SME stalwarts

SMEs are the 'work horses' of the global economy. They account for approximately 90 per cent of businesses and 50 per cent of employment around the world and yet they have been too often ignored by press and pundits alike as they look for any kind of solution to the issues of business development and job creation. They've rarely been invited to sit at the strategy table and yet they remain key players in the potential economic stability and market growth of communities and countries.

To a certain degree the fact that they are not part of strategy discussions can be understood. There is a need for them to gather together and speak, with one voice, of their position as key players and, equally, what their requirements are to continue in this position. Obviously, as they are relatively minuscule in number, it is much simpler for Tier One organizations to gather as peers and influence policy and direction.

However, as the SME community increases its navigation and connection in the flat world of the DACE (Digital, Attention and Collaboration Economies) the potential for them to be a force to contend and connect with intensifies exponentially. The 2014 Deloitte report 'Democratizing Technology: Crossing the "CASM" to Serve Small and Medium Businesses' (Banerjee and Openshaw, 2014) notes that, 'In 2013, the National Federation of Independent Business stated that US small businesses collectively produced half of all US private sector GDP and employed more than half of the US private sector workforce'. They employ between 60 and 80 per cent of the formal workforce in the OECD. It is quite feasible that this 'constituency of capital', once connected, could change the economic direction of communities, countries and continents.

If you are the owner, investor, or member of an SME, now is the time to reach out to your potential partners, colleagues and collaborators. Equally, if you work with, for or in a large organization the time is ripe to build the bridges and business connections to engender the collaborative potential profits waiting to be shared between you and the SMEs within your own DACE ecosystem/flat world. Service providers, particularly those who have, to date, been focused on fighting in the highly contested arena of Tier One and Two provisioning should prime themselves to point their attention towards their potential SME clients and customers who are gearing up to being increasingly pivotal players in the DACE.

The acceleration of innovation and the massive decrease in infrastructure prices, due to the increased availability and shrinking cost of Cloud technology, are having an enormous effect on the business environment in general. Specifically, SMEs are, quite rightly, coming to expect access to levels of technology and service which were, until recently, the purview of organizations that have been the traditional tenants of the corporate top tier.

For their 'Crossing the "CASM"' report, Deloitte analysed 84 large tech companies. Of those, they found it was the organizations serving SMBs (small- to medium-sized businesses, aka SMEs), that 'consistently out-performed their counterparts in revenue growth and operating income margin' and 'experienced less volatility in revenue growth and operating margins.'

The next significant change, which is now appearing on the horizon and that is likely to be a major game changer in the near, medium and long term, comes from those providers that enable cooperation and collaboration between Tier Ones/Twos and their SME clients. It goes without saying that there will (almost) always be room found in a top tier budget for the rollout of new infrastructure and systems. However, they cannot expect their potential partners, who do not have the same budgetary leeway, to be able to access their infrastructure in a manner that is complementary, cost effective and consistent for all parties – things which are imperative for success, particularly in the global DACE.

Flat World Navigators share their stories

Chris Gabriel, *Chairman, Alive Mobile Group*

Collaboration and networking have been essential in my career and business to date, and will continue to increase in significance going forward. Operating across several continents, collaboration and networking are vital to establish credibility, leverage diversity and skill sets, secure and deliver global projects and initiatives, facilitate liaison and attract and recruit the best talent. We now operate in one global marketplace and therefore need to leverage the tools to compete and thrive.

Endusers now have instant unlimited choice at their fingertips – how you differentiate yourself to come up first in their ranking and manage your online presence is vital for ongoing survival. With online payment methods, international delivery and access to global markets, consumers are less concerned about where they source their product from – local sourcing is less of a priority for many. For the seller, therefore, it's all about marketing, reputation management, validation through case study examples, online presence, SEO, etc – constant reinvention of the business in order to establish and maintain credibility and stay ahead of the competition, without falling into the trap of competing on price. Business continues to move faster and calls for more agile and dynamic leaders – the pace of change will only quicken – all good fun though!

Operating in the startup and angel investment space, I am plugged into several select national and global networks and collaboration initiatives all aimed at increasing deal flow. Likewise I am plugged into the incubator and mentor scene, nationally collaborating with select universities and incubators again aimed at increasing deal flow. Furthermore, operating as a global advisor to several PE funds, it is vital to establish a global reputation and to leverage skill sets and resources to optimize outcomes. In addition, I leverage industry and professional networks more for visibility and reference, and recruitment of the best talent, as well as leveraging common tools such as LinkedIn, Google and other relevant software.

One of my startup companies is Alive Mobile Group – we have developed bespoke enterprise apps. We will never cut a line of code until we have first workshopped the pain points in an organization with all the critical stakeholders – redesigning their entire suite of business processes around human-centricity and mobility, and building in analytics to prove out benefits following rollout of the app. Up-front engagement of all key stakeholders builds rapid buy in, assures successful outcomes and drives repeat business.

Reputations are earned and outcomes, good or bad, are promulgated on social media. I was in a situation where I was requested to compromise my integrity – I declined to do so and walked away from the deal. Subsequently the power of social networks spread the word that I was a person of integrity, which immediately resulted in an influx of business and numerous other opportunities that otherwise would not have come my way. As a public figure, everything you do, say and stand for is open for comment, the nature of which is outside of your control. The learning was simple: never compromise your integrity for short-term gains. If you are in once, you are in for life.

The new gameplay of success – flattening your DACE

With the convergence of new technologies, technically savvy and empowered Endusers, and the advent of upstart startups, the status quo has forever changed. The challenge is to determine what can be gained from the new provisions while remaining focused on how those gains can be transferred into a growing value proposition for all stakeholders.

For many organizations this premise alone is a shift outside their normal perspective where being the General who musters the troops to go forth and conquer was the name of their game. Times have changed and the audience – those watching your work and work-place: customers, clients, etc – aren't giving the awards and rewards to 'he (or she) who shouts loudest' but rather to those that have the most interesting, informative, intuitive thing to say. Rather than focusing on marshalling 'the art of war' the future of business is likely to lean towards learning how to strategically work the windfall of win-win.

> Honesty and authenticity are the foundation for developing solid professional relationships. Be the best version of yourself, without apology. Let people see the real you and it's up to them to determine whether they will accept it or not. But, making a good impression isn't the end of your work. You have to nurture and maintain professional relationships by consistently showing up with integrity and delivering on the promise of results. If not, you'll find out fast how your reputation can precede you. Building solid, long-term professional relationships is not for the faint of heart. You've got to put some relationship-building skin in the game if you want results.
>
> Karima Mariama-Arthur, Founder and CEO at WordSmithRapport

To do this will necessitate not only evolving how your market and market partners think about you and your brand but, quite likely, how you think about these things too. It may take a quite fundamental change in perspective for the inherent problems and potential bene-fits to become clear but it is an alteration which, I believe, will pay substantial dividends.

The most effective way to make gains in the DACE is through an ROI (Return on Involvement). It will come as no surprise that I see Flat World Navigators and flat world navigational skills as powerful avenues through which any organization can strike a compelling and clear competitive advantage.

The Flat World Navigator effect – transforming operations into opportunities

Flat World Navigators and flat world navigation are the enablers of transformation in the globally mobile and social DACE. It stands to reason, therefore, that engaging and empowering these navigators to connect, communicate and collaborate with colleagues, consumers, customers and clients is sound strategy. This is particularly true when looking to reap rewards from the altered business models which encompass social, mobile initiatives and outcomes.

The flexibility and inherent agility – due to their ability to make quick decisions – of SMEs means that they can adjust their value and supply chains with far greater expediency and efficiency than larger behemoths. Additionally, they are in a position to take advantage of joint venture opportunities, which are becoming more easily embedded into the offerings presented to Endusers. Service suppliers can work with product developers who engage with delivery providers. By taking advantage of mobile/Cloud-based digital technology and tools – which are unlocked through vendor neutrality – and by embracing win-win business models, SMEs can transform their business strategies and trajectories towards success in the DACE through increased customer and client engagement.

According to a December 2014 Report, 'The Mobile Internet Economy in Europe', published by Boston Consulting Global, the mobile internet economy annually generates revenues of €92 billion in the EU5 (France, Germany, Italy, Spain and the UK). This is expected to rise to approximately €230 billion by 2017. Driven by lower cost and capability requirements, according to the report, the majority of EU5 consumers would 'give up alcohol and almost 50 per cent are willing to forgo coffee, movies, and exercise to keep their mobile internet access. One in five is willing to give up his or her car and 17 per cent would abstain from sex.' That kind of loyalty to the marketplace, coupled with the minimal costs involved in 'setting up shop' and connecting in the Cloud, is priceless.

This is the 'business end' of Social Business; the connections and collaborations between customers, clients, colleagues and, occasionally, competitors via social tools and technologies. Relational bridges are being built and, through them, bigger and better business is being done. Regardless of whether the relationships are being made and maintained across the world, across a country or across a departmental floor, whether externally focused or internally facing, the ROI is measurable and valuable.

Flat World Navigators share their stories

Carolyn Hardy, *Senior Advisor, United Nations Trust Fund to End Violence Against Women*

In the last two years, online community building and networking have become increasingly critical as forums for global communities to meet, engage, connect and innovate. I work in the area of gender equality and women's empowerment.

On a macro level, these issues have global communities engaging daily, sharing news and innovation and advocating for people to join the discussion and take a stand. On a more micro, day-to-day level, online digital collaboration is the way I get my work done across borders and time zones with innovative partners and teams working in different countries and communities. Right now I am based in Sydney and managing a global project with partners and stakeholders in London, Cyprus, Nairobi and New York.

My work involves advocacy and outreach to form partnerships. Social media is key to the mobilization of people for advocacy purposes and to deeper engagement with partners around issues. Social platforms have become integral for engaging audiences, supporters and communities. One essential thing that is often forgotten is that these social platforms are two-way and interactive; this can be prodigious if an organization is not strategic or prepared for it.

It is key to be clear about why you are using these platforms. In my case it is for very specific, professional use and I've been fairly structured in the way I engage and the issues I engage on. I keep my content within defined parameters. That way people know what to expect and what they will receive, and what content will be of interest and use for me. There is consistency of messaging and two-way interaction.

I've found that collaboration via various platforms around ideas leads to greater innovation, diversity of thought and bolder thinking. It is easier for people to be courageous and put their ideas out there, as people on those platforms welcome it and engage with it. Your audience has already been 'qualified', so to speak, so you don't need to go looking for an audience.

Social media supports innovation due to fast early feedback and the ability to revise early and re-test quickly. Platforms are data driven so it is easier to see results and tweak as necessary. It also enables rapid mobilization and organization. Movements are gaining strength and robust debate is more readily taking place. Additionally, analytics provide greater measurement and evaluation providing evidence to help innovate and reiterate as projects and innovations develop.

Clear policies about content, joining movements and hash tags need to be in place for organizations with multi-users. It is easy to get swept up in the emotion of a social movement but doing so from an informed, clear policy position is critical if your organization is to have impact.

For individuals:

- don't make it too complex;
- be clear about the objective of interaction;
- be open to inputs and insights from potential collaborators and engagement with a broader community;
- take advantage of opportunities to interact and contribute to discussions;
- find yourself a tribe of like-minded people who are engaging on the same issues. I have.

Smart social data can and should be used in determining strategies that directly respond to the wants, needs and wishes of the relevant stakeholders within these relationships. This data can be garnered from internal tools exemplified by company wikis – a user-built repository of company information and knowledge, which is the same format as Wikipedia but only available internally for company use – as well as blogs, forums, collaboration platforms and external social media arenas such as Twitter, LinkedIn, Facebook, Pinterest and Instagram. These connections are not discretionary, far from it. The demands and expectations of consumers, for instance, are such that lack of communication and connection on social media has moved far beyond surprise and now engenders both bewilderment and disappointment, and leads to a decision to take business elsewhere.

In times of crisis these lines of communication are invaluable in sharing news but are equally important in enabling those within the network to contribute to and, potentially, co-create solutions. Flat World Navigators are extremely adept at using this effective and efficient method of both educating and empowering stakeholders to share ROI dividends. This, in turn, is a powerful point of connection which can pay premium returns post crisis.

> In the aftermath of the Miami hurricane of 1992 a coalition of existing women's groups gathered together under the banner of Women Will Rebuild. Working 'collaboratively as a coalition with short-term goals and a shared vision' they successfully directed resources to the crisis needs of communities and families.
>
> (Enarson and Hearn Morrow, 1998)

Of course, outside of crisis situations it will be the organizations that embrace the Flat World Navigators within their midst and seize the opportunities inherent in the evolution of traditional roles by enhancing the flat world navigational skills of all their stakeholders, who will find themselves with an unprecedented competitive advantage during this time of change. The economies of scale that are afforded to those who use the positive potential of collaboration and the sharing of knowledge assets (KA) when developing ideas, innovations, services and products are unparalleled.

The importance of trusted, authentic relationships and the advantages they bring is perhaps best exemplified in the HR/hiring arena.

This is an industry in a state of huge upheaval as personal recommendations and online networks move to the heart of staffing strategies and the management of personnel performance issues. There are a number of online companies that are now fully focused on disrupting the industry and removing the need for recruitment companies altogether.

Their aim is to use the relationship nodes of online networks – the people who know people, who know people, who know people – as the arbiters of advocacy. In short, who you know and recommend is of much greater interest, and value, than a random prospect being pushed by a recruiter whose bottom line is more about their revenue than your internal personnel view and reviews. The 2014 MIT Sloan Management Review and Deloitte social business study, 'Moving beyond marketing: Generating social business value across the enterprise' (Kane *et al*, 2014), found that the majority of mature and maturing businesses (as reflected in 'the breadth and sophistication of its initiatives') have a strong awareness of the value of social business to their organizations; so much so that '83 per cent turn to social to improve leadership performance and manage talent.'

Every stakeholder can play a part in the navigation of the flat world and the potential collaborations and connections therein – be it in-house, in-industry or bringing together partners who have, to date, not had an accustomed affiliation: academia and SMEs for instance. However, it is the champions of the connections and collaborations, the Flat World Navigators, who bring attention to the ideas, innovations, products and services. This attention – which, as it crosses generational, gender, cultural and departmental boundaries has a greater chance of creating value – is critical to accumulating the advantages inherent in this changed and charged marketplace. It must be remembered that it doesn't matter how profound your product or imaginative your innovation if no one is paying attention to it. Paying attention is the core commodity in the DACE.

> Our collaboration model is not open to everyone. We have the right to select people that share our purpose and believe, as we do, that it is possible to employ inventiveness worldwide. Additionally, it is critical that they believe in the collaboration model that we call Dolphin Collaboration. In this model, smart people collaborate around a

common goal; they are, essentially, missionaries not mercenaries, dolphins not sharks.

Miguel Reynolds Brandão, President at Market Financed Inventions

Flat World Navigators are individuals who connect with a unique, authentic and honest voice. They are the accelerants who propel an organic, primary principal into an effective, purposeful, connection that engenders a buy-in from the community created around, and supportive of, the idea. However, for the greatest ROI, theirs cannot be a solo effort. The most cogent and compelling connections are those which are co-owned, to some degree, by all levels of an organization – with a particular buy-in from middle and senior management. It is with their backing that an innovative idea can be fully integrated into a corporate structure and have the best chance of fully realizing the competitive advantage – be it through the changed infrastructure, enhanced services and products or new clients, customers and partners – it promises.

Actions with intent

It is quite likely you already have most of the tools you need within your organization's daily operations. Take stock of what tools are currently being used internally and externally, by individuals and departments, to connect and collaborate.

Think about your own experience as an online Enduser and how you have, on occasion, not had your needs/wishes met. How would you have changed that experience and how can you incorporate that change within your own organization?

Determine a list of three key goals you want to accomplish, three key competencies you are eager to promote, three positive messages you want to bring attention to and three points of recommendation you are willing to share.

Support a space, either offline or online, where the Flat World Navigators at all levels within your organization are rewarded for exploring ideas that assist in achieving these goals. Be it through rewards or recognition, be sure to enable sustainable sharing of the connections and introductions these Flat World Navigators create.

Flex your own flat world navigating muscle by creating a wish list of potential partners and determine how many 'degrees of separation' there are between you. Delve into your network and ask for introductions, making clear what opportunity you see and how it holds potential benefits to all the stakeholders partaking in the transaction.

INTERVIEW   An interview with a Flat World Navigator

Patricia Greene, *National Academy Director of Goldman Sachs 10,000 Small Businesses Initiative and holder of the Paul T Babson Chair in Entrepreneurial Studies at Babson College*

Patricia Gene Greene holds the Paul T Babson Chair in Entrepreneurial Studies at Babson College, where she formerly served first as Dean of the Undergraduate School and later as Provost. She is the National Academic Director for the Goldman Sachs 10,000 Small Businesses initiative and advisor to the 10,000 Women programme. A founding member of the Diana Project, a research group focused on women's entrepreneurship, Patricia is a federal appointee to the National Advisory Board for the SBA's Small Business Development Centers. She loves to talk about entrepreneurship and changing the way the world does business with anyone who will listen.

Acknowledging that you've had quite an interesting career Patricia, how has collaboration been part of your career to date and do you envision it being important as you go forward?

I work much better as part of a team for a number of reasons. One is I believe in diversity of thought – learning how other people look at things, trying to have multiple perspectives and then building from there. And the other is just flat-out capacity; I tend to get things done for other people before I'll get them done for myself. I'm not sure that's a good thing, but it is a realistic thing. Lately I've tried to do more things on my own but I find that, while I can get it done, I don't enjoy it as much.

Do you think there is a particular personality type that works well collaboratively?

I definitely think there are people to whom it comes more naturally; however, that's not necessarily always the group with which I want to work.

In 10,000 Small Businesses, we do an exercise for our business owners about leadership styles. It's fine to know your style, but we stress that the more important thing is, what does that style mean for how you work with others? So, while it might sometimes seem to work better to work with people like yourself that's not necessarily the way to get the strongest product or service, no matter what it is.

What I've learned to do is recognize that, while it might sometimes be more comfortable, easier, or even more fun to work with people that think like me or that interact like me, it rarely gets the best results. I've also learned that you can actually have more fun if people are thinking about things strikingly differently.

So what would be your key insights for making collaborative opportunities simpler to take advantage of?

One of the things we do both in 10,000 Small Businesses but also at Babson [College], in the programmes we run for executive women, is getting them to think about the management of their network. I think a core of collaboration is to really think about who you're going to collaborate with and how.

I've asked many people over the years, 'How do you do it; what is your process?' I've heard some really good things but it comes down to this: you have to treat it like a resource. Which means it takes time and attention.

Yes, it is one more thing to do, but it's not going to do it itself. So, it can be anything from making sure that every other week you pick two people from your network and just give them a call or send them an e-mail. Or, once a month, run through your contact list and refresh.

I travel a lot and I admit that, in the past, when I'd get to a city I tended to go wherever I had to be then go to my hotel room and do my work. What I've started doing is to task myself so that every time I go to a city I connect with somebody I know there. Even if it's 30 minutes for a cup of coffee or even a call saying, 'I'm in town. I probably can't get together but I just say "Hi" while I'm here.'

We can all take on a responsibility for our 'social resource'. It takes care and feeding, but that's how it starts working for you.

Speaking of making things 'work' for you, I'm very interested in Goldman Sachs' 10,000 Small Businesses Initiative. This stems particularly from an Australian perspective, as 99 per cent of the businesses in Australia are SMEs. It's a nation of small business owners, and yet I wonder how many of those business owners take advantage of, or are even aware of, initiatives that look to enhance their enterprises. How did you come to be involved in the 10,000 Small Businesses Initiative and what is it looking to enable?

The programme is an economic development program situated at the intersection of entrepreneurship and economic development. Its overall objective is the creation of jobs through increasing the generation of revenues. When it was launched, in early 2010, jobs were needed — just like now. That's why it exists.

Ninety-nine point something per cent of the businesses in the United States also are small- and medium-size enterprises. You know, less than 10,000 businesses in the United States are 'big business'. Increasingly, especially over the last five to ten years, there's been more recognition of that. It's not complete, you still wouldn't know it from reading many of the major media, but there is more of a celebration of small- and medium-size enterprises... of a certain type.

I would still suggest that the emphasis is still on the thinnest slice possible, probably the 3 per cent of the businesses that are technology, equity funded, that type of thing. While 97 per cent of the businesses in the country are 'Main Street' types of businesses, they receive very little time and attention.

Do you think the attention given to SMEs is beginning to increase – not least due to the tools and technologies available to them? For instance, the 'microphone' that is social media is empowering them to be heard and make a bit more of a 'ruckus'?

I do think they can be heard more; but, I still think that it's a small slice of them that take advantage of those kinds of tools. I also don't necessarily think that being heard translates into policy. I'd still suggest that for the most part, policy is still made according to much larger-scale businesses. After all, that's where the money can be spent on policy support.

And yet, one could quite logically think: if the majority of the people who are voting are involved with an SME, and a vote is going to translate into getting a policy maker back into his elected seat, it would behove that elected person to pay more attention to SMEs.

It would. The challenge is there are 28 million of them (SME owners). It is much easier to focus on a few very large ones rather than the multitudes of much smaller ones.

In your LinkedIn profile you make a point of stating that you take advantage of the virtual soapbox. How are you using social media and the other tools and technologies to get your message across?

Not as effectively as I would like, I readily admit that. But I do try to point out where people are thinking differently – particularly when is it about the successes of small businesses. It's one of the reasons I really like the *Huffington Post* project, What is Working: Small Business.

I also try to point out that innovation is not just about new products and services, but how we can be more innovative about the way businesses work together – both the people inside those businesses and across businesses. So, overall, in my basically opportunistic, haphazard way, I just try to change the nature of the conversation.

I absolutely agree that there is a great advantage in businesses and business people working together. There is such a need for un-siloing knowledge and working towards win-win collaborations, particularly 'cross-cubically'. Such great savings, both in time and money, can be brought about by connecting and working together.

In a number of your positions you've been the connector between various entities that don't necessarily speak the same language. They may be from the worlds of academia and business, perhaps there are those who are more focused on profit and those who are less so. How do you find the common communication layer that ensures these different groups can understand one another and find common cause?

One of the skills sets I've intentionally tried to hone is that I'm multilingual. Not in languages from different countries and societies but I think that I'm 'organizationally multilingual' – probably because I have such an eclectic background.

I've spent time in for-profits, not-for-profits, on the educational side, practitioner side and, especially through my times at colleges and as a nursing home administrator, with a lot of different generations. I intentionally try and listen and think in what language 'they' are thinking in – and how I can best make that connection.

And I assume that if you are aware of, and concerned with, being heard, it makes sense to ensure that you speak a language that your listeners can not just understand but can connect to.

That's very, very important. I also recognize that SMEs are not a homogeneous group. So, even within SME, you can't just speak pure SME – there is gender SME, minority SME, immigrant SME. There's the sole proprietor SME and there's a high-growth 'I don't want to be an SME'; you name it. They certainly don't all speak exactly the same language.

It's interesting that you've brought up gender. I'm always excited to encounter anyone who wants to enhance women's entrepreneurship, so I'd love to know more about the Diana Project. I know that you're a founding member of the group, which aims to increase the awareness and expectations of entrepreneurial women. What are you hoping will be the end 'product' of the project?

This project came together largely because a group of us wanted to work together. So we looked for something we could do that would be really interesting. We've been working on it for a long time – 15 years. We started with a research and advocacy mission; you have to be careful about mixing advocacy and research but I think it's worked out OK for us.

What would we like to see is equality of opportunity. Nobody is saying, 'everybody should create businesses' and the Diana Project would never say, 'women should make their businesses look like those of men.' We'd like everybody to remember that 'gender' means men and women and then explore what we can learn from each other.

That ties us back to asking, what are better ways to do business that we can develop – rather than just replicate everything that's been done to date? Let's face it, until maybe two decades ago, almost everything we thought we knew about business was learned from studying businessmen in the businesses they created. That doesn't mean it was the right model, it was just the existing model.

Do you feel that in some way we need to be rebranding the discussion over gender and particularly feminism?

Frankly, I think having a discussion about gender is a really good starting point. The discussion is so different across generations; this is true across almost every type of diversity that you'd think about, but I think particularly across generations.

I'm always intrigued by young women, colleagues, undergraduates, who almost patronizingly say, 'We really appreciate what you did. Thank you very much. There's no need for this battle anymore. Everything is fine.' Then they come back to grad school seven, eight or more years later saying, 'Oh! Now I see what you mean!' Because it's when the resources get really worth competing for that the differences start showing up.

There is no doubt that there are women of all ages who don't think it's an issue. But the fact of the matter is there are far, far, far more women that have been on the 'less-than-healthy' side of some type of gender discrimination. So, 'the work' is not finished. At the same time, I have three sons – so I want the world to be wonderful for everybody.

FWN Keys from Patricia Greene

- Though it might seem better to work with people like yourself, that's not necessarily the way to get the strongest product or service.
- Treat collaboration like a resource, which means giving it time and attention.
- Innovation is not just about new products and services, but how we can be more innovative about the way businesses work together – both the people inside those businesses and across businesses.

In conclusion

Specific attention has been given in this chapter to the importance of leveraging any and all flat world navigational skills at your disposal to best support impactful DACE-based business strategies. Not for the first time, the importance of sustained, authentic ROI as the best way to create an ecosystem of credibility, clarity, respect and shared revenue has been emphasized.

The realities implicit in a connected, collaborative flat world of business, particularly as they pertain to markets – local, national and supranational – have been investigated at length. We also focused on the advantages available to those organizations prepared to take off the armour construct of command and control and instead reach out to work for win-win solutions for and with their partners. The position and potential of SMEs in the DACE is another aspect of this chapter that is given ample consideration, along with the economic developments engendered by entrepreneurship and self-employment.

The next chapter, 'Navigating the direction of the DACE', goes further into the exploration of the often drastic social, political and economic effects the DACE is having. It looks at what different nations and nation states, through legislation and engagement, are doing to take advantage of the opportunities the DACE offers them and their citizens. We will also give prominence to the importance of: supported innovation and educational infrastructures; filling a skills shortage gap; and adapting to the altered, interpersonal formats and formulas required to gain and maintain a highly skilled, flexible workforce.

Navigating
the direction
of the DACE

Advantage Attention
Authentic Business Change
Collaboration Communicate Connect
DACE Digital Economy Enduser Enterprise Flat
World Navigator Global Network Relationship Strategy
Success Technology Win-Win **Advocate Cities Citizen**
Community Discussion Funding Government Growth
Information Internet Language Local Million Services Support

Featuring

Peter Church (AFG Venture Group), Jeff Finkle (International
Economic Development Council), Peter Hewkin (Centre for Business
Innovation Ltd), Philo Holland (Authentic Collaboration Space),
Giorgio Prister (Major Cities of Europe), Robert Joachim Schiff
(City of Saarbrücken) and Liora Shechter (Tel Aviv – Jafo Municipality)

Without doubt flat world navigation has the potential to have drastic effects, not just on the individuals and businesses who embrace the opportunities therein, but at a community level – regardless of how large or small that community is. Frankly, the socio-political-economic ramifications of successful flat world navigation are incalculable. It is with collaborative solutions that communities and nations will find the wherewithal to do more, much more, with the lessened leveraging power inherent in the constrained budgets that all are faced with.

The competition is global in scope for highly skilled IT/DACE resources

Let's begin by looking at the exponentially increasing competition for highly skilled IT/DACE resources – especially people who possess the flat world navigational abilities, which enable profitable connections and collaborations. A good place to begin our exploration of this is by looking at the startup community, where the technology sector in particular is garnering considerable attention from governmental agencies, media and investment brokers. An excellent example of this competition can be found between the UK and Germany, each of which is working to establish itself as the major force of the European tech startup scene.

In Germany, Munich has long worked to position itself as that nation's Silicon Valley but it has healthy competition from Silicon Allee (Berlin), Silicon Saxony, IT Lagune e.V and a variety of 'Valleys', including BioCon, CFE, Isar, Measurement, Medical and Solar. Additionally, there are accelerator programmes at play such as the German Silicon Valley Accelerator (GSVA) – supported by both private sponsors and the German Federal Ministry of Economics and Technology (BMWi) – and the German Accelerator, with strategic partners including the Federal Ministry for Economic Affairs and Energy, Siemens and Telekom Innovation Laboratories. The latter mentor startups in their San Francisco/Silicon Valley and New York outposts. Both of these organizations are clear in their mandate to expedite the economic growth of the nation's tech- and communication-focused startups and to aid them in successfully accessing international markets – that of the United States in particular.

Silicon Fen – aka the Cambridge Cluster – and East London Tech City, otherwise known as the Shoreditch 'Silicon Roundabout', are two of the better-known areas where tech startups gather together in England. The regions are renowned for early stage investment, flexible job markets and higher than usual tolerance for 'fail-ful' useful failures as learning experiences in the run-up to success. One could also look to Bristol for a focus on robotics and Edinburgh for AI (Artificial Intelligence); for those interested in media technology, Manchester is the place to look for forward movement.

Both the German and UK arenas are also awash with what is commonly known as 'accelerators' – highly charged and competitive 'classes' which include mentorships, focused feedback and, occasionally, public pitching, potential investment and further funding. They are often cited as encouraging ecosystems for brainstorming, connection and collaboration as well as access to early-stage investors – though it should be noted that they are, more often than not, rather tech-centric. Tech City recently promoted the launch of its Digital Business Academy – a free joint venture between itself, UCL, Cambridge University Judge Business School and Founder Centric to provide courses focused on teaching the requisite, and not insignificant, skills necessary to start and run a successful digital business.

From the perspective of flat world navigation, as it pertains to collaboration and the DACE, what is most interesting about Tech City is its attention not just to accelerating the growth of digital businesses, but the fact that it looks to do so across the UK. In part, this is by engendering cooperation between different groups and encouraging the sharing of best practices and opportunities.

Tech City was founded by the UK government in 2010, and its focus on digital is important. According to its 2013 annual report, nearly 600,000 people were employed in London in either the technology or digital industries in that year. The report also asserted that those sectors, in London, increased by nearly 17 per cent between 2009 and 2012, with digital and tech companies increasing in number from just under 50,000 (49,969) to 88,215. The organization predicts that the UK digital economy will increase by 11 per cent annually through to 2016 and, in doing so, increase the value of the internet economy to more than £220 billion. In addition, the 2014 UK 'App Economy' report (Vision Mobile, 2014) suggests that app developers will generate more than £4 billion in that year, with 45 per cent of the growth in the sector to be found outside of the Greater London, South East area.

Flat World Navigators share their stories

Peter Hewkin, *Founder, Centre for Business Innovation Limited*

Networking has had a huge impact on my career. I started out running the Centre for Exploitation of Science and Technology (CEST), linking together blue chips, government departments and universities for the UK government and for the benefit of UK plc. Then I ran the Cambridge Network, linking diverse stakeholders in the Cambridge cluster for the benefit of the region. Most recently I have founded The Centre for Business Innovation (CfBI) and Connected Cambridge, which build on prior lessons learned and take networking to another level – spanning the world, engaging with like-minded communities and addressing specific grand challenges that community members want to work on.

Going forward I envisage the pace of change accelerating as players need to find partners (customers, employers, funders, stakeholders) quickly and on the basis of 'best in class'. The challenges include: 'how do you build trust?' and 'how do you build partnerships which endure?' I wonder if something akin to the Amazon 'readers also liked' might help; imagine a 'networkers' approval rating' which people would want to be credited with!

As a B2B marketeer, I use new media primarily for finding new, trending themes and buzzwords as well as for identifying the parties who are interested in these. As soon as I have a 1-2-1 dialogue going I will quickly extract this from social media (where I cannot tell if I am being spoofed by competitors) and move to phone and e-mail. Saying 'I want to send you an attachment' is a good way to make the jump over to e-mail.

As a connector of businesses, I find that there is value in delivering just that. I am more efficient at getting a group of companies together and facilitating a particular dialogue than they would be doing it by themselves. The value lies partly in 'know who' and partly in 'know how' – in this case, in being able to align expectations and provide a service that the users perceive as being hassle-free.

One of the biggest challenges for B2B relationships these days is access to people's time (rather than their money!). Corporate overheads can put the cost of someone's time up to $1,000 per day and they are expected to account for this in the finest detail. Is there time for real humans at the smaller end of the deal spectrum or will we soon have 'bots' networking and doing the large number of smaller deals on our behalf? The game for 'real people' becomes a continuous up-sell into spaces which justify real people's time.

Players need to ask themselves regularly if the effort (time, money, insight, help) they are putting into communities/networks is justified – either in benefit to themselves or to other parties they want to help. A long time ago a wise person advised me to always test, 'are you Net-working or are you Not-working?' Today that argument is more subtle but the basic idea behind the test holds true!

'Data manipulation' in the middle of the business sandwich is gaining in value – deciding what to do, where to do it, when to do it etc. This is the business process we target with leading-edge ideas around big data, open innovation, social media, medical adherence and more.

It is fortunate for marketers that there is so much searchable data in cyberspace. This can be used to target B2C messages right down to the individual level so that 'personal' data, such as who someone is, where they are and what they are doing 'right now' has real value. For good reason, laws are seeking to protect consumers from unwanted analysis – for instance, that which might affect their insurance premiums or credit ratings. However, in a world of big data the regulator is struggling to keep up with technology.

The scarier scenario is the perception of 'Big Brother' and the thought of a popular 'lock-down' of data which will hold back a variety of new business models. If this happens it is unlikely that it will impact equally all over the planet and I predict a trend towards 'data tourism' where data (and the value which can be derived from it) will migrate towards friendlier jurisdictions.

The value of networks ultimately lies in interpretation of data associated with that network. In a world of big data this value can move around the planet in a fraction of a second. Knowledge is one of those 'have your cake and eat it' things. Proprietary knowledge is not – once the other guy knows your secret it cannot be forgotten. Legislators will try to regulate the collection, manipulation and transfer of these 'data-rich assets', but if the regulation becomes too heavy, the data and its considerable associated value will 'walk' to a more acceptable regime. I think of this effect as 'data tourism' and it is something which governments, companies, entrepreneurs and individuals will need to come to terms with.

Outside of Europe let's take a look at the sector in nations such as Singapore, Australia, the United States and Canada. The Internet Association of Canada published a detailed report in September 2014 titled 'Reasserting Canada's Competitiveness in the Digital Economy'. Canada, an early internet adopter, has an economy which will increasingly depend on the DACE. The IA report notes, 'According to Canadian Internet Registration Authority (CIRA 2013), the digital economy already accounts for 3 per cent of Canada's Gross Domestic Product (GDP) or CA\$49 billion per annum.' However, the association also makes clear their concerns that there is work to be done to ensure the nation can take full advantage of the DACE. This necessary work includes:

Government use of online services, support for business uptake of technologies and consumer confidence building; promoting accessibility and affordability through investment in infrastructure and attention to competitive markets; and creating an enabling environment for growth by investing in workforce skills, knowledge clusters, crafting smart and enabling regulation, and supporting R&D and venture capital attraction.

In that same year (2014), Australia's Treasurer, Joe Hockey, announced the removal of a range of programmes equating to nearly AUS$845 million, which had been in place to assist the industrial sector. Included in those cuts were the Innovation Investment Fund (IIF) and Commercialisation Australia, which had previously been at the heart of the support system for the innovation and technology sectors.

Factoid

Of Australia's 'digital opinion leaders', 67 per cent believe the nation is in danger of being left behind due to the government's digital policy while 80 per cent of Australians believe the government should implement policies that force organizations to be more transparent about how they use the customer data they hold.

(Source: EY Sweeney, 2014)

Their replacement is the Entrepreneurs' Infrastructure Programme. With a five-year budget of AU$484.2 million its remit, according to the Australian Government Department of Industry discussion paper, 'Establishment of the Entrepreneurs' Infrastructure Programme', includes providing a range of services to SMEs, which 'aim to improve the capabilities of small to medium enterprises to become more [self-reliant], competitive and grow.' This support focuses on 'business management; research connections; and commercializing ideas'. Australia ranked 14th in the 2014 Global Innovation Index rankings. I wonder if this is a reflection of the drop in Venture Capital funding available in Australia, which was down to AUS$111 million – a 20 per cent decrease from 2013.

Conversely, Singapore, which ranked 7th in the Innovation Index, had VC funding top out at S$1.7 billion and approximately S$100 million government funding streaming into its early-stage startups community. Additionally, there are a raft of governmental initiatives designed to support those involved in the Singaporean startup scene. These include: MDA i.Jam, which provides matching funds; the

National Research Fund Technology Incubation Scheme, which co-invests up to 85 per cent of investments; and the SPRING programmes, which support beginning entrepreneurs with mentors, funding and co-financing. There is also the Infocomm Development Authority of Singapore (IDA), which makes a wide range of programmes available to startups. These include an acceleration programme for startups and an accreditation programme that focuses on assisting and encouraging governmental organizations and other large entities to adopt emerging technologies.

Factoid

Who's Who in the 2014 Global Innovation Index:

1 Switzerland

2 United Kingdom

3 Sweden

4 Finland

5 The Netherlands

6 United States

7 Singapore

8 Denmark

9 Luxembourg

10 Hong Kong

Other notables:

12 Canada

16 Korea

17 Australia

21 Japan

(Source: GII, 2014)

The United States are always keen to be seen as leaders in innovation and they often are. However, it is important that they – as is the case with all nations – are steadfast in their refusal to rest on past laurels. Rather, they must be ever vigilant in ensuring that their population continues to upgrade their skills base. This will go far in ensuring that their leadership position remains as the internationalism of the DACE reduces the importance of partisan borders and boundaries.

In his 2014 State of the Union address, President Obama went some way towards addressing the internationalism of the DACE by noting that, as 95 per cent of the potential customers for US goods and services live outside their borders, 'we can't close ourselves off from those opportunities.' He also spoke of the imperative of enhancing the skills of the US workforce by acknowledging the work of his Vice President, Joe Biden, and the educational and corporate institutions collaborating to aid in this endeavour:

> Thanks to Vice President Biden's great work to update our job training system, we're connecting community colleges with local employers to train workers to fill high-paying jobs like coding, and nursing, and robotics. Tonight, I'm also asking more businesses to follow the lead of companies like CVS and UPS, and offer more educational benefits and paid apprenticeships – opportunities that give workers the chance to earn higher-paying jobs even if they don't have a higher education.
>
> (whitehouse.gov, 2014)

It is quite normal for governmental legislation to be in the position of playing catchup in comparison to agile enterprises and forward-looking, enterprising entrepreneurs and business people. However, it is incumbent upon all governments wanting to empower their populations to grasp the brass ring of successful engagement in the DACE by investing in the building and maintaining of 21st-century digital infrastructure. Doing so will go a long way towards assisting their citizens – including the unemployed, underemployed and those whose years of employment may be curtailed due to skills and knowledge gaps – to engage with the DACE, as will the suggested move towards making community college tuition free.

Lengthening the odds when addressing the skills shortage in the DACE

Of course this need to enhance skill sets is not limited to the United States, nor are the problems that surround that thorny, often partisan issue. A recent survey of private sector organizations by Tech London Advocates (TLA) – referenced on their website in April 2014 – made clear that as the digital economy continues to grow and mature, the skills necessary for it to flourish are, quite plainly, in short supply. To be frank, 'Appiness' – the profusion of apps both free and otherwise – does not equate to economic happiness. This is underscored by the responses from 70 per cent of the TLA members, who stated that it is this shortage of skills which is holding back the sector's growth. They also suggest the same is true in Germany.

There are two types of skill shortages that we will look at here, chosen due to the impact they are having and could, if not addressed, continue to have on the DACE. The first skill shortage, or at least perceived shortage, is for Flat World Navigators; those who, as has been underlined in this book, are the connectors, the collaborators, the bridge and business builders. They are, undoubtedly, to varying degrees of course, replete throughout every business sector. It is likely, though, that to date these skills have not received the requisite understanding and acknowledgement they deserve for being of such immense import to successful strategies within the DACE.

The second set of skills in short supply are those focused on delivering compelling user experiences to Endusers/consumers, on the device of their choice, at a speed and scale never seen before. The raft of social media applications/platforms have shown how quickly consumers can flock to, or away from, a company's offerings. The ability to remain compelling to the consumer while ensuring both a massively scalable and highly secure, near-instantaneous rollout, has illustrated a huge misalignment between 'business' and the IT sector.

The new companies that will thrive in the DACE are likely to be ones that have a new synthesis of what was, traditionally, a set of vertical competencies that rarely, if ever, talked to each other. A lack of communication and collaboration is far more than a hindrance in the DACE. The success stories will be those told by companies with the talent to integrate everything that relates to the Enduser experience, aka their CXM (Customer Experience Management). This includes everything from the UI (User Interface) through to supporting millions of users in complex business scenarios.

This is a world away from the comparatively simple and insecure social media apps and platforms of today. As such, the skills requisite to create these ecosystems include the business acumen and complexity of existing enterprise technology platforms combined with the sale, economics and ease of use of new-school tech. The synergies of these disciplines and points of view are the growth area of the next ten-to-fifteen years. Without them you will be of increasingly marginal value – and certainly not invited to sit at any strategy table of note.

Suffice it to say that these tech talents are in short supply. Often, through no fault of their own, they have little chance of gaining the experience held in the heads of an older generation, which was instrumental in building the infrastructure we so readily take for granted. Added to that, it is extremely rare that those who have worked in the industry for more than twenty years are interested in 'topping up' their skill quotient by learning about tech such as Cloud, UI, responsive user interface design, etc – a decision that they may come to rue.

Philo Holland, *Director, Authentic Collaboration Space*

Collaboration, both highly effective and disastrously inefficient, has played a pivotal role throughout my entire career.

Over the past decade, I have led a continuously growing team of people (now totalling 1,647) from 123 professions, 65 academic fields and 91 cultures all focused on answering one question: what are the minimum amounts of skills and knowledge required to create and sustain a low-friction, highly productive collaboration and communication capability regardless of gender, age, professional, educational and ethnic background, religion or language?

This highly experimental, hands-on project known as the Authentic Collaboration Space (ACS) has identified, tested and sorted 121 components forming the world's first algorithmic collaboration productivity formula. The components alone are simple, easy-to-learn topics. As with most interpersonal group situations however, it's when we are faced with multiple topics simultaneously that things get quickly out of hand. The ACS team not only identified these productivity-enabling components, but also tested the minimum amount that each component must be understood and which sequence was most effective for the transformation process. As a result, we have already simulated over 700 per cent productivity gains within controlled project environments.

There are components relevant to business, the arts, science, philosophy, friendship, responsibility, etc. Due to the nature of our work, we intentionally embraced diversity by developing a framework (space) based on a pre-qualified global crowd inclusion approach.

Looking at the past 300 years of the industrialized and post-industrial eras of failed mergers and acquisitions (approx. 83 per cent fail rate, depending on which study one chooses), it was clear from the beginning that we had to create an entirely new approach.

Fortunately, it appears that we may have established the world's first solution that lowers interpersonal tension, negative social interactions, negative stereotypes, prejudice and social isolation so significantly that it can be sustained and thus results in extremely high levels of productivity.

We believe this project offers organizations of any kind the opportunity to greatly improve interpersonal communication and teamwork. To reach our next goal of 10,000 people from 120 cultures, we are inviting anyone who can demonstrate a sincere interest in improving interpersonal collaboration to join the ACS project. Contact us via e-mail to receive a New Participant Package.

To engage and retain consumers in the DACE there is a need for 'warp speed' agility and focus to deliver services in a way that excites and delights Endusers. From a delivery perspective this implies a capacity for tight, dynamic and fluid collaboration – from the business through to UX (User Experience) from design to Cloud deployment – potentially involving a large number of internal and external departments and companies. Without a complete rethink and re-engineering of this capability there is a great risk of appearing slow, outdated and dull to Endusers.

The talent in this space is limited, but extremely entrepreneurial, ambitious and exceptionally accomplished. As such it is increasingly unlikely that they are interested in any kind of traditional, 9–5 engagement. They will have to be enticed with flexibility both in working conditions (they don't always need to be in the office) and remuneration (a simple salary offering won't cut it). Your imagination and adaptability in this space will be reflected in your success. The 40-hour, five-day-a-week hierarchical organizational chart is industrial-age thinking; the DACE is flat, fluid, and 24/7 – to thrive there, you need to be as well.

Those rare and coveted individuals who do possess if not all of these skills, at least a bountiful subset of them, should be able to name their price and work wherever and for whomever they choose.

Unfortunately, all too often, immigration policies are in place which hamper, if not altogether hinder, the ability for locally based businesses to gain access to the skill sets they require to move forward in a highly competitive, if cooperative, DACE. Certainly this has been the case in the UK, where partisan politics have been known to lead to a ratcheting-up of polarizing, off-putting immigration policies.

Going someway to correcting this problem is the Exceptional Talent visa, which became available in April 2014. This visa is intended to ease the way for businesses to hire those individuals considered world-leading in the digital technology sector and who have previously developed successful businesses. This is a good start, but it should be noted that it does little to aid SMEs who are extremely unlikely to be able to afford the wages expected by such highly skilled, and corporately coveted, individuals.

Additionally, this visa may not be of any use for those 'whizz kids' who have created the tools and technologies that will create an underlying platform from which further DACE initiatives can be built. They are less likely to have the traditional experience that would enable them to tick the 'business development background' box required for the ET Visa.

In general, a visa to work in the Eurozone can be equally difficult to acquire; however, hiring those with an EU-based passport and the requisite skill set is a much simpler proposition. Even if you aren't in possession of the passport there are nations, such as Germany, that are moving towards loosening the restrictions that may once have burdened their businesses and corporations. An example is that nation's Blue Card, which eases immigration and aids skilled immigrants in settling through access to such things as free language lessons. Germany, it seems, has grasped the fundamentals of the DACE and is making moves towards becoming a central player in the opportunities that this implies.

There are at least three challenges in bringing together collaborators from different countries:

- The first is simple but important: the language; not everyone will be able to speak English well.

- The next challenge is convincing people that they will gain an advantage by participating in a good collaboration.

- And the third really depends on the individual standpoint of each person. While one may be very interested in getting new experiences, the other might not feel they have anything to gain from working together.

I overcome these challenges by taking into account only those who are interested and who have the ability to speak and understand a modicum of English. You don't need a deep knowledge of English; most of us make do with no more than 500 English words in our vocabulary.

Robert Joachim Schiff, Geschäftsführung
(Managing Director) for the city of Saarbrücken
(with translation assistance from Kerstin Engelhardt)

There is an additional shortage, one which could have a long legacy of economic after-effects if not addressed at governmental, educational and societal levels. This is the fact that far too few young women are choosing higher educational degrees focused on science and technology – the arenas that are key to economic transformation in the DACE. As a champion of flat world navigation and Flat World Navigators I am also, of course, a champion of those skills being embraced and their strategic importance acknowledged. However, at the time of writing (January 2015) more than 85 per cent of students accepted into engineering or computer science degree courses in UK universities are men. This polarization does not bode well for employers and governments looking to balance the economic power between genders.

Finding new formulas to foster growth

In January 2015 EU Digital Commissioner Günther Oettinger was extremely forthright in his call for increased investment in Europe's digital infrastructure. Certainly, at the time of commenting, his focus was predominantly on increased broadband/internet speeds and access as well as settling net neutrality and data protection issues. 'I want one standard of quality for all', he made clear, 'that is offered without discrimination.' At the same time, he stated that to his mind the question was:

> how to mobilize funds under public law and co-financing contributions so that the infrastructure can be realized within this decade. At a European level we have structural funds, which we would like to employ for co-financing, to a greater extent than has been done previously.
>
> (euractiv.com, 2015)

Frankly, this is hardly surprising; rather, it is a given in the reality of an upsurging DACE. Where we may extrapolate, I believe, is in looking to the potential of funding for businesses that are engaged in implementing innovative technology and building new, or strengthening older, collaborative initiatives.

There are already examples of funds being made available to take advantage of the DACE, by bringing advantage to the lender, the borrower or both. For instance, since 2008 German SMEs have had access to a syndicated loan mechanism which is engineered to be easily combined with securitization, for mid- to long-term financing for German SMEs (small and medium-sized enterprises). These Schuldschein fixed-rate, regulated loans, generally coming from more than one lender, have become favourite financing tools within the German SME community – and to investors who have greater access to the SME arena.

Increasingly, international companies are also benefiting from these loans as, along with supporting SMEs, they are viewed as a positive platform for encouraging cooperation and collaboration between multinational enterprises. In an article entitled 'The Schuldschein: An investment alternative for Europe' published on the EurActiv site on 26 September 2014, Jean-Philippe Brioudes, Director of Debt Capital Markets at HSBC France, is reported as stating that at least 'one third of current loans do not go to German companies'.

Certainly the economic situation within the Eurozone is focusing attention on the extreme need to enable economic growth; and, doubtlessly, the Digital and Collaboration Economies will be major factors in this endeavour. To that end, the European Commission has plans (at the time of writing) to build a single digital market to support its efforts to boost the zone's economic growth and reliance.

Factoid

In February 2015 Amsterdam was named Europe's first Sharing City, with 84 per cent of its residents saying they were ready and willing to participate in a sharing/collaborative economy.

(Source: Glind, 2013)

This focus on supporting the digital growth of Europe was underscored in November 2014 when Axelle Lemaire, the French Minister for Digital Affairs and Matthias Machnig, the German Economic and Energy Affairs Minister, released a joint statement making note of the fact that only 2 per cent of listed companies in Europe's digital sector were actually European. To redress what they perceived to be a monumental imbalance, they called for much greater support for the European IT sector as well as taking an in-depth look at the tax payment practices of non-European enterprises in the sector. The contested billions of dollars/euros could, conceivably, go a very long way to relieving budgetary constraints and enabling more support – economical and otherwise – for SMEs and entrepreneurs looking to make their move into the DACE.

Flat World Navigators share their stories

Giorgio Prister, *President of Major Cities of Europe*

My experience in sharing knowledge and objectives, as a community, was further enhanced many years ago when IBM, the company I was working for at the time, reorganized itself with independent lines of business such as hardware and software products, technology solutions, consulting expertise, etc. It designed a new way of managing business by balancing different, often contrasting requirements, to obtain optimal business proposals. The key challenge was to work inside a business community, understand each other's priorities and balance them in order to produce the best proposal for the client.

It is experiences such as this, as well as my own personal and cultural mindset, that underlined the value and effectiveness of communities for sharing and cooperation. Modern businesses, whatever those businesses are, are generally unaffordable if they are not cooperating and collaborating in a community with shared objectives – it is a matter of making people understand the importance of this change in business culture.

Major Cities of Europe is the independent organization of City and Local Government CIOs that I am now managing. It has the mission to provide high value to that community of CIOs belonging to a fragmented market, which comprises thousands of cities and local governments around Europe.

You might wonder why, for example, a city in France would be interested in cooperating with a city in Germany. What do they have in common, why and what would they want to share? They have in common the fact that they are all public administrations managing the needs of constituents who generally have the same overall needs – this is true even if local laws and regulations might be different. The focus of Major Cities of Europe is exactly this; it is about sharing, teaming, and bringing value to each other in an open, non-competitive way.

A key question is: what are cities and local governments sharing in Major Cities of Europe? Is it basic technology which is, for the most part, the same – or quite similar – everywhere? Is it specific software solutions that might differ due to there being different laws and regulations across countries? Yes, these might be topics to share.

More importantly, the mission of the association is to enable the community members to share their knowledge and experiences around the issues of introducing, governing and managing ICT innovation. It is about sharing knowledge and experiences regarding what works well and what does not. That is what makes our association so valuable. The members are all managers who all deal with ICT innovation. Though it is quite likely that our members won't be using the same tools, they can still share their experiences as to how they achieve their goals. These are knowledge assets that can be applied everywhere.

The role of the CIO in public administration has changed dramatically in recent years. This is because they must now work closely with all other departments to understand not only what these other departments need but, also, to establish a real, two-way, balanced collaboration within the administration. Certain cities have created real ecosystems to develop innovation, which include not just the city's administration, but local, national and international companies, universities, NGOs, and so on, as well.

The CIO in the middle of that, if he or she is prepared to work collaboratively, can have a major role to play. Those leaders who are imagining new, innovative services for the community cannot move forward without technology. Decisions must be taken which determine the level of difficulty or investment involved in implementing said service – the CIO must take a leading role in the decision-making process. The experiences of his or her peers, across Europe, are of high value for any CIO wanting to succeed in their work.

Mass unemployment is a possibility for those not able to gain access to, or collaborate effectively in, the DACE

The Eurozone's younger generations have been particularly hard hit by unemployment; average rates at the end of 2014 reached 22 per cent, hitting 50 per cent or more in Spain and Greece. With approximately 5 million under-25-year-olds out of work the Digital Economy is one that can have a potentially massive effect.

With so many traditional jobs being automated, digitized if you will, it is increasingly important that differentiation be found. The difference is uniquely human as, along with empathy (which as yet cannot be turned into an algorithm), jobs requiring creativity will be difficult to automate. Oxford professors Michael Osborne and Carl Benedikt Frey explore this issue in their white paper, 'The Future of Employment: How Susceptible are Jobs to Computerisation?' They too believe it unlikely 'that occupations requiring a high degree of creative intelligence will be automated in the next decades' (Frey and Osborne, 2013). By using the tools, technologies and techniques made more readily available via the Cloud, many of those millions, as long as they have digital access, can grasp the advantages that the human touch brings to collaborative connections.

Factoid

The 'ins and outs' of international internet usage in 2014. Over 3 billion people across the globe access the internet – this is a more than seven-fold increase from 394 million in 2000. The global spread is approximately:

- Asia: 1.4 billion;

- Europe: 580 million;

- Latin American and the Caribbean: 320 million;

- North America: 310 million;

- Africa: 300 million;

- Middle East: 112 million;

- Oceania and Australia: 27 million.

(Source: Internet World Stats, 2014)

Governments leading the way in redefining service and services in the DACE

Considering Singapore's high ranking on the Innovation Index, it is not surprising that it is, in many ways, also leading the way in connecting with and to its citizens with full awareness of the economic impact these connections can have. It is not alone in this as other nations within the Asia Pacific arena are also well aware of the importance of moving forward towards full implementation of 21st-century infrastructure.

A 2014 (July) FutureGov research paper, 'Government Connectivity, Citizen Engagement and Economic Impact' (Smith, 2014) surveyed senior government officials in Australia, India, Malaysia and Singapore. Connectivity, the foundation stone of 21st-century infrastructure, was acknowledged as being very important by 71 per cent of the respondents. This was due to it being a key factor in driving departmental communications, efficiency and quality of service. It was also acknowledged as being key to connecting to their Citizens/Endusers through public sector and community collaboration websites. By engaging with, and connecting to, their Endusers the respondents were able to deliver 'more relevant, reliable, convenient and faster' services.

Even Myanmar, not historically known for its 'open government', is building, with assistance from Vietnam, an open source eGov platform which aims to aid officials in managing data. This platform will certainly have the potential to increase interdepartmental and local government collaboration and cooperation capabilities, through information exchange and increased mobile, Cloud technologies.

Flat World Navigators share their stories

Liora Shechter, *CIO of the Tel Aviv – Jafo Municipality, head of the team which won the World Smart City Award at the Barcelona Smart Cities Summit in November 2014*

When you look at the relationship between a resident and a municipality it's usually around paying taxes and parking tickets, I think this is quite common for municipalities all around the world. Residents often find it difficult to see the 'value' of their municipality. Tel Aviv embarked on a different strategy. The goal is to create a city for all its residents and a resident-oriented government. The city actively involves residents in the urban experience and urban development, while emphasizing engagement in decision-making processes and wisdom of the crowd as a means for smart municipal management in the new age.

When we launched the Digi-Tel platform we understood that the people of Tel Aviv were becoming more and more technological – they are used to tools like mobile and the usage of social media and e-services. These tools are part of their life so we had to adjust our municipality to service this new 'age'. In fact, part of the motivation for Digi-Tel was that Tel Aviv is an extremely high-tech city. We are a startup city, and we have a very large number of bright young people – one-third of the population is young. So our strategy was to leverage the city's high-tech ecosystem to facilitate its transformation into a smart city.

One of our key projects is the Digi-Tel Residents Club; when people join the Residents Club they specify their hobbies and interests as well as their phone number and e-mail. With this information we're able to connect with our residents. That said, it's important to emphasize that the information is only used internally and for the purpose of bringing value to the residents.

The Digi-Tel Residents Club is an integration of many tools: CRM, ILM, distribution tool, campaign tool, mobile infrastructure and so on. We are using the platform to enhance our ability to organize campaigns that are directed to various sections of the population, characterized by age, the area where they live, or their hobbies. So our campaigns are really individually tailored.

We began our Digi-Tel initiative to try to change the residents' perception of the municipality and to bring them value. After just a one and a half years of operating the opinions are already quite different. Each time we launch a new project we see the positive effect it has on public opinion; we're feeling a very positive shift in public opinion about the Digi-Tel tools we provide for the residents.

That positive public opinion is great, but the real gain, from the municipality's perspective, is that the public understands that the municipality is here for them and brings them value. Digi-Tel offers them personalized and relevant information and services. For instance, if you specify that you like sports, we'll invite you to the Tel Aviv marathon with a discount. And if you have a small child, we'll invite you to a story reading that will take place today in the nearby community centre. Or if you specify that you are interested in culture, we'll invite you to a show taking place today in the city theatre.

An example of e-service is around kindergarten registration. We recently sent an SMS to parents with relevant-aged children, inviting them to register to their preferred kindergarten classes. The message included a link to the online registration site. We closed the circle in one SMS, so the residents didn't have to come to City Hall.

Another important aspect of Digi-Tel is engaging citizens to influence policy making. We strongly believe that leveraging the wisdom of the crowd is vital for smart municipal management, so as part of Digi-Tel residents are now directly influencing a range of municipality decisions.

The positive public opinion is the result of the citizens' engagement and of all the innovative and unexpected services the municipality is giving to the people of Tel Aviv.

Worldwide there is a growing movement towards open government, something that has been made much more economically feasible and easily accessible due to Cloud-based tools and technologies. In October 2014, the Open Government Partnership (OGP) – an international platform for domestic reformers in 65 nations, working to develop and implement open government reforms – ranked the top 10 open government citizen/Enduser engagement endeavours of that year. Taking the top spot, Denmark was lauded for the legal requirement placed upon local government councils to connect and consult with their local senior citizen councils before making any decisions that pertain to their senior population.

Montenegro was second in the OGP ranking due to its 'Be Responsible' mobile app campaign that encourages citizens to report illegal activities; and the Philippines came third for its participatory budgeting programme, which enabled civil society organizations to be part of the decision-making process regarding funding priorities. The remainder of the top 10 noted nations are: Italy, The Netherlands, the United Kingdom, Mexico, Peru, the United States and France.

While far too many governments are playing catch-up with legalities such as those surrounding data protection/privacy and corporate taxation in a digital landscape, many of the initial fears that were fostered by a lack of understanding to the potential of Cloud-based and mobile tools and technologies have been overcome. As such, these tools, tech and the skills base moving them forward at a rapid rate are now at the heart of a great number of government strategies.

An excellent case in point is the Philippines, and its Department of Justice in particular, due to their need to work and collaborate with others – both inter/multi-departmentally, with internationally based colleagues within their own organizations and with their peers in partnering enterprises. As these connections and collaborations must be accessible anywhere at any time, the department has prioritized the implementation of enterprise-level mobility by focusing on two economical and easily implemented approaches: BYOD (Bring Your Own Device) and COPE (Corporation Owned, Personally Enabled).

Another nation committing to connectivity for its citizens/Endusers is India, which looks to bring broadband to 50,000 villages in the first half of 2015 and wi-fi connectivity to 100,000 additional areas in each of the following two fiscal years. This connectivity commitment is compelled by their determination to extend the advantages available through access to the digital economy as well as a firm focus on both creating employment opportunities in rural areas and curbing the migration to, and thus over-population in, its already overcrowded cities. As Ravi Shankar Prasad, India's Minister of Communications and Information Technology succinctly stated, 'The calculation is simple. It is IT (India's talent) + IT (information technology) = IT (India tomorrow)' (Ng, 2014).

Factoid

Digital Decision: As part of his March 2015 Budget to Parliament, UK Chancellor George Osborne announced investment of up to £600 million in mobile networks and plans for ultrafast broadband to be available to nearly all UK premises.

(Source: Gov.uk, 2015)

Catching up, 2015 found Australian Prime Minister Tony Abbott and Communications Minister Malcolm Turnbull jointly announcing the launch of a national Digital Transformation Office (DTO). Designed to be a collaborative effort, which combines the expertise of developers, designers, researchers and content specialists, the department is said to have the task of ensuring 'government services can be delivered digitally from start to finish and better serve the needs of citizens and businesses' with a focus on 'enduser needs in developing digital services.' A week later Wellington, New Zealand announced its own Digital Team to manage the government's e-services and focus on the front-end, citizen/Enduser experience.

Flat World Navigators share their stories

Peter Church OAM, Chairman, AFG Venture Group

I have been living and working in South East Asia and India for nigh-on 40 years as a lawyer and corporate advisor. Over these years I have frequently read or heard 'experts' pronouncing that a deep knowledge of Asian cultures is essential or vital to successfully doing business there. Other than the fact that many of these 'experts' are running cultural training businesses and thus are somewhat conflicted, I believe the importance is far exaggerated.

The extent of the exaggeration varies from country to country. The more international and developed a country is, in my opinion the less knowledge of the local culture is important for doing business. Indeed, even in newly developing countries like Myanmar, one finds that even those who cannot speak English have a pretty good idea of western culture from daily doses of western movies and TV shows. So they understand more about how westerners behave and operate in business than we understand of them and their cultures.

And even if the founder of a business in one of these Asian countries speaks no English and has little understanding of the country from which the foreign businessman comes, these days his children, relatives or executives are likely to have been educated overseas or at least have adequate English to communicate clearly. In my opinion these days the local businessman is prepared to ignore our ignorance of his or her culture and is almost solely focused on whether the foreign business has the product or service needed for his or her business.

Of course it helps if one understands the local culture and respects it, but it is not the all-important ingredient some make it out to be. I have always found that if one treats others with respect and manners, presumably just as you would like to be treated, you cannot go too far wrong.

Flat world navigation, and the connections, collaborations and co-operative endeavours it engenders, particularly digitally, is being embraced by governments around the world. Though it may have different branding and titles, depending upon the area and arena wherein it is being used, what remain the same are the dramatic results it gives rise to. Flat world navigation is a potential antidote to the reality of rapidly disappearing sectors of work and the trans-formation of professions. By engendering a demonstrable depth of awareness and acceptance of other ways of life, and of doing business, Flat World Navigators can be instrumental in bringing together win-win solutions and benefits to those same businesses, communities and nations where resources are highly sought after and competition to attain them oftentimes crucial to short-, medium- and long-term strategies.

All of these strategies must take into account the findings of the December 2012 European Commission report, 'Digital Agenda for Europe: A Europe 2020 Initiative', which noted that mobile internet traffic was doubling every two years, that there would be 25 billion devices connected to the internet by 2015 and this number would likely double by 2020. There will be no let-up to the number of machines and devices connecting to the internet. But, as humans, we can ensure that the manner in which we navigate the flat world and connect, both to the internet and to each other, is personal, authentic, and uniquely our own.

Actions with intent

Take stock of how prepared you are to effectively take part in the Digital, Attention and Collaboration Economies by first determining how well your people, processes, applications and technologies work together.

If there are factors that are communicating, connecting or contributing, explore why that is and what you can do to alleviate any impediments in the way.

Make a 'wish list' of all the competencies you would like to be covered within your organization. Now look for those individuals or groups within your organization who either have those capabilities or are able to add them to their tool kits.

If you have a capability which you feel would benefit your organization but which is, as yet, undiscovered or under-utilized, bring this to the attention of the decision maker(s) and, with a plan of action in mind, offer to assist in moving a project or initiative forward.

INTERVIEW   An interview with a Flat World Navigator

Jeff Finkle, *CEcD, President and CEO of the International Economic Development Council*

President and CEO of the International Economic Development Council (IEDC) – the world's largest economic development membership organization – Jeff Finkle is an internationally recognized leader and authority on economic development. In cooperation with the US Economic Development Administration, IEDC has taken a leadership role in facilitating connections between federal agencies and communities, as well as providing technical assistance and expertise to local organizations nationwide. Under Jeff's direction, IEDC also managed the Association of University Research Parks (AURP) and the Association of Defense Communities (ADC) for three and ten years respectively, strengthening the structures and programs of each organization.

Jeff, I think it's safe to say that in your work with the International Economic Development Council and, before that, with the Council for Urban Economic Development you've faced the challenge of bringing different stakeholders together who are unlikely to speak the same language. That may be because they're coming from different countries or, perhaps, from different arenas such as the academic and commercial sectors. Either way, they use different vocabularies and have different drivers. I'd imagine that bringing them together, in a way that enables them to communicate and collaborate effectively, could be quite testing.

Frankly, I don't think that you can get started until you come up with a mutual language. I've been in meetings where people talked past each other because they didn't understand each other: they didn't understand the vocabulary, the goals or why things were being done in the way that they were. The only way you can get past that is getting some common goals, some common language, an understanding of what everybody is going to get out of 'something' and what they are putting in, in a way that they can perceive successfully.

The good news is that in my field economic developers have to do that all the time. Our members are trying to fit round things in square holes on a regular basis. For instance, many of our members work on this crazy notion called Public–Private Partnerships.

Now Private–Private Partnerships make sense. Everybody knows that they are trying to make a profit. They're trying to create a deal that creates some cash flow that creates some net positive return for the stakeholders involved in that deal.

A Public–Private Partnership has different requirements and different outcomes. The public sector may want jobs, they may want an investment made at a particular place, at a particular time. Their goal won't necessarily be the net financial benefit. They're trying to use their land, their resources, their money, their tax incentives, their zoning to leverage in private sector investment that may return taxes and/or infrastructure, such as a new cluster to a community.

The private sector has the same goal that they would've had in a Private–Private deal: to make money. The problem is that, often, the private sector doesn't 'get it'. They'll be asking, 'Why do you want to help me? What are you getting out of it? How much return are you looking for?' That's where the economic developer has to do some translation. At the same time, they may have to translate – for their city councils, to their Mayors, to the news media – why the city would do the deal in the first place.

You mentioned the word 'return', which could likely be a huge hurdle – for the public sector, at least. Their key driver is, in all likelihood, to be returned to office. So, they'll be looking for a translation – a 'sweet spot' or piece of candy – that they can take to their electorate. I'd imagine that it is not unusual for this to be a short-term 'return', and one which doesn't necessarily equate to the effective delivery of an overall project in a positive way. Is that a fair summary?

It is. In the economic development world, we can give politicians their desired return on investments: ribbon cuttings, press releases, job announcements. At the end of the day we can provide a variety of political capital that puts them in a position to get reelected.

A number of years ago, I worked with a member of the city council in my home region in Central Ohio. He got involved with a small economic development organization and, the next time he ran for office, he ran as the Economic Development City Council Member. The work that he had done with the organization was noted and gave him credibility.

You've referred to Return on Investment: I believe an equally important ROI is Return on Involvement. It's not uncommon for the public to look for, and reward, engagement. That citizen, that engaged Enduser, has become increasingly demanding, so much so that a politician could parlay even perceived involvement – rather than just rubber stamping – into political capital.

Exactly!

You've also spoken of people occasionally asking members within the group, for instance in a Public–Private Partnership, 'Why are you doing this? What are you getting out of it?' Do you find it difficult to explain the win-win equation as being genuine?

I have the elevator speech for a wider economic definition of Economic Development. In the elevator speech, economic development is the creation, retention and expansion of jobs, the development of a tax base and the enhancement of wealth. So, as long as that is our desire, it seems to me that I can – or any of our members can – explain to somebody with a straight face, what they are trying to get out of the Public–Private Partnership or an economic development deal.

They're trying to create more jobs in a community; sometimes the company might be thinking of relocating somewhere else, so we have to retain or sustain businesses and jobs in the community. We want to work with entrepreneurs – that's to create jobs as well as help them grow part of the tax base. A growing business concern is going to pay more real estate taxes, their employees are going to have to pay income tax, those same employees are going to buy things and so they'll pay a sales tax. By paying sales tax they'll support the social safety net. Those taxes can make the city safe, provide welfare services and pay for local education.

They can grow jobs and that puts more people to work so they can be a productive part of society. If those are your goals, I think most people would understand why we do what we do – and how we do it.

I understand that the International Economic Development Council was created through a merger of two fairly large membership organizations: the CUED and AEDC. That must have been an interesting exercise, bringing together two organizations that were very clear in their own roles and sure of their own importance. I'm sure that, particularly as almost all organizations are being asked to do more with less, nearly everyone in business is facing up to some semblance of a consolidation exercise. It could be interdepartmental, multi-industry, multi-corporation but, regardless of the size of the organization, there are merging exercises occurring, don't you think?

I spent a year working on this back in early 2000s and, here again, we were somewhat unique. We had three advantages: first, we had tried to merge a couple of times before and we were unsuccessful. Second, this time, I was running the Council for Urban Economic Development and the American Economic Development platform was having financial problems, so they were prepared to jettison their CEO. And third, both organizations' leases were ending at the same time, so AEDC was free to move from Chicago to Washington DC.

Had there been two reasonably good CEOs, where one of the boards was not willing to sacrifice their own CEO, I don't think we would have had a merger. The advantage was, they came to my board and said, 'We want Jeff Finkle as our new CEO.' My board would not have given me up, thank God!

FWN Keys from Jeff Finkle

- Come up with a mutual language.

- Find some common goals.

- Get an understanding of what each stakeholder is going to get out of 'something' and what they are putting in.

In conclusion

In this chapter we explored a global overview of the economic, social and political effects that the DACE is having locally, nationally and internationally. To that end geographic arenas – be they cities, municipalities, nations or unified states working in conjunction – that are taking advantage of what the DACE can offer them and, consequently, enhance their offering to their citizens is at the heart of this chapter. The focus, from a myriad of municipalities, on the imperative to empower their ever more engaged citizen/Enduser is correlative to the demands being placed on businesses, regardless of size or locale, in the DACE. Every minute of every day in the DACE there are Endusers voting via a ballot or a 'buck'.

We compared the offerings from a range of European, North American, pan-Asian and Oceanic nations. Areas analysed include their range of support for, and investment in: innovation and education; digital infrastructure; startup/entrepreneurial entities; SMEs; cross-border collaboration; and high-skill immigration. The skill shortage, due to a dearth of specialist/generalists focused on providing vendor-neutral, platform-agnostic, Enduser-centric products and services was noted, as was the underlying danger in undervaluing the advantages gained from placing the connections and collaborations brought to the strategy table by those adept at flat world navigation.

Which brings us quite neatly to the next chapter, 'Is flat world navigation the game changer for women in the workforce?' The inherent collaborative capabilities of women and their proclivity to choose cooperation rather than combat is noted. Further, focus is given to women's roles in business – particularly at decision-making, managerial, executive and ownership levels. Issues such as changing corporate KPIs, the one billion women entering the workforce, the long-term advantages to educating and employing women, and how their inherent flat world navigational skills may be the key different-iator for organizations looking to race ahead in the DACE are also explored. While referencing the past and taking stock of the present, this chapter addresses a future of great potential as it enjoys the benefits brought by working with empowered, engaged, economi-cally exalted, entrepreneurially minded women.

Is flat world navigation the game changer for women in the workforce?

Advantage Attention
Authentic Business Change
Collaboration Communicate Connect
DACE Digital Economy Enduser Flat World
Navigator Global Network Relationship Strategy
Success Technology Win-Win **Believe Billion Board**
CEO Confidence Community Directors Empowerment
Entrepreneurs Female Fortune Mutual Skills Value Women

Featuring

Shala Burroughs (Co-Founder and former COO at CloudPeeps), Anna Fälth (Knowledge Gateway for Women's Economic Empowerment), Natalie Goldman (Launch Pod and Peoplebank), Louise Guido (ChangeCorp) and Carolyn Lawrence (President at Women of Influence) et's call this the Belle Curve. It's the effect that entrepreneurially minded women are having on those organizations looking to gain the greatest advantage available from their engagement in the new, flat world of business. It is, generally, the natural inclination of women to be cooperative rather than combative and it is this capability that is so valuable in the DACE (Digital, Attention and Collaboration Economies). It is a tendency that should be taken advantage of by all stakeholders, including the women themselves.

There are fundamental steps which must be taken to attain this leading position, and the first point of action is recognizing and respecting the value of the innate cooperative and collaborative competencies inherent in many – if not most – women. In actual fact, this recognition and respect must first come from the holder of said skills. Let's face it, if an individual doesn't value their own skills it is highly unlikely that anyone else will value them either.

Too often women, who have a tendency to share, demean the value of this skill. They'll diminish it by saying something along the lines of, 'Oh I'm happy to do it', – which they may well be – or, 'It's just what I do'. Unfortunately, in the business arena, brushing off the level of skill it takes to create a cooperative, collaborative, safe ecosystem for sharing Knowledge Assets (KA) does a disservice both to the individual and the important role(s) and functions they fulfil.

Owning your position

Let's start at the heart of the matter. One of the most difficult challenges that women are confronted with is what has been colloquially called the 'Impostor Syndrome'. This affection – some might say affliction – is seen most frequently in the feeling, shared by far too many women, that they must be 'perfect'. Equally damaging, they believe that if they aren't faultless – particularly in their professional life – they will be 'found out' as being in some way fraudulent. In this way they are, in fact, often their own worst enemy and, as such, it is this syndrome that must be purged from their psyches.

Louise Guido, *CEO and Managing Partner of ChangeCorp*

The difference between men and women in the workplace is simply fundamental. Men just believe they belong. I think the challenge is that we defer to men; it's like an instinct, a knee-jerk reaction. I've often felt that every woman, if she wants to really get ahead and be comfortable in getting the pay gap reduced, should approach her job as a salesperson would. Who do I have to sell to, to get what I want?

If you think about the fundamentals of selling, you have to get people to like you so that you can communicate with them and sell to them. So the first thing is, strangely enough, like-ability. Men don't always need like-ability, but women definitely need it; that's just a fact of life. The second thing is that women have to believe that they are smarter than men and that they have more tools. The way you do it is through confidence and affirmation. When a decision has to be made or an opinion has to be voiced, stick to your guns and don't waffle.

As I have told many women: your strength and confidence comes from your capacity to be empathic, listen and compliment in ways that men either do not do, do not know how to do or, when they do, come off as insincere.

There are four different kinds of men in the workplace: the father, the brother, the lover, and the enemy. If you have a CEO who's a father figure... well, if you've experience as a daughter, you'll know how to work with him. The brother is the guy that protects you, supports you and tells you things no one else will tell you. The lover is the one you have to manage; he's kind of a creepy guy, but he may have power. If he tells you a dirty joke, say something like, 'That was great Charlie, aren't you clever.' And, finally, there's the enemy. He's the one you're never going to win over, so always compliment him when you're in public, but pay him no mind when you're in private.

Next is the wrong-headed assumption that women in business are weak – far from it. They are more likely to collaborate but don't be fooled; collaboration does not equate to yielding, support does not correspond to submissiveness and credibility is not naiveté. Nor is there any lack of authentic ambition or inclination to increase earnings – women are just as likely as men to have grand designs and ambitions.

> One fact that's come up in our research of senior executive women, which is a small but critical differentiator when networking for business success, is that while women are often natural networkers, they often forget about the strategic part of it. Men do it more for transactional reasons, while women do it more for relational reasons.
>
> For instance, let's says there's an industry conference or company meeting. You'll often see women making plans or expressing interests in re-connecting with colleagues or friends while the men in the room use their time more strategically, to connect with the most senior people or the people they're working on a deal with – or the people they'd love to work on a deal with. They have strategic purpose.
>
> We have a great partner in Deloitte, and one of their Senior Partners is a master networker. What I learned from her is invaluable: think about who you want to meet. How many business cards are you going to collect to make this a successful use of your time? How fast are you going to follow up with them and what's the 'Return on Cards' you're striving to hit? If you make a plan before you go it takes some of the pressure off 'upon arrival'.
>
> Carolyn Lawrence, President at Women of Influence

Nor is there any lack of opinion on the question of quotas – should there be a prescribed number of women required to be on company boards? If so, how many should there be? March 2015 found the German government weigh into the debate, legislating that 30 per cent of all corporate board seats must, by 2016, be filled by women – this will be an increase of more than 10 per cent on the current average (Deutsche Welle, 2014).

Considering that Germany is the home to a number of highly influential international companies – BMW, BASK, Bayer, Deutsche Bank and Siemens to name just a few – there are many watching this change with a view to how large a 'sea change' the 'she change' will be. In their *New York Times* article 'Germany sets gender quota in boardrooms', published on 7 March 2015, Alison Smale and Claire Cain Miller report on German Family Minister Manuela Schwesig's enthusiasm for the quota, which she called Germany's 'greatest contribution to gender equality since women got the vote' there in 1918. The nation has now joined Norway, which led the way, Belgium, France, Iceland, the Netherlands and Spain in the European quota club.

The UK has made some progress through voluntary methods, such as the 30 per cent Club, which was founded by Helena Morrissey, CEO of the Newton Investment Management Company. Since 2010 there has been a doubling of women on the boards of major British companies, with the number now standing at 23 per cent. There is a longstanding resistance to what is perceived to be quota 'restrictions' in the United States; however, representation of women on boards there now stands at 17 per cent.

Factoid

You can find the most favourable conditions for high-potential female entrepreneurship – defined as 'innovative, market expanding and export oriented' – in these countries:

United States

Australia

Sweden

France

Germany

Chile

UK

Poland

Spain

Mexico

(Source: thegedi.org, 2015)

The state of play – winning the numbers game

It is a curious thing: according to its analysis of data compiled by Factset Research Systems, in 2014 *Fortune* magazine found that those Fortune 1,000 companies with a female CEO had windfall returns of, on average, over 103 per cent (Fairchild, 2014). This is more than 33 per cent over the average return for the same period on the Standard & Poor 500 stock index. And yet, of those 1,000 companies, only 51 of them were led by women (24 of the Fortune 500 have CEOs who are women).

Now, it has been posited that one of the reasons for the lack of female members of this decidedly male-dominated club is that they are cooperative, compassionate, more thoughtful and less aggressive. While this may have been a problem in the days of 'mustering forces' and 'going in for the kill' in the boardroom, those days are, if not long gone, certainly on their way out as they hold little sway in the DACE.

> ### Factoid
>
> You can now rate how well you believe a company treats the women it employs by rating them on the InHerSight online platform, which ranks on data relating to issues such as maternity leave and management opportunities.

Though the trend for including women on boards is improving, the '2014 Catalyst Census: Women Board Directors' report (Catalyst, 2015) notes that, at the time of writing, there were still 18 companies in the S&P 500 with no female directors on their boards. And, according to the 2014 'Gender Diversity in Silicon Valley' report by law firm Fenwick & West, the number of female directors at the valley's 150 largest companies stands at a lowly 10 per cent.

Factoid

Diana Data for Investors

- US businesses with a woman on the executive team average higher valuations at first (64 per cent) and last (49 per cent) funding stages.

- Early-stage investment in US companies with a woman on the executive team has jumped from 5 per cent to 15 per cent in the last 15 years.

(Source: Brush *et al*, 2014)

If I was an investor, in the midst of a myriad of potential companies to plough my money into, I'd be looking for one that had a fair representation of women on the board. Why? Because, on average, those boards with women sitting at the table make it above the median. This is in comparison to those boards that are male-only bastions which are, on average, under performers who have, as made clear in the 2013 Thomson Reuters Study 'Mining the metrics of board diversity', '...higher tracking errors, indicating potentially more volatility.'

Additionally, a soon-to-be-released study from Wake Forest and the University of North Carolina, Wilmington, which examined board diversity over 20 years, found that having a female CFO and at least one female board member led to more ethical business and fiscal decisions being made. The same study revealed the US Internal Revenue Service estimation that corporate tax evasion cost the nation approximately $67 billion in 2006 alone (business.wfu.edu, 2015).

And yet, again looking at Fortune 500 stats, women only occupied 17 per cent of those corporate board seats. In Australia that number is slightly higher – but only just. According to the AICD (Australian Institute of Company Directors) as of November 2014, 19.2 per cent of the ASX 200 board seats were held by women. The UK numbers are comparable; as outlined in the 'Female FTSE board report 2014', women comprise 15.6 per cent of FTSE 250 and 20.7 per cent of FTSE 100 boards.

Factoid

At the current rate, women in America will not reach salary parity until 2058.

(Source: Institute for Women's Policy Research, 2015)

With numbers like that, you'd be forgiven for thinking that the number of women business owners is equally small. However this is far from the truth; in actual fact, women own one third of the businesses in the world. In the United States alone, according to the 2014 Womenable report published by American Express OPEN, there were over 9 million majority and/or privately-held businesses owned by women generating more than US$1.4 trillion annually. These women are part of what is now considered one of the fastest growing groups of entrepreneurs, potential entrepreneurs and wage earners – they are the Third Billion.

It is expected that one billion women will enter the global workforce in the next decade – equal to the populations of India or China. As they do so they will quickly become an economic force to be reckoned with and, as such, should be acknowledged as a wellspring of opportunity to be embraced.

Twenty years ago, in September of 1995, at the Fourth World Conference on Women, the Beijing Declaration and Platform for Action was agreed to and adopted. It included a wide range of declarations and recommendations for the General Assembly of the United Nations, including the following statements:

In countries that are undergoing fundamental political, economic and social transformation, the skills of women, if better utilized, could constitute a major contribution to the economic life of their respective countries. Women have increasingly become self-employed and owners and managers of micro, small and medium-scale enterprises. The expansion of the informal sector in many countries, and of self-organized and independent enterprises is in large part due to women, whose collaborative, self-help and traditional practices and initiatives in production and trade represent a vital economic resource.

Factoid

The Global Gender Gap report (World Economic Forum, 2014) tracks the correlation 'between a country's gender gap and its national competitiveness. Because women account for one half of a country's potential talent base, a nation's competitiveness in the long term depends significantly on whether and how it educates and utilizes its women.'

- Top 5: Iceland, Finland, Norway, Sweden, Denmark

- Other countries ranked include: Germany (12), France (18), Canada (19), United States (20), Australia (24), UK (26)

(Source: United Nations Department for Policy Coordination and Sustainable Development, 1995)

To mark the 20th anniversary of the Beijing Conference, the Bill and Melinda Gates Foundation published the 'No Ceilings: Full Participation Project' report (2015). The report states:

> An estimated, 200 million fewer women than men are online in the developing world, and 300 million fewer women own a mobile phone. This matters, because when women in the developing world get online, 30 per cent report earning additional income, 45 per cent report searching for jobs, and 80 per cent report improving their education.... women remain vastly underrepresented in senior management positions. The share of women CEOs in Fortune 500 companies was zero in 1995; now it is 5 per cent. Women's share of board seats varies – ranging from 8 per cent in Portugal to 36 per cent in Norway – but falls well short of parity.

I suggest that nations (and businesses, too) who take the opportunity to empower and exalt entrepreneurial women are actually investing wisely in their country's coffers. Strongest will be those who recognize the women of the Third Billion as a substantial part of their solution stack instead of a problem in need of a solution. Why? Well, as noted by the Clinton Global Initiative report, 'Empowering Girls & Women' (2015):

When women work, they invest 90 per cent of their income back into their families, compared with 35 per cent for men. By focusing on girls and women, innovative businesses and organizations can spur economic progress, expand markets, and improve health and education outcomes for everyone.

So let's break down the 'Third Billion Index Rankings' by country. This list, collated by Strategy& (formerly Booz & Company) ranked 128 nations on performance inputs such as Access to Work policies and Entrepreneurial Support. Australia topped the list, followed by Norway, Sweden, Finland, New Zealand, the Netherlands, Canada and Germany. What may come as a surprise are the rankings of the UK in 13th place and the United States, which only made it to the 30th spot – just one point ahead of Greece and two in front of China.

Factoid

The country with the highest percentage of female managers, at nearly 60 per cent, is Jamaica, followed by Colombia at 53 per cent and St Lucia at 52 per cent. America's percentage stands at 43 per cent while Japan sits at 11 per cent.

(Source: ilo.org, 2015)

One of the great gifts of the DACE is its ability to enable members of the Third Billion to connect, collaborate, engage and empower each other. This is clearly evidenced by the myriad of networks both online and off, which are centred around enabling just that – for women and girls of all ages, wherever they are located and whatever their current circumstances. These networks can be within companies, such as eBay's Women's Initiative Network (WIN), and/or those that are organizationally agnostic, such as Girl's CEO Connection. What they share in common is their perfect placement for prompting and perpetuating the collaborative offerings that are at the heart of the DACE.

Anna Fälth, *UN Women Manager – Managing the Knowledge Gateway for Women's Economic Empowerment*

Collaboration and networking is essential to all the work I do, both internally within UN Women as well as with organizations and individual men and women globally. With the establishment of UN Women in 2010, governments mandated us to be the conveners and coordinators for gender equality and women's empowerment within the UN system.

The online community that I am managing, EmpowerWomen.org, was conceived and funded with the objective of bringing together all types of stakeholders from around the globe to jointly drive women's economic empowerment.

The increased attention being given to women's economic empowerment by governments, NGOs, companies, academia and many others over the past five years, has been accompanied by a proliferation of initiatives by these individual organizations. However, limited notice was given to the importance of building coalitions to enhance the impact these initiatives could have upon the lives of women and girls. As such, EmpowerWomen.org has filled an important gap in ensuring improved collaboration and networking among all stakeholders. This remains our core mandate.

With EmpowerWomen.org, we continue to build coalitions of gender advocates to drive a women's economic empowerment agenda. To that end, we facilitate networking among our members so that they can team up and drive change for women and girls in their communities and countries, as well as globally.

Being a collaborative and networking platform, EmpowerWomen.org has benefited tremendously from social media, in particular Facebook, Twitter and LinkedIn (and soon Instagram). In fact, they represent the preeminent drivers of attention to our site, followed by our e-mail-based newsletter and our partners' websites.

Since we are seeking engagement, collaboration and networking with women and men in developing countries, where their access to computers and the internet is limited, we have used more traditional forms of communication, such as offline engagement, to get our messages across and to raise awareness of EmpowerWomen.org. We have also used radio broadcasting in an ad hoc manner (eg World Radio Day, UN Radio Day). More recently, we are providing free learning material (with no data charges) to women (so far in South Africa and Colombia and soon in India) with regular cell phones via our collaboration with Facebook's internet.org.

One of the key challenges that we face as a global community of many different stakeholders is the 'communication gap'. We address this by, as much as possible, simplifying the language we use to the lowest dominator of terms and concepts. As a next step in addressing this issue, we are engaging our Champions – our Flat World Navigators – in helping us to remove jargon and explain difficult terms and concepts so that the broader community, as well as the general public, can engage in the same discussions. The greatest challenge, I believe, has been language barriers, in particular for users in Arabic, French and Spanish-speaking countries. To overcome this, we are creating versions of our site in these languages, to facilitate collaboration.

Our approach is that the more people who access our knowledge the better. EmpowerWomen.org is an open platform available to anyone in the world. However, to engage, collaborate and network we ask that our users register as EmpowerWomen.org members.

As we launched EmpowerWomen.org in September 2013, we also launched a Champion Programme to engage online volunteers as the 'first adopters' of our platform. What we didn't count on was the amazing success this programme would have. Our Champions carried the messages of women's economic empowerment and the existence of our global online community, while they developed their own projects in their communities in countries such Canada, Nepal, India, Italy and the United States among many others. In doing so, they successfully contributed to our mission of promoting gender equality and women's economic empowerment. Some of them have joined forces to drive this mission through social media as well as connecting, collaborating and networking on EmpowerWomen.org. This has helped us as an organization to connect with stakeholders in their countries and to develop and implement a global campaign, which drives attention to the fact that everyone benefits from empowered women.

[The views expressed are those of the author and do not necessarily represent those of the United Nations, including UN Women, or their Member States.]

The skills already within reach

It is not uncommon for women to possess many essential skills elemental to the natural Flat World Navigator, which puts them in prime position to leverage these talents. As the DACE continues to progress and grow, it is likely that these skills will be ever more recognized by the investors of the future – perhaps becoming part of the KPI for organizations and their leadership structures. I say this as it is likely to be multi-party/department/company offerings and collaborative endeavours that take centre stage in the DACE in the near-, mid- and long-term futures. This is particularly so, as the technologies that engender and empower this cooperation become increasingly available and accessible at all cost and capability levels.

Let's say you were a digital marketer who was at the CMO level when you stopped working 10 years ago. If you've decided to try to reenter the workplace now and you don't know what Twitter, Facebook, Instagram, and Pinterest are, you're going to find the entire digital marketing landscape has totally shifted and your skills are no longer directly applicable.

It's like taking a pot of boiling water completely off the burner – wouldn't it be easier to leave it at a simmer and quickly ramp it up when you are ready again? [Tools and technologies] are enabling people to freelance and do just that, allowing them to keep their careers at a simmer. They're able to maintain their skills and an ambient awareness of what's going on. That way, when they're ready to return and turn their career back to a 'boil' they can do so instantly.

That will change their earning potential. They won't have to drop from CMO to a mid-level position; they'll be able to go back to what they were meant to be earning. I find that really exciting!

Shala Burroughs, Co-Founder and Former COO at CloudPeeps

The rate at which IT, sales, marketing, logistics and supply chains – and the tools and technologies they employ – will have to work together, simply, securely and with no vendor lock in/out, is accelerating exponentially. This will not diminish; instead it will further quicken and, as it does so, it will expedite those entrepreneurs and enterprises who have embraced this position in the flat world of the DACE and the Flat World Navigators – the key connectors and collaborators – within their midst.

Inarguably, the world has changed. From this point onwards, a cornerstone of success in the DACE will entail having an understanding of the importance of, and willingness to participate in, this co-operative, collaborative arena. Working for a win-win solution is a key element of this enterprise and this is a theatre wherein women, natural Flat World Navigators, are well set to take centre stage. Businesses, organizations and their senior-level leaders must recognize the importance of this. Their commitment to establishing a working environment that affords opportunities to take advantage of this strategy of authentic, accountable communication, connection and collaboration stands their businesses in good stead to create prosperous futures for all stakeholders.

Actions with intent

Decide what changes could create a more Belle Curve-friendly work environment and how you could effect, or help to effect, them. Decide on one change you could make within a week, one you could accomplish within a month, and one you could accomplish within a year. Plan the steps and step to your plan!

If you are a business owner/leader ensure that you (or your representative) interview a wide range of candidates for any position or promotion. You may want to undertake a policy of 'blind' applications wherein gender, age and ethnicity are removed from any application forms thus removing any potential unconscious and unwanted bias-based hiring and promotion decisions.

Look to join or become more deeply involved in two women-led/centric networks that extend your reach and, perhaps, your comfort zone. The first of these organizations should reflect your professional goals as an individual, the second the goals of your business or organization.

Know and name your top five strengths and spend time each day applying what you do best within your workday.

Develop a plan for your career, which includes what you need to do and who can help you do it. Search your network for potential mentors (and/or introductions to them) who can be of help. Ask for assistance – it never, ever hurts to ask... nicely!

If you are in a position of management/leadership reach out to a minimum of three women who you can give assistance to in developing their career plans or progression.

INTERVIEW   An interview with a Flat World Navigator

Natalie Goldman, *Founder and Managing Director at Launch Pod and Learning and Development Manager at Peoplebank*

Natalie is driven by making a difference in this world, through her passion for helping people. This is evident in her 20-year career through Learning and Development, Coaching, Organizational Development and Technology. It has now transformed with the birth of Launch Pod, which combines her career and her passion for empowering women. She is a believer in challenging the norm, being curious and innovating, finding better and different ways of doing things, connecting, collaborating and then disrupting. Her work experience spans corporate, government and the not-for-profit sector with a multitude of companies and industries.

Natalie, bearing in mind your expertise in the HR and corporate learning-tech arenas, I'd like to explore your perspective on social media, Cloud-based tools and how they've impacted the way you do business or would like to do business.

I've seen a dramatic shift in how technology impacts the way learning happens and what a learning development professional can access. I began pushing for Cloud-based solutions over five years ago and I've no doubt that in the next few years we'll see the number of people using these solutions increase as more and more telecommute, hot-desk and become more focused on a work-life balance.

How would you suggest people, who see the great benefits that Cloud-based tools and technologies bring, manage up and 'sell in' the concept?

Having a good business case is absolutely essential in any project. Of course it depends on what's happening in the business in question but in general, providing an example that can be replicated across business centres that are geographically dispersed is a great case in point to share. With this exemplar you could point out that travelling a lot is not very economical whereas having everything online is. Another business case is consistency – with Cloud-based tools it's possible that, no matter who looks at the material, there's a consistency around what people are accessing. This then leads to higher levels of control and 'trackability': knowing who's doing what.

Speaking of 'who's doing what', and bearing in mind our shared passion for collaboration and win-win strategies, how do you see those things – embodied in the role of a Flat World Navigator – enhancing the position of women within a corporate structure?

I've actually started a business called Launch Pod, which is all about empowering and working with female entrepreneurs to help them grow their businesses. So, that question is quite apt for me as I'm using all the collaborative skills I've developed over the years to help my business take off.

There are two sides to my answer: the corporate side and the entrepreneur/business owner's side. From the corporate side, when looking at the leadership competencies required to be successful, when tested across the general population of both men and women, women tend to have more of the core competencies necessary to be excellent leaders. One of those competencies is collaboration, which women do so well. I don't know if it's innate but women have a well-developed capability to collaborate and connect with others in a way that's meaningful.

However, women need to see that what they bring to the table is valuable. It's not just luck, it's not just by-chance situations; they really do provide value. With that knowledge they can go forward and break those glass ceilings.

From the entrepreneurial perspective I see it a lot more in action. There are a lot of great groups, locally and internationally, for women, coming from what I call 'a place of abundance'. This is where there's enough 'pie' for everyone and there isn't a fear of, 'You're stepping on my territory!' It's quite the opposite.

Coming from a place of abundance could be perceived as something of an anomaly when looked at from the 'command and control' point of view. Perhaps looking for the win-win is more of an entrepreneurial perspective.

I think it's interesting that more and more companies are taking on Stephen Covey's work and win-win habit. ['Think Win-Win isn't about being nice, nor is it a quick-fix technique. It is a character-based code for human interaction and collaboration' – (Stephen Covey, *Seven Habits of Highly Effective People*).]

A lot more companies are taking on his philosophies and his habits because people want more of that 'connection' – they're over the politics of it all. Interestingly, company politics are one of the key drivers for people deciding to leave their job. They want to do their job well, they want to be trusted as capable adults and they want to work in a highly engaged workforce because they want to give a hundred per cent themselves.

Entrepreneurs tend to be solo. They work alone and/or grow their business and then sell it to start another one... and once again they're alone. So, to them, their network is everything. They look at collaboration as an absolute essential in order to survive. If you don't know people who can help you and, in return, you help them, nothing ever happens.

It's interesting that you mention networking. There seem to be two different worlds of networking. There is the world where you go to networking events, pass your business cards around, have a few drinks and work the room. I'm not saying it's necessarily superficial but there is less depth there than within a collaborative network.

Absolutely. I have only started going to networking events as a female entrepreneur in the past six months and my experiences are so very different to the networking I did in the years before that.

It's exactly what you said. When I was networking from a learning and development perspective, it wasn't collaborative. It was all about 'Could you be my next boss?' or 'Who can you help me get to?' There wasn't a direct or deep connection.

When I started networking around entrepreneurs – predominantly women entrepreneurs – it was such a different experience. Immediate connections were made and friendships have developed. They are 'true' connections; we are helping each other in very different ways but in ways that make such a big difference! I've never seen this side of networking; it is so much more meaningful. I don't know if that's due to it being a 'women' thing or if it's an entrepreneur thing but my gut feel is that it's a combination of both.

Can you give me a couple of examples of how you are using collaboration to build your new business?

Sure, there's a lot of 'if you'll help me, I'll help you' collaboration going on! For example, I coach my Chief Financial Officer and in return she helps me with all my finances. I am also working with a woman who is helping me write my eCourse and develop a customer service programme. The three of us are all helping each other with the various projects that we're doing.

There's a give and take with no money being passed between anyone. And there's never a question of, 'I helped you with this, why aren't you helping me?' or 'I gave you more hours than you gave me'. It's all coming from a place of abundance.

These kinds of things are happening more and more now that I'm branching out into the entrepreneurial space. It's a space where I feel very comfortable... like I should have been here a long time ago.

FWN Keys from Natalie Goldman

- A corporate leadership competency required to be an excellent leader is collaboration – something women do very well.

- Women need to see that what they bring to the table is valuable; with that knowledge they can go forward and break those glass ceilings.

- Entrepreneurs look at collaboration as an absolute essential; if you don't know people who can help you and whom you can help in return, nothing ever happens.

In conclusion

This chapter was by the numbers – and what a lot of numbers there were on the Belle Curve; numbers relating to windfall dividends, diversity and directorships, ethics, equality, innovation and the importance of internet access. The gender gap – some might say gender gulf – was squarely addressed as were issues around cooperative and collaborative natures and the ability to nurture both businesses and business relationships. Further, we underlined the need for these key and core capabilities to be acknowledged and rewarded at both board and investor levels. We discussed the complexities around the Impostor Syndrome and quota systems as well as the importance of women to national economies and competitiveness.

Correlative to the population of India or China, the billion women entering the workforce in the next decade will be an economic and entrepreneurial force to be held in high esteem. They will be adding to the trillions of dollars already being generated by female business owners annually.

Flat world navigation and the skills embodied therein are key differentiators in the DACE. That these skills are part of the casual competence of women gives them a huge advantage. Entrepreneurially focused women must celebrate their own capabilities and, in doing so, assist their colleagues and compatriots to do the same.

It is an exciting time to be a businesswoman. With so many tools to hand, we are able to communicate, connect and, working in concert, capitalize upon our capabilities.

Twenty years after the Fourth World Conference on Women this chapter explored the unfolding of a flat world of cooperative, collaborative relationships at the heart of the DACE, both now and in the future. The next chapter, 'A collaborative conclusion' salutes the grounded spirit of Flat World Navigators – and does so by looking to the stars.

Summary
A collaborative conclusion

Advantage Attention
Authentic Business Change
Collaboration Communicate Connect
DACE Digital Economy Enduser Flat World
Navigator Global Network Relationship Strategy
Success Technology Win-Win **Achieve Astronaut**
Augmented Bill-Murray Create Dollar Enjoy Experience
Future Inspire Intellect Participate Possible Research

Featuring

Christopher Altman (Applied Physics, Global Leadership, Converging Technologies and The Future of Manned Spaceflight) and Francesco Calabrese (ExMG International, Inc, I2KI, International Institute for Knowledge and Innovation)

Y ou have walked with me through the flat world of the DACE – the Digital, Attention and Collaboration Economies. In doing so we have explored the importance of connecting, collaborating and working towards win-win strategies in an economic reality that demands that we create more – be it product, profit and/or partnerships – while we are constrained by increasingly tightened budgets. Fortuitously, we live in a time when the requisite tools, technologies and techniques necessary to flourish while working under these pressures are easily accessible and generally affordable to anyone who does business in the DACE. Ingenuity is occasionally called for – clear leadership and communication always is.

This is not the first time these traits have been called for and it is unlikely to be the last. That said, there is no doubt that when talented, committed and resourceful people are brought together to work towards a common goal, what is possible, while perhaps seemingly improbable at the outset, can be conceptualized and capitalized upon.

It is with these things in mind that I chose these final features to close this book with. They share a spirit of reciprocity, fraternity, teamwork and a total commitment to finding win-win solutions to whatever problem is placed in front of them. This golden time – when the world is your oyster and can be accessed at a lower cost – was all but impossible to imagine until just a few short years ago. It is a land of opportunity for those who seize the day, particularly for those Flat World Navigators leading the charge into the new frontier.

Flat World Navigators share their stories

Francesco A Calabrese, *DSc, CPSC, President at ExMG International, Inc, and Founder/Executive Director, I2KI, International Institute for Knowledge and Innovation*

As a PDG (Pre-Digital Generation) member I have retained a strong sense for putting old-fashioned relationship-building habits at the core of my evolving persona into the cauldron of social media's constantly seething digital era.

My realm of 'unintended consequences' since 1990 has become a cautionary theme in dealings with colleagues, students and customers in the academic, private and government sectors where my career has taken me. As essentially stated in various class syllabi and articles since 1997: 'The lure of what technology can do FOR YOU must also be weighed against what it may do TO YOU!'

We seem to have reached the *de facto* approach that we MUST accommodate human intellect, decision processes and time demands in 'technology' in all its manifestations. But because the 'way we do things around here', which is often defined as 'company culture' is human rather than technology-centric, I submit that if 'off-the-shelf technology' is the perfect solution, apply it. If not, we must be sure the empowered, knowledgeable Enduser, and not just the scientist or programmer, influences the outcome so that it may retain the dominance of human cognitive intellect over the digitized machine instructions.

This has been dramatically demonstrated by chess Grandmaster Garry Kasparov, who recently won a rematch against the pre-programmed moves of IBM's 'Deep Blue' using his own computer augmented by newly conceived moves. He coined the phrase 'Centaur Knowledge work' to aptly define the 'man/machine' roles of that mythical animal.

'Centaur Knowledge' capabilities can level the playing fields of BOYD, Cloud, Big Data, networking platforms, etc, which are helpful when they can be presented understandably and with a view to 'win-win' business models that look to ensure there is true Knowledge Transfer, mutually agreed to by all parties. Additionally, unless the discussions are explicitly 'by-the-numbers' processes, all parties should be prepared to adapt/adjust/improvise and 'tailor' outcomes during project performance. Of course, it is imperative that all involved guard against miscommunications every step of the way.

Clarity is greatly aided by the equivalent of a 'Commander's Intent Document' from the Enterprise CEO, which outlines an overall statement of expectations and governance. Though it may be something of an oversimplification, one could look to President Kennedy's 1961 powerfully stated intent for the NASA Moon Landing programme: 'I believe that this nation should commit itself to achieving the goal, before this decade is out, of landing a man on the moon and returning him safely to the earth' (jfklibrary.org, 1961).

This, followed by the identification of key plans, initiatives and expected results – along with clarity around how these will be prepared, monitored, evaluated and, where necessary, adapted is extremely effective. All of this should be shared internally to expand the CEO's Intent and reach all members of the Enterprise so they can be vetted and integrated in a strategic plan from which operational/delivery support teams will be drawn to successfully achieve the stated intent!

Reading *Innovation: How innovators think, act and change our world* focused my memories of multiple, strategic 'Innovation-events' that happened even before I knew, used, or could spell the word. The most economically impactful for me occurred at the age of six.

The business setting was in place: my 'Innovation-event'– my moment, if you will – was having the chutzpah to talk my immigrant, very poor and uneducated (but growing ever smarter in their 95-year life spans) parents into capitalizing my summer entrepreneurship itch with one dollar! I also convinced them to 'lend' me one small basket and one large jar of mustard so I could walk the streets of South Philadelphia selling palm-sized soft pretzels for one penny each. Buying two for a penny earned me two dollars and I was able to repay my 'capital debt' of $1 on the same day, leaving an operational positive cashflow of $1 to purchase the next day's inventory. I was debt free, except for the basket and mustard 'balance sheet asset items'! It wasn't that good every day, but when the 'inventory' wasn't completely sold, the residual augmented the family's rather meagre food supply – it was a true WIN-WIN!!

Flat World Navigators share their stories

Christopher Altman, *Applied Physics, Global Leadership, Converging Technologies, The Future of Manned Spaceflight*

I began my scientific career at a Deep Future, multidisciplinary research institute, Starlab, located deep in the serene and secluded forests outside Brussels. The Institute, co-founded by MIT Media Lab founder Nicholas Negroponte and established in partnership with MIT, Oxford and Ghent University, was created as a 'Noah's Ark' to bring together brilliant, creative scientists to work on far-ranging projects that held the potential to convey a profound, positive impact on future generations. Projects actively pursued onsite included neuroscience, robotics, time travel, stem cell research, quantum computing, artificial intelligence, biophysics, materials science, genetics, protein folding, and nanoelectronics. Our group's artificial intelligence project was recognized by the *Guinness Book of World Records* in 2001 as the 'World's Most Complex Artificial Brain'. I lived and worked at the Institute, taking up research collaborations with the principal scientists of our NASA and USAF-sponsored time travel division, profiled in a prominent Discovery Channel Special. Our work, which was widely published, featured in a *Discover Magazine* cover story and continues to this day.

In the aftermath of the September 11 attacks I was elected to serve as Chairman for a UN Disarmament and International Security Committee, leading more than 500 diplomats to address and combat the threats of international terrorism, global and regional nuclear security, and information warfare. I was subsequently tasked to advise US national policy and principal funding agency directors as part of the US Government's fast-track research programme in the global race to harness the revolutionary promise and potentials of quantum technology, travelling to leading research institutions around the world. I was fortunate to participate in spaceflight training at NASA Ames, NASA JSC and commercial providers around the country, and to conduct analogue fieldwork on the slopes of Mauna Kea in Hawai'i, where next-generation spacesuit prototypes, in-situ resource utilization, augmented reality interfaces and robotics field tests are being conducted for the next series of manned lunar and Mars missions. My present-day research and academic collaborations integrate these experiences to explore some of the more revolutionary space-based applications of quantum technology.

As an early-stage innovator in the nascent field of commercial spaceflight, I helped shape the strategic direction and astronaut training programme for the world's first commercial astronaut corps, which counts former NASA astronauts, astronaut trainers and instructors in its ranks of flight members and on its board of advisors. We're comprised of over 170 PhD-level scientists, researchers and engineers based in 58 countries around the world. Our members have completed several successful 'Zero G' microgravity research campaigns, directed research experiments in orbital satellites and on the ISS, and received NASA funding to conduct manned research experiments on the first generation of suborbital vehicles as soon as they come online.

The first race to space was driven by national competition: a race for supremacy between the United States and the USSR. The achievements of the Apollo space program gave us countless spinoff technologies, inspiring the creativity and intelligence of an entire generation. Today's generation needs its own inspiration, its own Sputnik moment – its own Moon shot. That inspiration will be a widespread access to space, for the wider public, as more of us are able to go, and to share this experience with each other. This perspective will bring us together in innate recognition of our inherent fragility, our unity and responsibility to steward the Earth for ourselves, for our children, and for our children's children. As we expand our reach outwards to other worlds – and other stars – Earth becomes a destination, no longer limited as a point of origin.

Authentic, clear and honest communications – open sharing based on mutual trust, empathy, and compassion – are absolutely essential for bringing about a better tomorrow. There is no clear division between 'us' and 'them', no real separation. We live in an increasingly interconnected world. No one is unaffected by the events occurring around the world today; we are all interconnected, and we are all interdependent upon one another to create a better future.

New technologies already connect us, empower us, inform, influence and permeate our everyday lives – from platforms like Twitter, Facebook, and Wikileaks, to the seamlessly integrated virtual reality platforms just over the horizon, such as Oculus Rift and Magic Leap. Each of these technologies reflects a singular, fundamental human desire: our desire to share, to inspire, to participate and reach out to each other. They express our desire for unity and belonging, for transparency and connection, our yearning to break down the walls of separation. Our desire to transcend our differences and divisions, expand beyond boundaries to share our personal moments of joy, our everyday experiences with our loved ones, our families, and our communities – to be a part of something greater than ourselves. We are collectively participating in the development of a global awareness; in the collaborative creation of a brighter future and a better world.

I've been fortunate enough to be an early part of several groundbreaking, pioneering initiatives that broke the mould in transcending disciplines; be it my early experience living and working at Starlab, or bringing together corporations and nonprofits, global policymakers and diplomats, scientists and academic researchers. Other examples include conducting field operations with interagency government and military teams working to deploy disaster relief and humanitarian aid; harnessing the most radical and counterintuitive aspects of quantum entanglement and teleportation to enable unconditionally secure communications for the International Space Station and for NASA space assets; and training the next generation of commercial astronauts. What all of these 'adventures' share is first-hand leadership experience coupled with a global perspective. It's a view that spans multiple sectors and fields, conveys empathy, understanding and attunement, and opens the door to authentic communication, allowing you to bridge the gap between the differing perspectives and vocabularies that each stakeholder brings to the table.

My present initiatives span commercial spaceflight, advanced physics, science and technology research and development, next-generation government transformation initiatives, policy, advocacy, outreach and advising as well as global humanitarian aid and disaster relief efforts.

Increasingly rapid, recursive advances in science and technology, in fields such as 3D printing, artificial intelligence, biotechnology, nanotechnology, neuroscience, renewable energy, spaceflight, supercomputing and quantum technologies – each enabled by the rapid technological progress of Moore's Law doublings in computer processing power, speed and complexity – will converge to confer radical changes to our society over coming decades. We're quickly approaching a critical influx point, a collective transition towards the dawn of a post-scarcity economy.

The responsibility falls upon us to ensure that the limitless potential embodied by that transition is filled with dreams of hope, happiness, freedom and fulfilment. Drawing from my own multidisciplinary background and experiences, I strive to bridge the gap, to play a positive role, to leave a lasting impact in the initiatives that I'm fortunate to contribute towards, in the hope of creating a brighter future – to ensure that the world is a better place for the generations to come. This is reflected in my work with the QUIST Project, exploring the revolutionary potentials of quantum technology to transform society, business, and commerce – to radically accelerate progress in medicine, manufacturing, materials science, biology and more.

Through global policy, advocacy and outreach efforts, I aim to raise awareness, open up access, break down hierarchies and remove barriers – to encourage active participation so that others are equally empowered to explore their dreams, to harness their creativity and imagination, and play an active role in the collective creation of a brighter tomorrow.

At the end of this collaborative journey I will leave you with a question: could Bill Murray's lifestyle make your style better?

Why Bill? Well, I remember reading Jada Yuan's Vulture.com interview with him in September of 2014 and thinking: I like the way that man navigates his world!

In short, Bill's seven steps are:

- *Sing. And be really into it.* Yep – if you're enjoying what you're doing, really enjoying it, it's pretty likely others are going to want to join you in singing your song.

- *Just be honest.* There's no point in lying – social media will tell... everyone.

- *Always make room for your friends.* They keep you honest. And, when you're dancing to the music of life they're unlikely to step on your toes.

- *Be spontaneous.* Be flexible and it's likely that the winds of change, though they may bend you slightly, won't break you.

- *Leave yourself open to magical moments.* You never know where an audacious, innovative idea will come from so be open to connecting and collaborating with anyone who crosses your path.

- *Stay relaxed and success will follow.* Stress breeds more stress – in yourself and those around you. Taking a few moments to breathe, think and connect with others whose experience and expertise you can learn from will lead to a longer life – both professionally and personally.

- *Remember that you are you and no one else.* Authenticity. It's just that simple.

Thanks Bill!

Why do I share this with you? Because if you keep these tenets close to you, either professionally or personally, you will undoubtedly enjoy your own flat world navigational adventures and be a Flat World Navigator that others seek out to connect and collaborate with. Win-Win-Win!

REFERENCES

Abbott, Tony PM and Turnbull, Malcolm MP [accessed 27 January 2015] Digital Transformation Office to Deliver 21st Century Government [Online] http://www.malcolmturnbull.com.au/media/digital-transformation-office-to-make-it-easier-to-connect

ACCA (2014) [accessed 28 February 2015] Back in the Game – Global SME Performance Review 2013/2014 [Online] http://www.accaglobal.com/gb/en/technical-activities/technical-resources-search/2014/october/back-in-the-game.html

Aron, Dave, Waller, Graham and Weldon, Lee [accessed 27 November 2014] Executive Summary: Flipping to Digital Leadership: The 2015 CIO Agenda (No. 7), *Gartner* [Online] http://www.gartner.com/imagesrv/cio/pdf/cio_agenda_execsum2015.pdf

Australian Bureau of Statistics (2013) [accessed 4 November 2014] Business Use of Information Technology [Online] http://www.abs.gov.au/ausstats/abs@.nsf/mf/8129.0

Australian Communications and Media Authority (2014) [accessed 27 January 2014] Australian SMEs in the Digital Economy [Online] http://www.acma.gov.au/theACMA/engage-blogs/engage-blogs/researchacma/SMEs-key-drivers-of-the-digital-economy

Australian Government Department of Industry (2014) [accessed 3 January 2015] Establishment of the Entrepreneurs' Infrastructure Programme [Online] http://www.industry.gov.au/industry/Documents/EntrepreneursInfrastructureProgrammeDiscussionPaper.pdf

Banerjee, Dr Preeta M, and Openshaw, Eric (2014) [accessed 8 April 2014] Democratizing Technology: Crossing the 'CASM' to Serve Small and Medium Businesses, *Deloitte University Press* [Online] http://dupress.com/articles/dr14-democratizing-technology/

Blau, Andrew (2014) [accessed 5 January 2015] Deloitte on Disruption, Changing Course in a Disruptive World, *Deloitte* [Online] http://www2.deloitte.com/us/en/pages/risk/articles/deloitte-on-disruption

Boston Consulting Global (2014) [accessed 15 January 2015] The Mobile Internet Economy in Europe [Online] https://www.bcgperspectives.com/content/articles/telecommunications_digital_economy_devices_mobile_internet_economy/

Brush, Professor Candida G, Greene, Professor Patricia, Balachandra, Professor Lakshmi and Davis, Professor Amy (2014) [accessed 29 March 2015] Diana Report: Women Entrepreneurs 2014: Bridging the Gender Gap in Venture

Capital [Online] http://www.babson.edu/Academics/centers/blank-center/global-research/diana/Documents/diana-project-executive-summary-2014.pdf

BT (2014) [accessed 5 January 2015] Art of Connecting: Creativity and the Modern CIO [Online] http://www.globalservices.bt.com/uk/en/insights/creativity_and_modern_cio

Business Insider Australia (2014) [accessed 7 January 2015] The Future of Digital [Online] http://www.businessinsider.com.au/the-future-of-digital-2014-slide-deck-2014-12

Catalyst (2015) [accessed 17 February 2015] 2014 Catalyst Census: Women Board Directors [Online] http://www.catalyst.org/knowledge/2014-catalyst-census-women-board-directors

CCS Insight (2014) [accessed 19 February 2015] *Smartwatches and Smart Bands Dominate Fast-Growing Wearables Market* [Online] http://www.ccsinsight.com/press/company-news/1944-smartwatches-and-smart-bands-dominate-fast-growing-wearables-market

Cisco® (2015) [accessed 8 February 2015] Cisco® Visual Networking Index™ (VNI) Global Mobile Data Traffic Forecast for 2014 to 2019 [Online] http://www.cisco.com/c/en/us/solutions/service-provider/visual-networking-index-vni/index.html

Clinton Global Initiative (2015) [accessed 16 March 2015] Clinton Global Initiative: Empowering Girls & Women (90%) [Online] http://www.un.org/en/ecosoc/phlntrpy/notes/clinton.pdf

ComScore (2014) [accessed 2 August 2014] 2014 US Digital Future in Focus [Online] http://www.comscore.com/Insights/Presentations-and-Whitepapers/2014/2014-US-Digital-Future-in-Focus

Crowdtap (2014) [accessed 8 January 2015] Social Influence: Marketing's New Frontier [Online] http://go.crowdtap.com/socialinfluence

Deutsche Welle (2014) [accessed 6 January 2015] Germany to Legislate 30 Percent Quota for Women on Company Boards [Online] http://www.dw.de/germany-to-legislate-30-percent-quota-for-women-on-company-boards/a-18088840

Domo/CEO (2014) [accessed 19 May 2015] Social CEO Report [Online] https://web-assets.domo.com/blog/wp-content/uploads/2014/09/SocialCEO2014Report-2.pdf

Eggers, William and Macmillan, Paul (2015) [accessed 28 January 2015] A Billion to One: The Crowd Gets Personal [Online] http://dupress.com/articles/personalizing-customer-experiences-analytics/

eMarketer (2013) [accessed 12 April 2014] Social Networking Reaches Nearly One in Four Around the World [Online] http://www.emarketer.com/Article/Social-Networking-Reaches-Nearly-One-Four-Around-World/1009976

Enarson, Elaine and Hearn Morrow, Betty (1998) [accessed 29 January 2014] Women Will Rebuild Miami: A Case Study of Feminist Response to Disaster [Online] http://gdnonline.org/resources/women_will_rebuild_miami.pdf

Etherington, Martyn (nd) [accessed 6 March 2014] @Etherington_CMO [Online] https://twitter.com/etherington_cmo

EurActiv (2014) [accessed 19 May 2015] The Schuldschein: An investment alternative for Europe [Online] http://www.euractiv.com/sections/innovation-enterprise/schuldschein-investment-alternative-europe-308755

EurActiv (2015) [accessed 16 January 2015] Oettinger Playing 'Catch-Up' on EU Digital Infrastructure [Online] http://www.euractiv.com/sections/innovation-enterprise/oettinger-playing-catch-eu-digital-infrastructure-311325

European Commission (nd) [accessed 13 January 2015] Digital Agenda for Europe: A Europe 2020 Initiative [Online] http://ec.europa.eu/digital-agenda/

EY Sweeney (2014) [accessed 19 February 2015] EY Digital Australia: State of the Nation 2014 Report [Online] https://digitalaustralia.ey.com/

Fairchild, Caroline (2014) [accessed 8 July 2014] Women CEOs in the Fortune 1000: By the Numbers [Online] http://fortune.com/2014/07/08/women-ceos-fortune-500-1000/

Farrall, Frank, Simes, Dr Ric and O'Mahony, John [accessed 21 July 2014] The Collaborative Economy: Unlocking the Power of the Workplace Crowd [Online] http://www2.deloitte.com/au/en/pages/economics/articles/collaborative-economy-unlocking-power-of-workplace-crowd.htmlc

Female FTSE Board Report (2014) [accessed 19 May 2015] [Online] http://www.raeng.org.uk/publications/other/the-female-ftse-board-report-2014

Fenwick & West (2014) [accessed 17 February 2015] Gender Diversity in Silicon Valley: A Comparison of Silicon Valley Public Companies and Large Public Companies [Online] http://www.fenwick.com/FenwickDocuments/Gender_Diversity_2014.pdf

Frey, Carl Benedikt and Osborne, Michael A (2013) [accessed 27 September 2014] The Future of Employment: How Susceptible are Jobs to Computerisation? [Online] http://www.oxfordmartin.ox.ac.uk/downloads/academic/The_Future_of_Employment.pdf

Friedman, Thomas L (2005) The World is Flat: A brief history of the twenty-first century, Farrar, Straus and Giroux/Allen Lane, USA/UK

Fry, Richard (2014) [accessed 17 January 2015] This Year, Millennials Will Overtake Baby Boomers [Online] http://www.pewresearch.org/fact-tank/2015/01/16/this-year-millennials-will-overtake-baby-boomers/

GII (2014) [accessed 13 January 2015] The Global Innovation Index – The Human Factor in Innovation [Online] https://www.globalinnovationindex.org/content.aspx?page=GII-Home

Glind, Pieter van de (2013) [accessed 5 April 2014] The Consumer Potential of Collaborative Consumption [Online] http://www.collaborativeconsumption.com/2013/08/20/what-is-the-consumer-potential-of-collaborative-consumption-answers-from-amsterdam/

Global Entrepreneurial and Development Institute (2015) [accessed 16 March 2015] Gender GEDI Index [Online] http://thegedi.org/research/womens-entrepreneurship-index/

Head, Beverley (2015) [accessed 29 April 2015] Jumping Off a Cliff for Your Customers [Online] http://www.itnews.com.au/CXOChallenge/400935,jumping-off-a-cliff-for-your-customers.aspx

Hong Kong Commerce and Economic Development Bureau (2013) [accessed 26 November 2014] Public Consultation on 2014 Digital 21 Strategy: Smarter Hong Kong, Smarter Living [Online] http://www.digital21.gov.hk/eng/relatedDoc/download/2014D21S-booklet.pdf

Hootsuite (nd) [accessed 3 March 2015] Social Customer Service: The Future of Customer Satisfaction [Online] https://socialbusiness.hootsuite.com/whitepaper-future-of-customer-satisfaction.html

Iñárritu, Alejandro G (Dir) (2014) *Birdman or (The Unexpected Virtue of Ignorance)*. New Regency Pictures [movie]

Institute for Women's Policy Research (2015) [accessed 16 March 2015] The Status of Women in the States: 2015 Employment and Earnings [Online] http://www.iwpr.org/publications/pubs/the-status-of-women-in-the-states-2015-2014-employment-and-earnings

Instituto Nacional de Estadistica (National Institute of Statistics – Spain) (nd) [accessed 17 February 2015] [Online] http://www.ine.es/en/welcome.shtml

International Labour Organization (2015) [accessed 17 March 2015] Women in Business and Management: Gaining Momentum [Online] http://www.ilo.org/wcmsp5/groups/public/---dgreports/---dcomm/---publ/documents/publication/wcms_334882.pdf

Internet Association (2014) [accessed 12 January 2015] Reasserting Canada's Competitiveness in the Digital Economy [Online] http://internetassociation.org/wp-content/uploads/2014/10/September-2014_-The-Internet-Association-Canada-Digital-Economy-Paper.pdf

Internet World Stats (2013) [accessed 8 October 2014] Top 50 Countries with the Highest Internet Penetration Rates [Online] http://www.internetworldstats.com/top25.htm

Janssen, Cory (nd) [accessed 20 November 2014] Techopedia: What is the Maker Movement? [Online] http://www.techopedia.com/definition/28408/maker-movement

John F Kennedy Presidential Library and Museum (nd) [accessed 15 February 2015] NASA Moon Landing [Online] http://www.jfklibrary.org/JFK/JFK-Legacy/NASA-Moon-Landing.aspx

Kane, Professor Gerald C (Jerry) (2014) [accessed 19 February 2015] Can You Really Let Employees Loose on Social Media? [Online] http://sloanreview.mit.edu/article/can-you-really-let-employees-loose-on-social-media/

Kane, Gerald C, Palmer, Doug, Phillips, Anh Nguyen, Kiron, David and Buckley, Natasha (2014) [accessed 5 September 2014] Moving Beyond Marketing:

Generating Social Business Value Across the Enterprise [Online]
http://dupress.com/articles/social-business-study-mit-smr/

de Kok, Jan, Vroonhof, Paul, Verhoeven, Wim, Timmermans, Niek, Kwaak, Ton,
Snijder, Jacqueline and Westhof, Florieke (2011) [accessed 16 November 2014]
Do SMEs Create More and Better Jobs? [Online] http://ec.europa.eu/
enterprise/policies/sme/facts-figures-analysis/performance-review/files/
supporting-documents/2012/do-smes-create-more-and-better-jobs_en.pdf

Kulkarni, Aditi, Rybkowski, Zofia K. and Smith, James (2012) [accessed
9 February 2014] Cost Comparison of Collaborative and IPD-Like Project
Delivery Methods Versus Competitive Non-Collaborative Project Delivery
Methods (Paper for the 20th Annual Conference of the International Group for
Lean Construction) [Online] http://www.iglc20.sdsu.edu/papers/wp-content/
uploads/2012/07/79%20P%20076.pdf

Malik, Om (2014) [accessed 8 June 2014] Online & Connections [Online]
http://om.co/2014/06/03/online-connections/

McDonald, Kim Chandler (2013) *Innovation: How innovators think, act and
change our world*, Kogan Page, London and Philadelphia

McGrath, Benjamin and Mahowald, Robert P (2013) [accessed 7 July 2014]
IDC 2013 CloudTrack Survey: An Evolving Set of Cloud Drivers [Online]
http://www.idc.com/getdoc.jsp?containerId=244624

Meeker, Mary (2014) [accessed 17 November 2014] Internet Trends 2014:
Code Conference [Online] http://www.kpcb.com/internet-trends

Morrissey, Brian (2013) [accessed 18 May 2015] 15 Alarming Stats About Banner
Ads, *Digiday* [Online] http://digiday.com/publishers/15-alarming-stats-about-
banner-ads/

Ng, Kelly (2014) [accessed 10 October 2014] How This Country Plans to Connect
50,000 Villages in Six Months [Online] http://www.futuregov.asia/articles/
4701-broadband-to-connect-50000-indian-villages-by-march-2015

Nielsen (2013) [accessed 8 August 2014] Nielsen: Global Trust in Advertising
Report [Online] http://www.nielsen.com/us/en/insights/reports/2013/
global-trust-in-advertising-and-brand-messages.html

Nielsen (2014) [accessed 4 October 2014] Nielsen: China Sees More Sophisticated
Online Shoppers [Online] http://elitepdf.com/page/nielsen-china-sees-more-
sophisticated-online-shoppers.html

No Ceilings: Full Participation Project (2015) [accessed 14 March 2015]
No Ceilings: Full Participation Project Report [Online] http://noceilings.org/
report/report.pdf

NSW Business Chamber (2014) [accessed 30 July 2014] Industry Research
Collaboration Discussion Paper [Online] http://www.nswbusinesschamber.com.au/
NSWBC/media/Forms/Final-Report_-Thinking-Business-Industry-Research-
Collaboration.pdf

Obama, President Barack (2015) [accessed 24 January 2015] Remarks by the
President in State of the Union Address [Online] https://www.whitehouse.gov/

the-press-office/2015/01/20/remarks-president-state-union-address-january-20-2015

Open Government Partnership (2014) [accessed 14 November 2014] Open Government Partnership: Citizen Action, Responsive Government [Online] http://www.opengovpartnership.org/sites/default/files/attachments/2014%20OGP%20HLE%20-%20Full%20Transcript%20FINAL_0.pdf

Oxford Dictionaries (2015) [accessed 20 November 2014] [Online] http://www.oxforddictionaries.com/definition/english/google

Oxford Economics (2014) [accessed 13 January 2015] SMEs: Equipped to Compete [Online] http://www.oxfordeconomics.com/recent-releases/smes-equipped-to-compete

Philipson, Graeme (2015) [accessed 25 February 2015] eBay and Woolworths Sign Collection Deals [Online] http://www.itwire.com/it-industry-news/deals/67084-ebay-and-woolworths-sign-collection-deal

Popken, Ben (2011) [accessed 9 July 2014] You're 475 Times More Likely To Survive A Plane Crash Than Click On A Banner Ad [Online] http://consumerist.com/2011/07/01/youre-475-times-more-likely-to-survive-a-plane-crash-than-click-on-abanner-ad

Raik-Allen, Simon (2015) [accessed 16 March 2015] The Future of Business Australia 2040 [Online] http://files.myob.com.s3-ap-southeast-2.amazonaws.com/news/MYOB-Future-of-Business-Report-AU.pdf

Rubel, Steve (2015) [accessed 15 January 2015] Storytelling in the Age of Social Consumption [Online] http://www.edelman.com/post/storytelling-age-social-news-consumption/

she-conomy (2009) [accessed 9 May 2013] Marketing to Women: Quick Facts [Online] http://she-conomy.com/facts-on-women

Smale, Alison and Miller, Claire Cain (2015) [accessed 7 March 2015] Germany Sets Gender Quota in Boardrooms, *New York Times* [Online] http://www.nytimes.com/2015/03/07/world/europe/german-law-requires-more-women-on-corporate-boards.html?_r=0

Smith, James [accessed 1 August 2014] Government Connectivity, Citizen Engagement and Economic Impact [Online] http://www.futuregov.asia/ext/resources/digital_assets/Government-Connectivity-Citizen-Engagement-and-Economic-Impact.pdf

Strategy& (2012) [accessed 12 December 2014] Third Billion Index Rankings [Online] http://www.strategyand.pwc.com/media/file/Strategyand_2012-Third-Billion-Index-Rankings.pdf

Sweney, Mark (2015) [accessed 19 March 2015] Guardian, FT, CNN and Reuters in Ad Deal to Take On Facebook and Google, *Guardian* [Online] http://www.theguardian.com/media/2015/mar/18/guardian-ft-cnn-reuters-ad-deal-facebook-google-pangaea-alliance

Tech City (2013) [accessed 17 October 2014] Tech Powers the London Economy, The Tech City 3rd Anniversary Report [Online] http://techcity.s3.amazonaws.com/press/Final-2013-Tech-City-Report.pdf

Tech London Advocates (2014) [accessed 2 May 2014] London Tech Growth Hampered by Talent Shortage [Online] http://techlondonadvocates.org.uk/london-tech-growth-hampered-by-talent-shortage/

Thomson Reuters (2013) [accessed 12 February 2014] Mining the Metrics of Board Diversity [Online] http://accelus.thomsonreuters.com/sites/default/files/mining_the_metrics_of_board_diversity.pdf

United Nations Department for Policy Coordination and Sustainable Development (1995) [accessed 4 March 2015] Report of the Fourth World Conference on Women: Beijing Declaration and Platform for Action [Online] http://www.un.org/esa/gopher-data/conf/fwcw/off/a–20.en

Vidyasekar, Archana Devi (2014) [accessed 12 May 2014] Connected Living Connected Homes, Work, and Digital Cities to Create a $731.79-billion Market Opportunity by 2020 [Online] http://www.frost.com/sublib/display-report.do?id=M94C-01-00-00-00

Visa/UMR (2015) [accessed 19 April 2015] Tokenisation: Why Australia, why now [Online] http://www.visa.com.au/aboutvisa/research/include/Tokenisation_Why_Australia_Why_Now_FINAL.pdf

Vision Mobile (2014) [accessed 11 August 2014] UK App Economy 2014 [Online] http://www.visionmobile.com/product/uk-app-economy-2014/

Wake Forest University School of Business (2015) [accessed 15 February 2015] School of Business Professors Find More Female Executives Means Less Tax Evasion [Online] http://business.wfu.edu/newsroom/school-business-professors-find-more-female-executives-means-less-tax-evasion/

Weber Shandwick (2013) [accessed 17 August 2015] The Social CEO: Executives Tell All [Online] https://www.webershandwick.com/uploads/news/files/Social-CEO-Study.pdf

Womenable/American Express OPEN (2014) [accessed 18 January 2015] The 2014 State of Women-Owned Business Report [Online] http://www.womenable.com/content/userfiles/2014_State_of_Women-owned_Businesses_public.pdf

World Economic Forum (2014) [accessed 18 November 2014] The Global Gender Gap Report 2014 [Online] http://reports.weforum.org/global-gender-gap-report-2014/

Yuan, Jada (2014) [accessed 17 September 2014] 7 Steps to Living a Bill Murray Life, by Bill Murray [Online] http://www.vulture.com/2014/09/7-steps-to-living-a-bill-murray-life.html

INDEX

Note: for more information on interviewees please see biographies in preliminary pages.